KIDNAPPED IN YEMEN

ONE WOMAN'S AMAZING ESCAPE FROM CAPTIVITY

MARY QUIN

THE LYONS PRESS
Guilford, Connecticut
An imprint of The Globe Pequot Press

For Andrew, Margaret, Peter and Ruth,
who did not live to tell their stories.

The Lyons Press is an imprint of the Globe Pequot Press.

10   8   6   4   2 1   3   5   7   9

Printed in the United States of America

This title was published in slightly different form by Random House New Zealand.

Library of Congress Cataloging-in-Publication Data

Quin, Mary.
Kidnapped in Yemen : one woman's amazing escape from captivity / Mary
Quin.
    p. cm.
ISBN 1-59228-728-X (trade cloth)
    1. Kidnapping—Yemen. 2. Terrorism--Yemen. 3. Terrorism—United
States. I. Title.
HV6604.Y46Q85 2005
364.15′4′092--dc22

2005003118

CONTENTS

	Acknowledgments	v
1	Tell Me Again Why You Went to Yemen?	1
2	Touring the Land of Sheba	11
3	Ambush on the Road to Aden	21
4	Surviving the Rescue	37
5	MASH in Mudiyah	57
6	Getting Out of Yemen	65
7	Fallout—Personal and Political	75
8	A Networking Opportunity	89
9	"I Only Gave Orders to Kill the Men"	95
10	The British Boys	103
11	Arrow from Cupid's Bow	111
12	Verdicts in Aden	117
13	Justice in Zinjibar	121
14	Fighting Back with Feminism	131
15	Pursuing the Promised Lands	143
16	The Mullah of Finsbury Park	149
17	Jihad Britannia	163
18	Controlling the Camps	175
19	Inside al-Mansoor Prison	183
20	Return to Abyan	201
21	North to the Future	215
22	Becoming the Hunter	225
	Afterword	237
	Sources	241
	Relevant Names	243

ACKNOWLEDGMENTS

This book is about a journey to Yemen. It is also about a journey through four years of my life. I did not make this journey alone. A remarkably diverse group of people has been there to offer advice, information, perspective, expertise, support, friendship, memories, and love. It would not have been possible to make this journey or to write and publish this book without their help.

In the early days of writing the manuscript, it was my U.S. literary agent, Andrea Pedolsky, who taught me the techniques of blending personal experience, research and secondhand reports into an integrated story. Andrea believed in me as a writer and believed my story deserved to be published. This book would not have happened without her patient coaching, encouragement and advice.

I would like to thank the team at The Lyons Press for their editing, designing, proofing, and production work. Special thanks to my editor, Jay McCullough, who contributed numerous improvements and insights.

My writer's group in Anchorage—Karen Benning, Dawnell Smith, Judy Stoll, and Tara Witterholt—provided valuable feedback during the many months I spent researching and writing this book. Our monthly Sunday meetings were a wonderful source of friendship and humor.

Many people provided me with leads and information that helped me to piece together the events that preceded and followed the kidnapping. In particular I would like to thank Peter Bergen, Sheila Caripico, Nick Childs, Brad Deardorff, Max and Nasrine Gross, Lisa Hughes, Fred Humphries, Duncan Jarrett, Mark Katz, Mike Marks, Malcolm Nance, Kevin O'Shea, Robert Young Pelton, Anna Wuerth, and my Arabic-

English translator. Pat Morris and Margaret Thompson were particularly helpful in sharing their recollections of the kidnapping and filling in details I had missed.

My return research trip to Yemen would not have been possible without the generous support and assistance of former Yemen prime minister Abdel Karim al-Iryani, and Yemen's ambassador to the United States, Abdulwahab Abdulla al-Hajjri. For spending time meeting with me and answering my many questions I would like to thank Badr Basunaid, Khaled Tarik, Bashraheel H. Bashraheel, Mustafa Rajamanar, Martin Lamport, and Barbara Bodine. The governors of the provinces of Aden and Abyan were prominent among the Yemeni government leaders and officials who assisted me in my search for information. Special thanks also to Sameer and to Mohammed Mozeid, who facilitated my meetings and transportation in Yemen, and to the Yemeni soldiers and police who ensured my safe travel.

This book recounts my best recollections, records and research of the kidnapping and the context in which it happened. I recognize that some of my tourmates may remember certain aspects differently but I trust this account will provide new insights and contribute to a sense of closure for them and their families. The remarkable composure and courage demonstrated by all of the hostages in the face of violent death were a great source of strength to me and for that I extend deepest thanks and admiration to them all—Andrew, Brian, Catherine, Chris, Claire, David, Eric, Gill, Laurence, Margaret T, Margaret W, Pat, Peter, Ruth, and Sue.

While many have questioned the wisdom of the rescue operation, it is nonetheless true that dozens of Yemeni soldiers put themselves at risk on my account. For this I am profoundly grateful, especially to those who were wounded, and to the unknown sniper who likely saved my life.

This is also an opportunity to thank the many people who came forward with expressions of concern and acts of caring immediately after the kidnapping and in the subsequent weeks. I am most grateful to the diplomats and staff of the American and British embassies in Sana'a and the British consulate in Aden, whose professionalism and sensitivity were so impressive. The assistance of David Pearce, Margaret Scobey, and Dr.

Chuck Rosenfarb was particularly appreciated. I would like to acknowledge and thank my friend Marilyn Sadler-Bay for taking charge at my home in Rochester during the kidnapping crisis. My thanks also to my family in New Zealand, colleagues and friends at Xerox Corporation, and friends and travelers from all over the world who contacted me.

Lastly I would like to thank my dearest friend and life partner, Ray Kaufman, for the love and adventures we have shared during the years since the kidnapping—and for having the courage to send the fateful e-mail that changed both our lives.

—MARY QUIN
ANCHORAGE, ALASKA
JANUARY 2005

TELL ME AGAIN
WHY YOU WENT TO YEMEN?

The waters separating Africa and Arabia moved with a slow and heavy swell, slapping against the shores of a tiny island 30 miles from the coast of Eritrea. The island was little more than a sandbar, shaped like a grain of rice and seeded by sea oats. Waves broke both ways across the island's pointed tips. On the surface, the water of the Red Sea glittered in the African sun, and I closed my eyes against its brilliance. Floating on my back, I could sense the power of the swell deep below me. Above, the sky was infinite blue, the same relentless blue I had come to expect every day in my short journey through the Horn of Africa.

Voices of fishermen drifted across the water from an open boat moored offshore. Images of Ethiopia flickered through my thoughts: men and women with skin like polished bronze, dressed in garments light and white as cheesecloth; a priest arrayed in vivid yellow robes, standing in the doorway of a church, his hand clutching a jewel-encrusted cross; books depicting black Madonnas, saved for centuries in dusty trunks, their pages leafed with gold. Ethiopia—poor beyond belief, rich beyond measure. In a mere two weeks, I had journeyed back two thousand years. Tomorrow I would travel home.

I rolled off my back and swam a slow breaststroke out from the shore, savoring my last hour at this isolated beach. Apart from this scrap of an island, there was nothing but water in every direction. Behind me to the west was the coast of Eritrea, a country newly carved by will and weapons out of the kingdom of Haile Selassie. One hundred miles ahead, beyond the eastern horizon, lay the land the British called "The Yemen." With my trip through Ethiopia and Eritrea coming to a close, my thoughts were already turning to my next adventure. My curiosity about Yemen was aroused by the stories I had heard from fellow travelers. It was a land of great beauty, they said, and still traditional in its customs. Bordered by Saudi Arabia to the north and the Gulf of Aden to the south, Yemen has a history that lives on in legends shared from generation to generation among its tribal peoples: the home of the Queen of Sheba; the burial place of biblical Job; the source of gold, frankincense and myrrh; *Arabia Felix* ("Fertile Arabia")—an irresistible lure to any adventure traveler. Here, off the coast of Africa, there was nothing separating me from Yemen but the waters of the Red Sea.

Someone called my name. The fishing boat that had delivered me and a dozen other visitors to the tiny island was ready to return to the Eritrean port city of Massawa. I already knew where my next vacation would take me. I would return to this part of the world and visit Yemen, the land that beckoned from beyond the far horizon.

My journey back home took me from the warmth of Africa to the bitter cold of upstate New York. Flights between such distant worlds were the portals between my two lives. My "normal" life was on the course that I had planned: a challenging career in corporate America, a comfortable income, a beautiful 1930s home in the preservation district of Rochester, many good friends, and the independence of being single. My other life was lived in the small pockets of time when I could disappear to the farthest corners of the earth. Feeling alien and anonymous, I could step off a plane into a totally different world and be free to explore at will all the sounds, sights, and smells of a totally different culture in a totally new landscape.

The memories of more than fifty journeys were on display at my Rochester home. African masks and a warrior fetish, embedded with rusty chips of iron, dominated my sunroom. A Bedouin face veil trimmed with coins and a Sumatran ceremonial skirt threaded with gold took pride of place in the formal living room. Heavy silver jewelry, embedded with cerulean and amber, lay on a sideboard in the dining room, a ready reminder of my travels

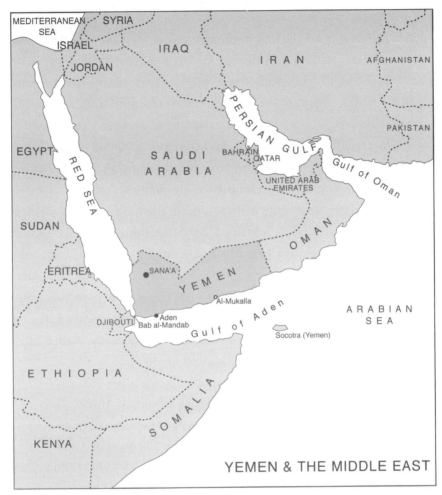

Figure 1

through the Silk Road countries of Central Asia. A photograph of a Burmese woman, sifting rice in the doorway of her thatched hut, greeted me with her smile each time I came through my own kitchen door.

Even with four weeks of vacation each year, it was increasingly difficult to get time away from my job for these journeys of discovery. I envied the Europeans for their more civilized attitude towards vacation time and travel. It would probably be another year before I could escape on my next adventure. As soon as I returned from Ethiopia in the first week of January 1998, I was quickly swept back into the day-to-day urgencies of managing a business unit at Xerox Corporation.

My career had always been important to me and I had never felt much interest in raising a family. I grew up in a small town in New Zealand, the seventh of nine children, and knew from a young age that I did not want the life of domesticity my mother had chosen. There was too much else to see in the world, and my ticket to discover it was education. When Northwestern University in a suburb of Chicago offered me a place in its materials engineering PhD program, I worked evening and weekend jobs, washing dishes in a university cafeteria and sorting glasses on a factory production line to save enough money for my airfare to America.

After my early career years in metallurgical engineering and research, I went back to university and obtained my MBA from Harvard Business School. Ten years later, in 1998, I had achieved the goal I had originally set for myself—to run a business unit or division in a Fortune 500 company—but I had given little thought to what might lie beyond that goal. Unexpectedly, at forty-five years of age, I was beginning to feel an itch to veer off the traditional corporate career path. Entries in my journal captured the early stirrings of uncertainty about my future.

> I'm feeling very at risk of failing in my job due to lack of focus. Questions about whether I'm doing what I should/want to do with my life are distracting me from putting heart and soul into the job. I see the possibility of losing future promotions to much more singularly focused colleagues . . . Do I have the courage to walk away from the financial handcuffs at Xerox? I'm not ready to do it now because I don't know what I want to do instead . . . Is there a different industry (one I would have more passion about) where my curiosity about the unknown, the diversity of the world, the creation of totally new ideas, recognition for changing the world—would have more chance for expression?

I jotted down some of the possibilities I could imagine: stay at Xerox; buy a company; go after a CEO job at a smaller company; take a year off to study and travel; run a nonprofit; politics?

There was no urgency to choose one of these options. In fact, from a stock-option perspective, it made sense to stay at Xerox—at least for another couple of years. Perhaps by then it would be obvious what I wanted to do next.

Early in the summer of 1998, I began to think seriously about planning my next vacation. The Christmas and New Year holidays were a quiet time at work and many employees took time off. Except for the sales reps frantically closing year-end deals with customers and the factories loading every last copier order onto trucks, Xerox facilities would empty out over the vacation period. With my relatives far away in New Zealand and little interest in spending Christmas alone, it was a good time for me to travel—preferably to somewhere warm, with limited e-mail or voice-mail access. Yemen fitted the bill perfectly.

I contacted a travel agency in California that represented a British tour company, Explore. I often traveled independently—either alone or with a friend—but had found tours a more efficient way of seeing some countries, especially where driving a rental car is not an option. I had used Explore for Burma, Uzbekistan, and Ethiopia, having found its tours reliable and good value for the money. I was in luck, my agent told me. Explore had a two-week tour of Yemen scheduled for a December 21 departure. The tour was limited to nineteen travelers, and there were a few places still available. I faxed in my reservation with a credit card number for the deposit.

Once I had booked the trip to Yemen, I gave it little further thought apart from reserving my flights to Sana'a, Yemen's capital city. It was still too early to apply for a visa and, mentally, I moved Yemen on to the back burner. My management responsibilities at Xerox and my involvement in two nonprofit initiatives kept me busy through the summer months. Between working on a fund-raising plan for Garth Fagan Dance, where I served on the board of trustees, and running the 100 Heroines Project, there was neither time nor need to think about events as far into the future as December.

The situation changed on August 7. The American embassies in Kenya and Tanzania were attacked with massive car bombs, leaving

224 people dead and over five thousand injured. The two coordinated explosions took place just minutes apart. I watched on CNN as rescuers struggled to recover survivors and bodies from devastated buildings and burning cars in Nairobi and Dar es Salaam. Although the attacks targeted Americans, local Africans suffered by far the worst in terms of casualties. All but twelve of the dead were non-American victims. The terrorists' van, loaded with explosives and left in an alley near the United States embassy in Nairobi, did far more damage to the adjacent Ufundi Cooperative Building (housing offices and a secretarial school) than it did to the embassy. As windows shattered in buildings up to half a mile away, many Kenyans were injured by flying glass.

No one claimed responsibility for the car-bomb attacks, but investigators' suspicions quickly focused on Islamic Jihad in Egypt. Its leader was Dr. Ayman al-Jawahiri, who was believed to be in Afghanistan and working in association with Osama bin Laden. According to a *Washington Post* article, Islamic Jihad had warned that it was planning to retaliate "in a language [Americans] will understand" for the role the U.S. had played in extraditing three jihad members out of Albania and back to Cairo. A May 26 statement by Osama bin Laden had threatened terrorist action against United States military and civilian targets. Americans were advised by the U.S. State Department to avoid travel in countries where bin Laden was known to have affiliations—countries such as Sudan and Yemen. I was aware of these advisories but did not cancel my trip. After all, the State Department received about thirty thousand such threats every year. My departure date was still four months away, giving me time to monitor the situation and keep my options open.

I was vaguely aware of Osama bin Laden prior to the embassy bombings, but the events of August 1998 marked the point at which (in my household at least) he became a household name. I was less concerned about bin Laden upsetting my personal travel plans than angered by the threat that he and his like-minded fundamentalists presented to the cause of global women's rights. During 1997 and 1998 I spearheaded the 100 Heroines Project to recognize and assist women around the world who were putting themselves at risk on behalf of women's rights. Along with several other Rochester women who, like me, had attended the United Nations Fourth World Conference on Women in Beijing in 1995, I launched the project to coincide with the 150th anniversary of the first women's rights convention held near Rochester, in Seneca Falls. As we gathered data on women's rights activists around the world, it became clear that the most extreme repression of women was taking place in Afghanistan under the Taliban. Extremist, militant Muslims were using Islam as their excuse to wage war on the freedom and independence of Afghan women. Thirteen million Afghans were banned from education and employment, and sentenced to virtual house arrest. The situation seemed to get very little news coverage in the U.S., even though it should have deeply concerned at least one half of the American population. Osama bin Laden and his Taliban hosts emerged on my radar screen in 1998 as much in the context of their war on women as of their terrorist acts against the United States.

Far from discouraging me from visiting Muslim countries my involvement in women's rights increased my desire to see more of the Middle East and experience its cultures. I find much to admire in the elegance of Arab architecture, the warmth of Middle Eastern hospitality, and the beauty of the Arabic language—not to mention that Middle Eastern food is my favorite cuisine. I particularly value any opportunity to speak with Muslim women, and to understand their varied points of view about their roles in society and the meaning of religion in their lives. The trip to Yemen offered a chance to explore all these aspects in one of the most intriguing and beautiful countries of the Arab world. Moreover, another nonprofit organization on whose board I serve, the Center for Development and Population Activities (CEDPA) in Washington DC, was considering introducing programs for women and girls in Yemen. I was hoping while there to meet a diplomat from the Dutch embassy who was strongly advocating CEDPA's involvement. With so many personal interests driving me, there would need to be a strong indication of a specific personal risk before I would abandon my trip to Yemen. I continued my effort to learn some basic Arabic by listening to language tapes in my car.

After the embassy bombings, the situation did not improve. On August 20, the United States launched cruise missiles against a paramilitary training camp in Afghanistan and the Shifa pharmaceutical factory in Sudan. U.S. officials selected both targets on the presumption that they were part of bin Laden's terrorism infrastructure. The Afghan training camp was located at Khost, near Afghanistan's border with Pakistan, and U.S. officials thought that bin Laden and many of his senior staff might be in residence there. The Sudanese factory was believed by American intelligence to be doing double duty as a chemical weapons plant. Although U.S. administration officials later described these strikes as the start of "the real war on terrorism," some members of the U.S. Congress questioned whether the military action was merely an attempt to divert public attention from the Monica Lewinsky affair that continued to haunt President Bill Clinton and dominate every news broadcast. Regardless of motive, the unleashing of seventy-five Tomahawk missiles was hardly a war on terrorism. At best, it was an isolated retaliation that served little purpose. It failed to eliminate bin Laden and wasn't followed up by sustained antiterrorism action.

Toward the final two months of the year, I reached the point when I needed to apply for a Yemen visa. Before doing so, I contacted Explore's representatives in California to confirm that the tour was still going ahead. There did not appear to be any terrorist-related developments in Yemen, but I wanted to gauge whether the tour was at risk of being cancelled before paying the fees for a visa. Explore planned to proceed with the tour, my agent told me, and if I cancelled I would lose the full cost of the trip. It was not the financial loss that mattered to me. Had I really felt there was more than a miniscule chance of anything going seriously wrong, the $2,100 land-tour fee would have been a small price to pay for taking the prudent course. The reality was that I had always taken risks traveling, and this trip was no more risky than many other destinations I had enjoyed. In fact, it was probably far less risky than some. In the spring of 1994, I had spent over a week in Rwanda, leaving the country only a few days before a horrifying genocide engulfed that Central African nation. In the church grounds where I had camped in the capital city of Kigali, I had watched a joyous Tutsi wedding celebration. Within weeks, hundreds of Tutsi were slaughtered by their Hutu countrymen in that same church. By comparison, Yemen did not seem too risky.

Thus far, 1998 had been a stressful year at work and I was in need of a break from relentless meetings. The three small businesses I had been assigned to manage at Xerox that year were proving to be an awkward mix, with major political and ego battles getting in the way of real accomplishment. Although the 100 Heroines Project was going extremely well, it demanded a much greater investment of time than I had ever imagined when I started it. Spending two weeks in a warm, sunny, and remote location was just what I needed. I filled in and mailed the paperwork for my Yemen visa. By November 18 when the visa was issued, I perceived that the only unusual risk about Yemen—beyond the normal risks of travel in any third-world country—was the incidence of kidnapping. Yemen's tribes had a reputation for kidnapping foreigners and demanding some benefit from the government in exchange for the hostages' release. But over seventy thousand tourists visited Yemen annually and perhaps a dozen were kidnapped. None of these hostages had ever been harmed. The odds of being kidnapped were about one in ten thousand; hardly a risk at all.

On December 17, I had already started packing for my trip when the United States and Britain launched a four-day air offensive against Iraq. In an interview the next day with Katie Couric on the Today Show, U.S. Secretary of State Madeleine Albright explained that the purpose of the air strikes was "to degrade Saddam Hussein's ability to develop and deliver weapons of mass destruction and to degrade his ability to threaten his neighbors." The attacks on Iraq were triggered by a breakdown in the United Nations' weapons inspection program. This was one more step in the decade-long standoff between Iraq and the UN that had started with Iraq's invasion of Kuwait on August 2, 1990. Trade sanctions were immediately imposed on Iraq by the UN, with the condition that weapons of mass destruction must be eliminated before the sanctions would be lifted. In the spring of 1991—after a 44-day war between Iraq and an American-led coalition force over Iraq's invasion of Kuwait—a drawn-out process of weapons inspections by UN personnel was initiated. Inspections proceeded slowly for seven years, with Saddam Hussein using every possible means to conceal, distract and delay. In February and again in October of 1998, Iraq totally blocked the weapons inspection effort, only to allow resumption after further negotiations and threats. When Iraq still failed to cooperate as promised, weapons inspection teams finally left the country in mid-December, and the United States made good its earlier threats of air strikes.

Direct hostilities between the United States and a Muslim country clearly did little to reduce the threat of anti-American violence by Islamic terrorists. But, from my perspective, Iraq was a long way from Yemen—Baghdad and Aden are 1,400 miles apart—and the attacks on Iraq had no direct connection with Osama bin Laden or with Islamic Jihad. The risk of traveling in Yemen remained highly generalized. Yes, it was possible that terrorists might attack an American facility in Yemen while I was there, but the odds that such an attack would happen during my trip—and that it would happen in the exact place where I happened to be—were even smaller than the risks of a tribal kidnapping. What kind of wimp lets a remote chance of something bad happening dissuade her from an adventure? Not me. I continued packing. As I usually do when visiting countries with anti-American factions (and that's a long list of countries), I packed both my New Zealand and American passports.

On my last day of work I received a phone call from one of the executive vice presidents at Xerox. Effective January 4, 1999, I would be put in charge of running the $1.5 billion Color Solutions Business Unit. It was an unexpected and very big jump in responsibility and visibility. Color was the future of the company. I had previously led a corporate team that developed the company's color strategy. Now I would have the chance to implement a big part of Xerox's vision for the future. Perhaps this was the break I needed to move beyond my growing sense of dissatisfaction and boredom with life in corporate America. I boarded the first of the three flights that would take me from Rochester to Sana'a, feeling on top of the world. Ahead of me were two weeks of freedom to explore a fascinating country, followed by a great new job to sink my teeth into when I came home. It doesn't get much better than this, I thought, as I settled down for the long flight with a good book and a glass of wine.

2

TOURING THE
LAND OF SHEBA

Early afternoon on December 21, I joined eighteen other jet-lagged travelers from Britain, Australia and the United States in the top-floor restaurant of the Sam City Hotel in Sana'a. Many of us had arrived together at about 4:00 AM on the overnight flight from London. By the time we reached the hotel and were assigned rooms, we were glad to have the morning hours free to catch up on sleep. I was assigned a room with another American woman, Margaret Thompson, who was a little older than I and also employed by a large U.S. company. My first impression was that the blonde, softly spoken woman with a calm demeanor and similar professional background would be an ideal roommate.

Dave Nott, an outgoing, sandy-haired 29-year-old from England, would lead the tour using the local services of the Al-Mahmoun Travel Agency in Sana'a. Dave had picked us up from the airport that morning and taken us by minivan to the hotel. At the orientation meeting after lunch, he explained that he had several years' experience leading tours for Explore but that this was his first assignment in Yemen.

Dave ran through the logistics of how the tour would be conducted. We would travel around Yemen in five Toyota Land Cruisers, owned and operated by Yemeni drivers who were employed by Al-Mahmoun. The lead driver, Sammi (the only one who spoke English), and the other four drivers, Abdul and three Mohammeds, grinned and nodded cheerfully at their new batch of passengers. Like all Yemeni men, they carried ornate curved daggers, called jambiyas, in the front of their belts, and wore shabby sports coats over colorful wraparound skirts known as futas.

Our convoy of five vehicles would follow the itinerary described in the Explore catalogue, and we would stay in hotels along the way, Dave explained. Detailed information on each day's program, including departure times, would be posted in the hotel lobby the night before. Dave mentioned that the holy month of Ramadan was in progress and created some constraints regarding meals. Although non-Muslims were not expected to observe the practice of not eating and drinking anything (not even water) between sunrise and sunset, it would be wise to avoid obvious consumption in public places. After checking that we all had the required health and travel insurance, Dave led us out of the hotel for an afternoon walking tour of Sana'a's Old Quarter.

Tourism was emerging as an important, if fledgling, industry for Yemen. The country's exotic traditional culture, unique architecture and dramatic scenery attracted adventure travelers from western Europe, New Zealand, Australia and, to a lesser extent, the United States. After Yemen's brief civil war in 1994, European tour companies cautiously began to offer organized tours, enabling visitors to access remote areas of the country that would be difficult to reach independently.

Yemen's government encouraged the tourist industry. It provided much-needed jobs and a source of foreign capital. Developers built new hotels and Yemeni-owned travel agencies sprang up to provide local services and serve as subcontractors to the European tour operators. Typically, visitors to Yemen were experienced travelers seeking destinations "off the beaten track," and those of us gathered at the Sam City Hotel were no exception. Most had traveled independently in dozens of countries. Like me, several of our group were repeat customers of Explore. The timing of the tour, over the Christmas and New Year holiday period, made this particular trip attractive to business professionals and educators who were able to get time away from work. The tour was fully booked and only one passenger had yet to arrive: Andrew Thirsk, a 35-year-old Australian who was expected on a flight early the next morning.

Like a bunch of overage schoolkids, we trailed along behind Dave for our first look at the city we had all dreamed of seeing. My instinctive dislike of being herded in a group kicked in, but I needn't have worried. No sooner had we reached the edge of the Old Quarter than Dave suggested we should go off on our own if we wished. We quickly spread out, mingling with the crowds flowing through Bab al-Yemen, the great entrance gate built by the Turks in the 1870s. Old Sana'a is a walled city with enchanting seven- and eight-story tower houses that have changed little in centuries. Tradition holds that the city was founded by Shem, the son of Noah, over four thousand years ago. In the souks (markets), women shrouded in black chadors drifted among the huge sacks of pungent spices or fingered the bolts of fabrics unraveling softly in the breeze. In the gloomy darkness of a shop lit only by an open window, a camel plodded in circles driving an olive mill. Men sitting on their haunches in the narrow alleyways haggled over the quality and price of qat, the mildly narcotic leaves Yemenis love to chew. Handcarts piled with denim jeans or pirated cassette tapes were the only reminders that we had not been transported back several thousand years to a scene from the Arabian Nights.

Built of stone and clay, the reddish brown walls of the tower houses taper inward toward the upper floors. Delicate patterns drawn in white gypsum plaster decorate the wood-framed windows and balconies. At street level, massive foundations of volcanic rock enclose the family livestock. Each of the floors is occupied by one branch of an extended family and all share the use of the rooftop kitchen. The top floor is the preserve of the men, who while away the late afternoon and early evening hours chewing qat as sunlight filters through the stained-glass windows. It was not hard to see why travelers are drawn to Yemen. The mystery to me is why anyone would miss it.

Margaret and I wandered around together, getting to know a little about each other as we absorbed the sights, sounds, and smells of this extraordinary and ancient city. Originally from Texas, Margaret was living in London, where she worked in information technology for the oil company Conoco. I learned she was divorced with one adult daughter. As the sun dropped lower in the sky and the narrow streets darkened in the shadows of the tall houses, we realized we had no idea where we were or how to get back to our hotel. Our first attempts to ask directions met with little success but, using our map of the city, we determined from the position of the sun the likely direction of the Sam City Hotel. Leaving the Old Quarter walls through an unfamiliar gate, we stopped again to ask directions. Half a dozen Yemeni men crowded around us, jostling to look at our outstretched map and offer their opinions. None of them spoke more than a few words of English, which limited their ability to read our map and our ability to understand their explanations. Amid much laughter and good-humored debate, they seemed to reach consensus, so we walked in the direction they pointed and within a few blocks saw the Sam City sign.

Over dinner, I had a chance to get to know the other people on the tour. Our group consisted of four couples and eleven solo travelers, a total of eleven women and eight men. Only Mohammed Babiker, who was traveling with his wife Susan, was Muslim and spoke Arabic. Babiker, a physicist with British citizenship, was originally from Sudan. Not surprisingly, since Explore was a British company, the tour group was predominantly British. In addition to the fourteen Britons, there were two Australians and three Americans (who included me and my roommate Margaret Thompson); my dual citizenship meant New Zealand was also represented on the tour.

Looking around the restaurant, I noted that most of my fellow travelers appeared to be in their forties and fifties. Two younger faces belonged to the Australian Catherine Spence and a Scottish woman, Ruth Williamson. Catherine was vivacious and confident, with long black hair pulled back from her pretty, slightly plump face. Softly spoken Ruth was classically Celtic with freckles and short red hair. It crossed my mind that Ruth and I could have passed for sisters, although Ruth was taller than my 5 feet 3 inches. The group included a second Margaret: Margaret Whitehouse, a tall, slim woman with curly gray hair and sparkling blue eyes. She and her husband Laurence Whitehouse—both teachers—shared sunny dispositions, natural enthusiasm for life, and many interests. They appeared to be still in love after many years of marriage.

The two other couples in the group were less obviously well matched. Peter Rowe, a slender, scholarly man, was a mathematics professor with a sharp wit and (I suspected) little tolerance for fools. I assumed Peter was British but would discover much later that he was originally from Canada and, like me, held dual citizenship. His wife Claire Marston was fifteen years younger and had dark hair and olive skin. She was a university lecturer, too, specializing in business. Immediately after the trip, Claire would be transferring to a new position at Durham University where Peter was already tenured. Chris Cheeseman, a warehouse worker, had a typically English sense of humor and friendly, forthright manner but seemed a little distant from his partner Gill, a moody woman who did not seem totally happy to be coming on this trip.

Two other English women, Sue Mattocks and Pat Morris, were cordial and self-contained. I would later find dry humor and warm hearts behind their classic British reserve. Pat was a professional musician with a major orchestra and Sue taught religious studies at a girls' high school.

Brian Smith, a genial 52-year-old postal worker with thinning grey hair and ruddy complexion, was doing his best to set at ease the chemistry teacher Eric Firkins, who never seemed quite sure where to direct his nervous glances or position his awkward, gangling frame. The stern and officious David Holmes clearly had no such social uncertainties and it came as no surprise to learn that he was the retired headmaster of a high school.

There seemed to be an abundance of Davids. The third American, Carolyn Gay, was accompanied by her boyfriend David Leadbetter, who had not been able to get a place on the fully booked tour and had made independent transport arrangements: he would travel by private car along the same route as the tour while not formally being part of it. The couple hoped that there might be a cancellation at the last minute, but their hopes were dashed when the delayed Australian did indeed turn up.

I met Andrew Thirsk when I went to the lobby looking for bottled water early the next morning. A tall, tanned young man with an Australian accent was politely trying to make himself understood to the receptionist. Guessing he was our missing passenger, I introduced myself and offered to show him the way to the dining room where Dave Nott and the

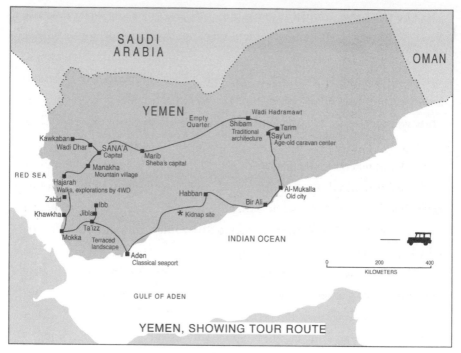

Figure 2

group would soon be gathering for breakfast. My attempts to make conversation with Andrew generated little response, but I remembered how exhausted I had felt when I arrived the previous day and figured he was just too tired and jet-lagged to talk. Unlike the rest of us, Andrew would not have the luxury of a free morning to sleep before heading out in the Land Cruisers for a day of sightseeing.

The first week of our tour proceeded according to plan, following the route illustrated in the map in Figure 2. From the beginning, Dave Nott encouraged his clients to swap around and travel with different passengers each day. The idea was to ensure everyone in the group got to know each other, including all the drivers, and to avoid the formation of cliques.

Although only Sammi spoke English, our drivers soon communicated their distinct personalities as they expertly drove the Land Cruisers through all manner of road and traffic conditions. The smallest of them earned the nickname "Mad Mohammed" for his heart-stopping driving techniques and feisty attitude. "Yellow Mohammed" was older, with a

16

stocky frame and weathered face. His nickname reflected the unusual color of his khafiya, the commonly red or black checked cloth worn as a head-covering throughout the Arab world. I noticed Yellow Mohammed kept an AK-47 assault rifle on the seat beside him, loosely covered with a blanket. He seemed like a man who could hold his own in any fight. The third Mohammed, "Mohammed with Glasses," had the look of a college professor and a genteel manner. Abdul seemed the quietest, but when the wind whipped up his travel-worn jacket I glimpsed a concealed handgun in a hip holster. The drivers stayed in the same hotels as we did, but usually took their meals separately and went off on their own in the evenings.

Yemen was everything we hoped it would be: palaces perched on top of rocky outcrops; camels moving silently across the vast desert of the Empty Quarter; skyscrapers built of mud in the walled oasis towns of the Hadramawt valley; freshly caught fish cooked with spices in the sea-side town of Al-Mukalla. In spite of diesel fumes and satellite dishes, Kalashnikovs and cell phones, Yemen was still truly *Arabia Felix*. One of my favorite days was the journey across the Empty Quarter. This vast sandy desert occupying much of central and northern Yemen is a favorite hunting ground for bandits and kidnappers. As a result, most of the private and commercial traffic crossing the desert gather together on the outskirts of New Marib early in the morning to join an armed convoy. Dave stressed the importance of being on time, because we would not be able to cross the desert if we failed to rendezvous with the convoy and our Bedouin guides.

Not long after sunrise, our five vehicles pulled up on the main road north of New Marib, alongside about three dozen trucks and cars. This bustling small town 125 miles east of Sana'a, in the province of Marib, is the gateway to a number of ancient archaeological sites—including Sabaean temples and the Great Dam of Marib, dating from the eighth century BC. After waiting nearly an hour, the mélange of well-used and heavily laden vehicles started out along the road. Twenty miles on, just beyond the village of Safir, the road simply disappeared. Abdul and the three Mohammeds immediately set to reducing air pressure in the tires, so that the Land Cruisers would travel more easily on the unpaved sandy surface.

With no road to constrain us, the convoy spread out and within an hour or two we had lost sight of all vehicles, other than our own Land Cruisers and the pickup truck driven by our Bedouin guide.

The idea of traveling in a protected caravan seemed to have disintegrated.

I truly felt we were in the desert lands of Arabia when we came across a small herd of wild camels. They seemed indifferent to us as we drove slowly towards them and stopped to take photographs. Further into the vast, featureless landscape, we came upon a single camel mothering a baby. Less than a day old, according to our guide, the charcoal-gray newborn struggled to keep its balance on knobby, wobbly legs as it reached for its mother's milk. That any life could survive in this dry and treeless place seemed remarkable. During the eight hours we drove across this wilderness—known in Arabic as Ramlat as Sab'atayn—we saw only two signs of human habitation. One was a nomad's tent in the distance, the other a deserted military outpost where we stopped to eat the bread and fruit we had brought with us for lunch. To the immediate south was the town and province of Shabwah, but our destination was further east in the magnificent oasis towns of the Hadramawt region.

The Wadi Hadramawt is a broad valley, 100 miles long and a mile wide. Its year-round ground water and seasonal flooding create a fertile valley in an otherwise arid landscape. Our tour allowed time for us to explore several of the ancient towns in the valley. Outside Shibam we scrambled up the face of a rocky plateau for a view of the town's five- to seven-story high skyscrapers. About 500 of these remarkable, closely packed buildings rise up from the desert floor, their whitewashed upper floors a brilliant contrast to the dun-colored earth. I handed my camera to Andrew who obligingly photographed me in front of the famous backdrop.

In Say'un, the largest town of the Hadramawt, we explored elegant mosques and palaces. Walking from one imposing building to another, I was grateful for the shade of Say'un's many palm trees. Children would approach us with shy smiles and giggles, but the few women we saw were often wrapped in black chadors or colorful tribal veils and quickly disappeared behind the brightly colored doors of their family compounds.

On Christmas Eve, we crowded into Laurence and Margaret White-house's hotel room. They had brought duty-free bottles of wine and sherry and traditional English fruitcake to share. Drinking from polystyrene tumblers or, in my case, a battered metal Sierra Club cup, we celebrated our Christmas in Yemen. Ruth Williamson joined in, although she was still suffering from a stomach upset that had caused her to miss most meals and subsist on little more than oranges. In the spirit of Yuletide cheer, even the overbearing headmaster David Holmes and the awkwardly anxious Eric Firkins were tolerated with good humor.

Christmas Day dinner was a modest affair in a seafood restaurant where clean newspapers, spread on rickety wooden tables, served as table-cloths. Since the newspapers were in Arabic, we did not even gain the benefit of catching up on news. Past experience of traveling in non-Christian countries during Christmas holidays had taught me to bring along a touch of tradition and I shared my box of Christmas crackers. At the Christmas dinner table during my childhood in New Zealand, my family had always followed the English custom of pulling these brightly colored paper tubes filled with trinkets, paper hats and jokes. Wearing paper hats looked ridiculous enough back home at a traditional Christmas meal, but even more absurd while eating fish in a Yemen restaurant during Ramadan. Our drivers were enjoying cigarettes at a table near the entrance to the restaurant. I offered crackers and tried to demonstrate how two people each grasp an end and pull them apart. From their confused expressions and the difficulty they had pulling the crackers open, I decided that this is one tradition that does not translate easily across cultures.

From the oasis towns of Hadramawt, we traveled south out of the mountains toward the Gulf of Aden. We could already sense the salty breezes from the ocean when our drivers pulled off the road not far from the town of Bir Ali, and followed a rough track that led to a beach. An expanse of brilliant white sand and blue water beckoned. After our travels through arid mountains and deserts, the opportunity for a swim was irresistible. We were several miles from the nearest village or road and there was no one around who might take offence. While our drivers went to one side of the vehicles for their midday prayers, we found privacy behind some rocks to change into swimsuits. The water was divine: crystal-clear and warm. I drifted on my back, buoyed by the gentle swells. The sky arched in a perfect blue dome above me. It was the same cloudless sky I remembered from one year before, when I floated in the Red Sea off the coast of Eritrea and first dreamed of visiting Yemen. I would be perfectly happy, I thought, to blow off the rest of the tour and simply camp out and swim here for the rest of my vacation. Those few idyllic hours on the beach near Bir Ali proved to be our last safe haven.

3

AMBUSH ON
THE ROAD TO ADEN

Our convoy of Toyota Land Cruisers left the town of Habban in Shab-wah province at 8:30 AM on December 28 as planned. I chose to travel in the fourth vehicle that morning, sitting directly behind Yellow Mohammed. Ruth was next to me in the middle of the back seat with Gill to her right and Pat in front. I was pleased to be in the same vehicle as Ruth. The Scottish redhead had been quiet during the trip so far but she assured us that she was getting over her early stomach upset. This long travel day might be a chance to get to know her better. Our tour leader Dave was in the front vehicle as usual with lead driver Sammi. Mo-hammed and Susan Babiker were traveling with them. While waiting for everyone to get their luggage into the vehicles, I casually asked Dave if we would have a police escort that day. Dave replied that he didn't know; the escort decision would be left up to the authorities in each region we passed through.

According to the itinerary, we would travel 200 miles on December 28, driving west across the harsh deserts of Shabwah and Abyan provinces, to reach the port city of Aden by nightfall. Crossing the barren beauty of Shabwah, we stopped a couple of times to photograph stunning views of mountain plateaus and canyons. The scenery reminded me of the Ameri-can Southwest. As usual during these photo stops, I would try out my few words of Arabic on our drivers. At one lookout point, I passed by the vehi-cle driven by Mohammed with Glasses and he called me over. Sitting in the driver's seat, he pulled out photos of his children and showed them to me through the open window. In my limited words of Arabic, I was able to ask the names and ages of his two sons and Mohammed beamed with pride as he replied. But he shook his head when I asked if he had a photo of his wife: it would not be proper to show a photo of his wife in a land where most women were still fully veiled in public.

Continuing toward Aden our convoy drove through a bustling market in a small village. We paid little attention to the sound of a single gunshot as our vehicles eased through the jostling crowd of tribesmen, merchants, and donkeys that spilled over into the road. Members of another tour group buying food in the market were visible in the crowd, and one of them waved to us. The crowd thinned out and the convoy accelerated out of the village into the open desert again. Several miles away to our right, the broad, flat expanse of desert was bounded by a mountain range, its peaks reaching to about three thousand feet. The faded yellow rock faces were streaked in ferrous pinks and shimmered in the hazy dust stirred up by passing trucks. To our left, the land stretched south toward the Gulf of Aden, a landscape rumpled with eroded hills and canyons that camel trains and nomads had passed through for millennia. This main route from the Hadramawt valley to Aden was now well used by a steady flow of trucks and battered cars. We thought nothing of it when a white pickup truck, its bed crammed full of men, pulled onto the road between our first and second vehicles. The men's faces were covered by their khafiyas, but this was the way travelers in open trucks usually protected themselves from the dust. The pickup traveled with us toward Aden for about half a mile, then swerved sideways, blocking the path of our second Land Cruiser. Suddenly, several rifle shots cracked across the emptiness of the desert. Yellow Mohammed downshifted fast and, muttering a few words of Arabic, reached for the AK-47 on the seat beside him. Looking past Yellow Mohammed's shoulder, I saw our third Land Cruiser had stopped some hundred yards in front of us. Three armed men were surrounding it and gesturing to its driver, Mad Mohammed, to get out. We were too far back to hear their voices, but body language conveyed their aggression. Our lead vehicle continued on ahead, unaware that anything was amiss.

Yellow Mohammed's powerful shoulders were tense. His left hand grasped the door handle and his right closed around the stock of his rifle. The veins were taut under his leathery skin. Gill, Ruth and Pat were silent, their bodies leaning forward, watching. I knew at once that this was an ambush and we were about to be kidnapped. My first instinct was to escape, now, before anyone saw me. The passenger door to my left opened on to the middle of the road where there was no shelter. Ruth and Gill blocked my way to the other door. Could all three of us get out unobserved? Unlikely. I looked back to my left. Could I drop down beside the vehicle, then crawl under it and hide in the scrappy shrubs at the right side of the road? The skeletal trees there afforded little cover. I turned to check the road behind us. The last of our convoy, driven by Mohammed with Glasses, had also stopped. Yellow Mohammed eased the Land Cruiser into reverse and edged slowly backwards. For a few moments, I thought he might be able to back up far enough to make a turn and escape the ambush but more armed men came running toward us from all directions, shouting and firing shots into the air. I abandoned any idea of escaping unseen. I did consider taking photos with the camera I had on my lap, but quickly thought better of that idea, too. These guys probably wouldn't appreciate being caught on film while conducting an armed ambush.

A tall Yemeni in a green fatigue jacket, his face covered by his red and white checked khafiya, rapped the barrel of his automatic weapon against Yellow Mohammed's door, shouting and demanding the driver's gun. Yellow Mohammed shouted back angrily and showed no sign of giving up his weapon. Another kidnapper opened Pat's door and reached across her lap to grab the rifle, but still Yellow Mohammed fought back. Pat shrank back against the seat as the two men on either side of her wrestled with the automatic rifle. More armed men surrounded our four vehicles from all sides. A short, chubby one, who was swaggering down the middle of the road with two belts of ammunition slung bandit-style across his potbelly, seemed to be giving directions. Another carried across his shoulder a 3-foot-long metal tube, which I later learned was a rocket-propelled grenade-launcher. I counted about eighteen men, most of them wearing headscarves wrapped across their faces. Suddenly, I remembered something my detective father

23

had told me many years before: If you ever witness a crime, pay attention to the time that it happens. I glanced at my watch. It was three minutes before 11:00 AM. Against the desert background, the scene reminded me of a B-grade cowboy movie. My reaction was fascination rather than fear. After all, I knew no foreign hostages had ever been harmed in a Yemen kidnapping.

Yellow Mohammed lost the struggle over his rifle and was dragged out of the Land Cruiser and onto the road. Two attackers were now shouting at him and grabbing at the jambiya in his belt. Yellow Mohammed pushed them back, refusing to part with his only remaining weapon and the symbol of Yemeni manhood. Behind us, Mohammed with Glasses was being frog-marched from his vehicle and forced up onto the rear bumper of ours. Abdul, driver of the second vehicle, walked slowly past us, blood running down the right side of his face. The tall Yemeni who had demanded Yellow Mohammed's gun got in the driver's seat of our vehicle and stashed his Kalashnikov between the seat and the door, its barrel pointing directly toward me. Another kidnapper climbed in beside Pat in front and a third crammed into the back seat next to Gill, squeezing us all to the left and pushing me hard up against the passenger door. At least one of the gang was on the roof, his dusty sandaled foot dangling down outside my window. Yellow Mohammed had joined Mohammed with Glasses on the rear bumper. Our convoy was on its way again. The ambush had taken between five and seven minutes.

Only the front vehicle in our convoy of five Land Cruisers had escaped. In it was our tour leader with the only driver who spoke English and the only tourist who spoke Arabic. Dave would later explain to me that, as soon as he and Sammi realized something was seriously wrong, they quickly debated what to do. Seeing the number of armed men surrounding our vehicles, Sammi urged Dave to flee the area and get help, knowing there was nothing they could do to assist us. The best thing they could do was to find police and raise the alarm as quickly as possible.

A mile down the road our captured convoy approached one of the security checkpoints that punctuate Yemen's highways. The kidnappers mounted on the roofs of each vehicle fired shots into the air and the convoy barreled straight through the flimsy barricade. Soldiers abandoned their post and ran for their lives towards a shack at the side of the road. So much for security. We continued along the main road toward Aden for about ten minutes, then the convoy swerved left onto a rock-strewn track, which cut south into the desert. As the Land Cruiser lurched over the rutted path, I was conscious of the dull eye of the renegade driver's automatic rifle, which he had stashed between his seat and door, its barrel pointing casually at my chest. I wondered if an AK-47 had a safety lock and whether its owner would bother to use it. I badly wanted to reach out and push the barrel away, but I knew any attempt to touch the gun could be dangerously misunderstood. During that jolting, forty-minute journey across the desert, my greatest fear was death by accidental discharge.

Gill, Ruth and I exchanged a few words but the kidnapper in the back seat stabbed his forefinger toward his mouth, gesturing for us to be silent. The Land Cruiser behind us became stuck in the winding gravel track several times, until the kidnappers replaced their incompetent driver with one of ours. I tried to watch for landmarks in the terrain in case I should need to find my way back to the road on my own. Focusing on the landscape also helped distract my thoughts from that gun. After about half an hour, the vehicles came to a stop and six of the kidnappers climbed out. The chubby one shouted directions and a small group armed with a machine gun was left behind to set up a defense post. The site they chose was on an isolated hill, about 150 feet high, providing a view of the incoming track and surrounding desert. I was becoming increasingly convinced that this was not a conventional tribal kidnapping. This gang seemed too well armed, too militaristic. Of course it was hard to judge what was "normal." I had never been kidnapped before.

Our four vehicles bounced along the track for a further ten minutes before coming to a stop near a cluster of trees—at Point 1 in my sketch of the camp in Figure 3. Beyond the trees was an open area cleared of rocks and brush. Low dirt walls, about two feet high and broad enough to stand on, identified this open space as fields, used for crops in the rainy season. The berms would hold in the irrigation water when the fields were cultivated but I could see no sign of any human habitation. At gunpoint we

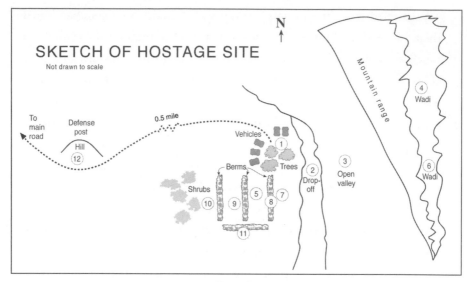

Figure 3

were all ordered to get out of the vehicles, leave everything behind, and sit under the trees where two blankets were laid out on the ground for us. The gesture of hospitality amused me. We noted that the kidnappers had with them what looked like a laptop computer. I would learn later that the flat metal case contained a satellite telephone.

Two of the men, who had been sitting apart from the others and studying a white piece of paper, came over and asked for our passports. Margaret, my roommate, was clearly worried. Since Carolyn Gay had quit the tour two days earlier to travel independently with her boyfriend, Margaret and I were the only Americans among the tour group. Whoever our captors were, we knew the United States was unlikely to have "favored nation" status. Having dual citizenship, I often carried both passports with me, precisely for situations where one nationality might prove more useful than the other. I might be able to conceal my American citizenship, at least for a time, but Margaret had no such option. The kidnapper who appeared to be the leader approached us again. He was relatively young, perhaps in his early thirties, with intense eyes and thick wavy hair. Although I did not know it then, this man was Zein al-Abidin abu Bakr al-Mehdar, better known by his *nom de guerre,* Abu Hassan. Another man, wearing bright yellow sweatpants under his futa, spoke reasonably good English and acted as the official interpreter for the kidnap gang. We soon nick-named him "Yellow Pants."

We sat on the blankets, still unable to believe the new twist our tour had taken. "Who Americans?" Abu Hassan asked, as he bent down on one knee in front of us. His interest in Americans was not a good sign. I recognized the danger of being immediately singled out for "special treatment" if I revealed my American citizenship now. Yet there was also the possibility that concealing my United States passport could make things worse for me if it were discovered later—surely they would search our luggage. Several of the group handed over their passports while others, including me, pointed to the Land Cruisers, indicating our papers were still in the vehicles. One by one, we were directed to go and retrieve them. I took one passport from my daypack and returned to sit on the blanket.

Abu Hassan approached us again, demanding the remaining pass-ports. "Who Americans?" he asked again, looking closely at each of us as though guilt of citizenship would be evident in our faces. I had decided to buy myself time and, saying nothing, handed over my New Zealand pass-port. We sat together on the blankets for some time, perhaps an hour, with instructions not to talk. Hassan and two others mulled over the pass-ports before coming back.

"Any more Americans?" According to the passports, they had cap-tured only one American—a woman at that—and clearly had been ex-pecting or hoping for more. I wondered if the white piece of paper they were holding was a passenger list and they already knew there should be three Americans on the trip: Margaret Thompson, Carolyn Gay and me. The preoccupation with identifying Americans reinforced my suspicions that this was not about a tribal grievance. In tribal kidnappings any for-eigners will do. Germans, Italians, Scandinavians, French, Asians, and Africans have all been kidnapped by Yemen's tribes to enforce their de-mands on government. These kidnappers had a specific interest in finding Americans among the hostages, implying a different agenda.

Most of the kidnappers were dressed in typical Yemeni style—a shabby suit jacket and wraparound futa. A few wore green military-style jackets. Many had jambiyas tucked in their waistbands and kept their khafiyas wrapped across their faces, revealing only their eyes. With no introductions offered and little else to distinguish the gang members, we gave them names based mostly on differences in clothing—Purple Skirt, Yellow Pants and Gray Shirt.

The manager in me was instinctively assessing their performance. Most of them were milling about in a nervous, disorganized way and seemed unsure what they should be doing. I could run a kidnapping better than this, I thought.

Satisfied that they now possessed all sixteen passports, the kidnappers ordered us to get our daypacks and water bottles from the vehicles, one at a time. I took the opportunity to switch from my sandals to sturdier walking shoes and to stuff a fleece sweater in my daypack. One of the youngest kidnappers, a bright-eyed boy in his mid-teens, noticed me changing my shoes and pointed toward my sandals. Never one to argue with anyone holding a gun, I handed the sandals over. "Be my guest," I smiled at him.

The boy happily put on my sandals and was delighted that they fitted him. He modeled his new footwear—handmade in upstate New York—for his colleagues, who laughed and joked appreciatively. I figured anything we hostages owned would be considered fair game by our hosts if they wanted it, and there was no point getting hurt or killed over a pair of sandals.

Led by a half dozen armed guards, we left the vehicles parked beside the trees and headed out in single file across a broad valley—Point 3 in the hostage site sketch. Chris and I were the first to reach the top of the hill on the far side of the valley. The land dropped away below us into a narrow ravine or wadi. In the rainy season, water would flow down from higher elevations through this dry riverbed to the plain below, but now, in late December, it was dry. We waited over the crest of the hill for the slower members of the group to catch up. I noticed Peter Rowe wore only flimsy orange flip-flops and he was having difficulty navigating the uneven terrain strewn with sharp volcanic rocks. We continued down into the ravine and, turning left, followed the wadi upstream for twenty minutes along a lightly traveled goat path. Where the wadi narrowed and curved to the right, we stopped under the shade of overhanging rocks—Point 4. The two blankets were again laid out for us to sit on.

We waited in silence for about half an hour until Abu Hassan arrived and crouched in front of us with Yellow Pants at his side. Another gang member squatted to the left of Hassan, nervously tossing a hand grenade from one hand to the other. His eyes glittered with a menacing excitement and I had the feeling he would love an excuse to use that grenade. I don't recall us assigning a name to this character, so I'll call him Grenade. Unlike the rest of the kidnappers, Hassan did not bother to cover his face as he spoke.

"You want to know why we have taken you? I will tell you. We are mujahiddin." He paused while Yellow Pants translated. "You are not responsible for the bombings in Iraq but your countries are." The political nature of the kidnapping was confirmed. This was not about the usual tribal grievances. "Our friends are in prison. When the government releases our friends you can go. Don't be afraid."

"How can I not be afraid with that guy playing with his hand grenade right next to me?" Catherine, the young Australian woman, angrily pointed to the offender. Hassan spoke abruptly to Grenade, who stood up moodily and moved around the bend in the path where we could no longer see him.

The terse explanation for our capture was over and we remained sitting together on the blankets. From a small cave under the rocks to our right, there was an occasional flash of light as one of our guards played with a camera taken from our luggage. Yellow Pants placed a plastic jerrycan on the ground near the blankets and told us it was water for us to drink. Most of us still had our own water bottles and preferred not to risk drinking the water Yellow Pants had provided. If there is one thing worse than being a hostage, it's being a hostage with diarrhea. I planned to make my water last as long as possible. To pass the time and keep a record of events, I began to jot down what had happened in the notebook I carried in my daypack. Chris cautioned me to be careful what I wrote.

We spoke little to each other, sharing only a few whispered exchanges. The afternoon sun still burned its harsh light into the narrow valley, reflecting off the bleached walls of the wadi and the dust-covered leaves of parched, stunted trees. In the shade of the overhanging rock, the temperature was comfortable enough. A heavy stillness filled the air and there was little we could do but wait and watch. The kidnappers took turns to kneel and pray, doing so in pairs so that some of them would always be maintaining armed guard over us. To our suppressed delight, we noted that the first pair must have faced the wrong direction because the second pair decided on a different orientation toward Mecca after consulting a compass.

After half an hour, Hassan returned with Yellow Pants and the one we had named Purple Skirt for the distinctive color of his futa. "Andrew, you come. You rest stay here."

"We rest" exchanged looks. Perhaps Hassan planned to use Andrew Thirsk as a spokesperson for our group and would put him on the satellite phone as part of the negotiations. If so, I liked their choice. The good-looking young Australian had impressed me with his intelligence and calmness. Alternatively, the kidnappers might have decided to execute one of us just to prove the seriousness of their resolve. If Andrew had thought of that possibility, he showed no sign of fear as he disappeared behind the bend in the path with our captors. We waited, listening. My greatest fear was of hearing the sound of gunshot. Minutes passed. We sat in silence, each of us coping alone with our private thoughts. After five minutes, the kidnappers returned and took another of the men, but Andrew did not return. One by one, all the men were led away and only we eight women were left under the overhanging rocks.

"Just be glad we haven't been kidnapped in Africa," Catherine whispered. "At least in an Arab country women are less likely to be raped." She had spoken the word on all our minds.

Several kidnappers then reappeared from behind the rocky overhang and told us to hand over our daypacks with all our jewelry inside.

"You know why we need the money," Hassan said, in an apologetic and confidential tone. "It is for the oil." It was not clear to me if he meant they needed money to buy gas for their vehicles or whether it was a more symbolic reference, implying payment for the Arabian oil exploited by western countries. I removed a gold chain from around my neck, remembering how I had purchased it, and another just like it for my mother, in the gold market of Istanbul. I placed the chain in the outer pocket of my daypack together with a bracelet wrought out of intertwined silver threads, that I had bought through the J. Peterman catalogue. It occurred to me that my situation would have been a perfect vignette for the catalogue's adventure travel theme. Pulling down my shirtsleeve to hide my watch, I handed over my daypack. I would never again see those two mementos and, even today, wonder if some Yemeni woman enjoys wearing my gold chain and bracelet, ignorant of their origins. My thoughts turned to my mother and how her identical gold chain had also been stolen, most likely by staff at the nursing home where she lived in New Zealand. The only redeeming thing about her having advanced Alzheimer's is that she would not be worrying about what is happening to me, I thought sadly.

We could hear the kidnappers going through our packs just out of sight around the bend in the path. After five minutes, Hassan returned with Yellow Pants.

"Mary? Who is Mary?"

"I guess they found my other passport," I said softly to Catherine and Pat, who sat nearest me. I stood to face Hassan at eye level, noticing my American passport in his hand.

"What is your nationality?" I chose simple, clear words and spoke slowly to ensure that Yellow Pants would understand me and interpret correctly. "I was born in New Zealand. All my family live in New Zealand." I paused to allow Yellow Pants to translate. "But I work in America. I have an American passport so I can work there." Again I waited.

The two men exchanged a few words in Arabic. Then, to my surprise, Hassan handed me my American passport and walked away. I was only a woman, after all, and not even a "real" American—hardly worth his time and trouble. It was exactly the reaction I wanted.

All the men in our group returned unharmed. They had each been interrogated with the same list of questions: "Is this your first visit to Yemen?" "What is your religion?" "Where do you work?" "Have you served in the military?" Some of the men were also asked how they liked Yemen. Even terrorists, it seems, are concerned about customer satisfaction. The kidnappers, blinded by the limited roles of women in their own culture, did not bother to assess the bargaining value of their female hostages. As employees of large American corporations, Margaret Thompson and I were potentially more valuable to the kidnappers than some of the male hostages who did not have employers with such deep pockets or influence. I found out later that the CEO of Xerox had put the corporate jet on standby to evacuate me if needed.

Evening approached and it seemed we would be spending the night on that narrow goat path, the sixteen of us crowded together on two blankets. As the sun set, the sky turned to a pale, translucent blue and the air chilled. My fleece had been taken along with my daypack and I began to feel cold. It was Catherine who again spoke up, demanding of Yellow Pants that our sweaters be returned. A few minutes later several sweaters were handed back to us, my fleece included. We tried to get comfortable on the blankets. Two of the men seemed intent on stretching out at full length, regardless of how much space they occupied. Pat made it clear to one of them that, no, he was not welcome to lay his head on her leg. Even for hostages in the desert, British decorum applied. I had a spot near one edge of the blankets, glad of the extra space it allowed me but uncomfortable with my exposure to scorpions or spiders. I had seen both while camping in the desert terrain of West Africa and had no wish to find an aggressive camel spider or scorpion crawling on me in the dark. After an hour of trying to sleep, I sat up. Andrew was lying next to me and he sat up too. We watched the night sky.

"When you decided to do this trip to Yemen," I whispered, "what did you think were the chances of being kidnapped?"

"About one in a million."

"Yeah," I replied. "Me too."

The beams of flashlights suddenly spilled onto the blankets and the kidnappers called to us to get up. My watch showed it was close to 9:00 PM. We followed the flashlights back along the path, retracing our steps through the darkness of the wadi. A half-moon lit up the valley. The kidnappers seemed light-hearted and one of them bantered a few English words with Catherine. "Don't worry. Tomorrow, Britannia," he said.

Perhaps they had already negotiated a deal with the Yemen government, I thought, and we would be set free in the morning. The prospect that this would soon be over, that the day's events would be little more than an inconvenience and an exciting travel story to tell friends back home, was reassuring. We scrambled up the embankment to where our tour vehicles were still parked and pushed through the cluster of trees to the open field beyond—Point 5. A long row of blankets had been laid out and our sleeping bags were stacked in a heap nearby. Spending the night in the warmth of my own sleeping bag, with plenty of room to stretch out, seemed like a four-star hotel compared with trying to sleep cramped together in the wadi. About 30 yards away, several of the kidnappers sat around a campfire, their faces glowing bronze in its light, showing no concern that the fire could disclose their location.

Yellow Pants came over and asked if anyone needed any medicines from their luggage. He seemed quite concerned that some of us might be critically dependent upon prescription drugs and might lapse into a catatonic state through medicinal deprivation. Several hostages requested that items be brought from their luggage. In a scene worthy of a Monty Python show, Brian requested that his green and pink toilet bag be located. Yellow Pants dutifully went over to the Land Cruisers to find it.

"No, that's not it," exclaimed Brian when Yellow Pants returned. "It's green and pink, not red. About this big." Brian illustrated with his hands. Yellow Pants went off again and returned with another smaller bag.

"No, no." Brian was becoming exasperated. "It's a pink bag, green and pink. That one is all green."

"Brian," I laughed, "he may not understand the English word for pink." At that point, Yellow Pants solved the problem by suggesting we all get what we needed from our luggage ourselves. All our suitcases were brought over from the Land Cruisers and placed in a heap near our sleeping bags.

Before retiring for the night, I casually walked across the field toward some bushes at one end of the open field, seeking a private bathroom spot. The kidnappers seemed to understand my purpose and showed no sign of stopping me. Squatting out of sight, I considered the possibility of escaping right then, by simply disappearing into the surrounding darkness. Was anyone watching to see if I came back? Would some of the kidnappers be standing guard in the desert surrounding the camp? Then another thought crossed my mind. This was southern Yemen and many minefields had not yet been cleared since the 1994 civil war. Tripping a landmine as I ran across the desert was a scarier prospect than remaining a hostage. I decided it was wiser to wait until our situation became clearer and I knew more about how carefully we were guarded. Until I could see some pattern in our captors' behavior and could choose a time when the moon had set, it was better to remain with the group. After all, I told myself, we would probably be set free in the morning.

Returning to the camp area, I stuffed my shoes down inside the toe of my sleeping bag to ensure they would not be taken during the night, and slithered inside the bag, fully clothed. Catherine lay to my right and we talked in whispers. Yellow Pants was on guard, either walking along the row of sleeping bags or sitting on top of my Samsonite suitcase, the only hard-sided bag among the luggage. He scolded Catherine and me for talking and asked what we wanted. Catherine explained that she had a bad cold and was asking me for some tissues. From time to time, another kidnapper strolled down Hostage Row scanning our faces with his flashlight. As he approached I closed my eyes, pretending to sleep.

At midnight we were woken again. Dinner time. One of the men brought a big plastic bag of stew to us from the campfire. I was not hungry but felt I should eat to keep up my strength and knew that cooked food should be safe enough. About half the hostages got up to eat. The meat was hard to identify. Goat? Camel? Mutton? It was tough but I chewed through two rubbery chunks and took a handful of the dates offered for dessert. A smaller plastic bag contained what Yellow Pants called sauce and he encouraged us to try it. As I crawled back inside my sleeping bag, I heard Brian genially explaining to Yellow Pants the difference in meaning between the English words "sauce" and "gravy." Our captor was delighted at this opportunity to refine his English.

The campsite was quiet now and the campfire burning low. Above me, the sky was a mass of stars, their brilliance diluted only by the moonlight. An occasional shooting star flashed across the constellations. The

Southern Cross, so familiar from my New Zealand childhood, was visible low above the southern horizon and the Big Dipper marked the northern sky. At least it would be easy to determine direction if I had to escape at night. Still unable to sleep, I sat up and took in my surroundings, but I could see little beyond the dark outlines of our row of sleeping bags.

Yellow Pants looked over at me from where he sat on my suitcase. "Why you not sleeping?"

I gestured toward the stars to indicate I was enjoying the incredible night sky.

"Yes," said Yellow Pants. "It is good to praise Allah." I lay back down, relaxing in the warmth of my polyester cocoon, and soon drifted off to sleep. A quiet stillness settled over our desert camp.

4

SURVIVING THE RESCUE

It was early when I woke. The sky was glowing a soft and fluid blue toward the east. Dips and valleys in the eroded hills were filled with charcoal shadows and their peaks flushed pink and gold, reflecting the first rays of an unseen sun. It took a few moments to remember where I was and all that had happened the previous day. The outside of my sleeping bag was drenched with dew but I must have slept for a few hours at least, warm and dry in the chill desert air. Propping myself up on my elbows, I looked around. Most of my traveling companions were still in their sleeping bags, but one of the men was up, heading toward some nearby bushes. Several of our captors were moving about near the campfire and the vehicles.

In the next few minutes, everyone began to stir and pull themselves from their sleeping bags. We didn't speak much, just exchanged looks of disbelief as each realized it hadn't been a dream. We really were hostages.

The atmosphere in the camp was much more relaxed than the day before. The kidnappers did not seem to be in any great hurry and let us go into our luggage to retrieve toiletries and clothing. Opening my hard-sided suitcase, I noted how much was missing. Binoculars, flashlight, warm London Fog jacket, the leather belt an old boyfriend had brought back for me from Afghanistan years ago. Any items useful to our kidnappers had been taken. Remembering how my skirt had caught on the branches of thorn bushes the day before, I decided to take the opportunity to change into long trousers. No one seemed to be paying much attention, so under my skirt I stepped into a change of underwear and drew on some dark brown pants. I thought about changing my long-sleeved T-shirt but that would involve a greater degree of exposure. A swish of deodorant under my existing shirt would have to do. I put away my skirt and pulled out my wide-brimmed straw hat for protection from the sun. Putting it on at a jaunty angle, I heard Margaret Whitehouse laughing at me. "You are looking very smart today, Mary," she joked, her warm eyes twinkling.

"It's what all the best hostages are wearing this season," I replied, tilting my hat for the right Indiana Jones effect.

A couple of kidnappers approached us carrying armfuls of small orange-juice cartons and packets of cookies. There were not quite enough cartons of juice to go around so we shared them. At least our captors were making some effort to feed us.

Several of our group discovered their boots or sturdy walking shoes were missing from their luggage. Catherine marched over to a man dressed in a spotlessly clean ankle-length white robe, called a dishasha, and complained firmly about the missing boots. I didn't expect it would do any good but I admired her guts. To my surprise, five minutes later Purple Skirt came over to us and dropped a half-dozen pairs of boots, plus my sandals, on the ground. "I am sorry," he said, "some of our people are criminals."

"No kidding," I laughed to myself.

Whatever the plans were for the day, no one seemed to be in a big rush to get us moving. I figured we would be taken back to the ravine, so I sorted out what to take with me in my daypack. Reading material was essential for what would likely be a long and boring day. I had already finished two of the three paperbacks I had brought with me to Yemen, leaving only *War and Peace*. Purchased on the spur of the moment at the airport, it looked like a perfect choice for the occasion. My small photograph album was still in my luggage so I removed from it a picture of my five brothers and my sister, tucking it in a pocket of my daypack. I wondered what they already knew about my circumstances. Was the kidnapping a news item on CNN yet, or was my family still completely unaware of what had happened? I had almost forgotten to tell anyone where I was spending Christmas. Only when I was at the airport waiting for my connecting flight to Yemen had I thought to call New Zealand and tell one of my sisters-in-law about my trip.

I added a fleece sweater, an extra pair of socks, a T-shirt and a change of underwear to my daypack, along with my water bottle and Sierra Club mug. This multipurpose metal dish had served me well all over the world. I smiled as I thought of how everyone had laughed at me for drinking wine from it at our Christmas Eve party in Laurence and Margaret's hotel room. It's always tough to pack when you don't know where you are going or for how long. We might come back to this campfire location tonight but maybe not. Maybe the kidnappers would take us someplace entirely new or keep us moving day after day. We might be living in the clothes we were in for weeks. Hey, I thought cheerfully, as long as I can rinse out my undies some place and put on a clean pair from time to time I can cope with anything.

About 7:00 AM we were rounded up by six of the kidnappers and motioned to head down the embankment again—Point 2. As an afterthought, I grabbed my sleeping bag too, wanting to spread it out to dry during the day and have the use of it if we did not return to the campsite tonight. Several others also took sleeping bags along with them. We set off in a slightly different direction from the route we had taken the day before. After a forty-minute walk, we went up over a moderate hill and into a wadi. This gully, which was wider than the one we had been in the previous day, may have just been further downstream in the same ravine, but I did not have a good sense of where it was located relative to the narrow goat path we had walked on before. We crossed up and over a low hill to a place that was out of sight of the road and the vehicles—Point 6. Three kidnappers stayed nearby to watch us and a couple of others were stationed at lookout points up on the ridges above the wadi.

The sun was still low in the sky and did not yet cast its warmth into the ravine. Our guards seemed fairly relaxed about where we sat, letting us spread out over the dry riverbed and its banks. Chris, Gill and Margaret Thompson climbed partway up the higher opposite bank of the wadi, which was already in sunlight. Others found spots to sit or stretch out in the lower and flatter riverbed. It surprised me how casual the guards were, compared with their tense vigilance the day before, but I felt glad that we were not forced to sit in a tight group on the blankets for another day. Peter and Claire had found a cozy spot together under an arbor of tree branches. I sat a bit downstream of the others on the bank we had just climbed over. I spread out my sleeping bag to dry and settled down for a long day. It was not yet 8:00 AM.

The next couple of hours progressed uneventfully. I tried to concentrate on *War and Peace* but it was not the easiest book to absorb under the circumstances. At this rate, it will last me quite a while, I thought, fully aware our hostage status might drag on for weeks. At one point, I saw three men come up from the lower end of the wadi to my right. They carried Kalashnikovs and were dressed in typical Yemeni clothes. Their arrival seemed to be welcomed by the two guards sitting opposite me on the far bank of the wadi. They greeted the newcomers with hugs and an animated conversation took place between the five men. I recognized the Arabic word for sixteen, and guessed the guards were telling the new arrivals about the number of hostages.

After they had talked for some time, the tallest of the newcomers looked over toward me and called out, "Are you the spy?"

"No," I replied, cheerfully gesturing towards the plain below. "I'm just sitting here to enjoy the view."

"Some hostages have been set free," he said.

"Do you mean the Germans?" I was referring to four German tourists who had been kidnapped and were still in captivity at the time I arrived in Yemen.

"Yes," our guards' visitor confirmed.

"Is your group responsible for that kidnapping too?"

"No, not us. Others."

"Seems like kidnapping is your national sport," I told him. The humor was lost on him.

"What are you reading?" the tall one asked me.

"A Russian story, called *War and Peace*."

"This is not a war," he replied.

You could have fooled me, I thought, then returned to my book, preferring to keep a low profile. The five men turned back to their own conversation until two of the visitors left, retracing their steps down the wadi. The third one remained to talk for another ten minutes, then also returned the way he had come.

As the morning dragged on, I gave up trying to read and wandered over to sit with Sue, Pat and Brian. Yellow Pants sat a short distance away and Brian decided to pursue a strategy of building rapport with our kidnappers. He moved over and sat down next to Yellow Pants, who seemed happy to engage in English conversation. Somehow the conversation developed into a discussion about religious conflict, not only between Muslim and Christian but between different Christian sects, notably in Northern Ireland. When Brian started discussing the medieval Hanseatic League of German trading towns, the rest of us, listening in to this unlikely dialogue, broke into broad grins. Brian was into territory that far exceeded Yellow Pants' limited English skills, but we gave them both credit for trying.

From time to time, one of us would get up and move around the ravine, stopping to see how others were doing and speculating on how long it would take to get a deal negotiated that would set us free. No one in the group seemed unduly anxious. We knew how other kidnappings had turned out. Even though this was obviously more political in intent, we had no reason to believe the outcome would be much different from that in other kidnappings in Yemen. And some of our guards seemed quite solicitous of our welfare. Only little Grenade bothered me. He was still tossing a plastic explosive from hand to hand as he watched us. I moved away and took up a spot near Pat. We watched as a man approached from the bottom of the wadi where the hills flattened out and merged with the plain below. He climbed slowly toward us carrying a cardboard box. As he came closer, we could see he was not armed. The visitor spoke to a kidnapper standing near us. The box contained more cookies and containers of juice, which were handed around to us. The delivery man seemed ready to leave when one of the kidnappers turned to us and asked, with his limited English, "Go market. You want something?"

Pat and I looked at each other in amusement. We were actually being asked for our shopping list, presumably with free delivery in the wadi.

"Some AK-47s with ammo would be handy," I commented to Pat, "but I don't think that's what he has in mind." Somehow I had never envisioned, as a hostage, being able to place orders at the local market. Once again, the entire situation felt like a scene from a Monty Python movie. We asked for bottled water, oranges and bananas, bread and—oh yes—how about some rolls of toilet paper? The kidnapper tore the top flap off the cardboard box and wrote our grocery list on it, then handed the cardboard to the delivery man, who dutifully headed off towards the market.

Figuring it would be hours before he returned, I decided to climb further up the right bank of the wadi where Chris, Gill and Margaret Thompson were sitting. The hillside was quite steep and the loose sharp rocks made it tricky to scramble up to them. When I reached their position, I could see why they were sitting there. They had a view directly across to our campsite of the previous night.

"There have been vehicles coming and going all morning," Chris commented, having noticed flashes of sunlight reflected from vehicle windshields in the distance.

I had been sitting up there for about ten minutes when we heard the sound of gunfire coming from somewhere beyond the campsite. At first there were isolated shots and I thought it might be just one of the kidnappers signaling to the others. In the next couple of minutes, the gunfire became more frequent. I looked at my watch. It was three minutes before 11:00 AM—exactly twenty-four hours since the ambush. As the intensity and frequency of the gunfire increased, I instinctively felt worried.

"Oh shit," I said to the others, "I think someone is trying to rescue us." I did not know it then, but my fear was well founded. Of all hostages killed in a kidnapping, 79 percent die during an armed rescue attempt.

The kidnappers in the ravine with us were clearly as surprised by the gunfire as we were. They shouted to each other and to the lookouts at the top of the opposite bank. For a few more minutes we sat there waiting to see what would happen next. The kidnappers were becoming quite tense and excitable again. One of them ran up the bank towards us and motioned to us to come down. There was urgency in his voice and gestures. We scrambled down the hillside toward the rest of our group, who were gathering together. As we got to the riverbed, we were told to head down the wadi. I had my daypack with me but my sleeping bag was lying about five yards away. I stepped out of the single file and took a few steps toward my sleeping bag, making eye contact with one of the kidnappers who stood between it and me. I pointed to the bag.

"No," he shouted. "Go! Go!" It definitely wasn't a good time to argue.

We walked quickly a short distance further down the wadi. When the kidnappers shouted to stop and motioned to us to sit down right where we were, Margaret and Laurence Whitehouse with Chris, who were some distance ahead of the rest of us, continued on. I thought they had not heard the direction to stop. A few moments later one of the kidnappers came back towards us and pointed to Andrew.

"You come," he said. "And David, you come."

I noted that he had used David's name. Andrew and David continued on down the wadi, catching up with Margaret, Laurence and Chris. A couple of the kidnappers went with them and we had no idea where they were being taken. The remaining eleven of us continued sitting on the ground. The sun was high overhead and there was no shelter from it. Grenade sat a few feet away watching us intently, his face tense and his eyes flashing. The ominous green block of explosive rested in his hand. He did not speak.

We sat there for about twenty minutes in the direct sun and I was glad of my straw hat. I could see sweat breaking out on Eric's face and he seemed increasingly agitated. Of anyone in the group, I felt he was most likely to lose control. Slowly, so as not to alarm Grenade, I unzipped my daypack. Inside I had a scarf, a fine cheesecloth-like white fabric with a beautiful band of embroidered ribbon at each end. I had bought several pieces of this cloth in Ethiopia the previous year and found it ideal for protecting my hair and face from flies, sun and blowing sand. Pulling the scarf slowly from my pack and keeping one eye on Grenade, I handed it to Eric.

"Here, use this to keep the sun off you."

Eric took it from me and tried to put it around his head. His hands were clumsy and shaking and he seemed unable to unfold and drape the scarf. In frustration, he handed the scarf back, shaking his head wordlessly.

The distant sounds of automatic machine guns and rifles became more repetitive and intense, but the ridge of hills prevented us from seeing who was shooting. Someone further down the wadi shouted to Grenade. He got up quickly and, with his rifle, motioned to us to continue down the ravine. We were joined by a couple more kidnappers, who helped Grenade hustle us back across the flat plain toward the campsite. Several times I noticed a puff of gray smoke in the sky ahead of us, followed a second or two later by the sound of a shell exploding in the air. We scrambled up the loose boulders—Point 2—back to the higher ground of the campsite and saw our tour drivers sitting next to the vehicles. It surprised me the drivers were still there: I had imagined the kidnappers would have let them go. But there was no sign of Andrew, David, and the other three. We were herded at gunpoint over behind a low dirt wall that defined one side of the field—Point 7. Suddenly, a shell exploded right overhead and instinctively the eleven of us threw ourselves down on the ground. At that point, we realized our extreme vulnerability to the ammunition being let loose around us. The gunfire was no longer somewhere else. We were right in the line of fire. A couple of the kidnappers shouted to us to get up and, waving their rifle barrels towards us, directed us to stand side by side in a line. I felt sure their intent was to shoot us all in a mass execution. The sense of complete vulnerability, that I could do absolutely nothing to prevent it, was as shocking to me as the immediate prospect of dying. We had just dropped our daypacks and formed a ragged line when our captors seemed to change their minds. We were hustled back down the embankment—Point 2. On my way down, I looked over my left shoulder and saw that our drivers had moved. They were now huddled partway down the embankment, protected from the crossfire by the overhanging rocks. I was hoping the kidnappers were intending to put us in a protected place too, but even before all eleven of us had descended, they changed tactics again and hustled us back up the embankment. As we were hurried back over the jagged black boulders toward the campsite, I tried to make eye contact with the drivers. What was going through their minds? What were they thinking about the bizarre scene in front of them? Did they care about what was happening to us? Were any of them implicated in the kidnapping? I could not fathom the looks on their faces. They seemed apart from us, part of a different story, a movie being filmed on an adjacent but unrelated set.

Back at the top of the embankment, we were now pushed at gunpoint onto the top of the low dirt wall—Point 8—that bordered the long edge of the field, parallel to where our sleeping bags had been laid out the night before. Half a dozen kidnappers were taking shelter behind the berm and others were sitting over near the Land Cruisers behind the grove of trees to our right. Now I understood what was happening. We were being used as human shields, to protect the kidnappers from the incoming gunfire. Surely the shooting will stop now, I thought. Surely whoever is rescuing us will not risk hitting us. The kidnappers made it clear we should keep our arms up in the air. Glancing over my right shoulder, I noticed Purple Skirt apparently pulling the pin on a grenade right behind me. I was fascinated by how he seemed to wait.

"Throw the mother," I breathed. Something to my left distracted me and, when I looked back, Purple Skirt had moved away. I do not know what happened to that grenade, but I found myself wondering whether it is possible to change your mind and reinsert the pin. I felt acutely conscious of how little I knew about guns and weapons of any kind. Suddenly, that ignorance seemed like a huge handicap. In this surreal situation, more like movies and television than real life, I did not know how to interpret actions or anticipate consequences.

The incoming gunfire did not stop. We stood on the dirt wall for about ten minutes, hearts pounding and feeling intense disbelief at what was happening. The bullets flying past made distinctive zinging sounds. Just like in the movies, I thought. I had to remind myself that these were real bullets, that I could get killed at any second.

The kidnapper we called Gray Shirt shouted to us to go forward. We were unsure what he wanted, but the forward thrusts of his gun seemed to imply we should go out into the open field towards another dirt wall, about 30 yards in front of us, which defined the other side of the field. We had reached about halfway across the field—Point 5—when Grey Shirt shouted to us to stop but to keep our arms up. We stood in a loose cluster together, within reach of each other, our arms in the air. The bullets kept flying, and shells and grenades were exploding in the sky around us, creating small gray clouds against a perfect blue sky. The midday sun was intense and the glare off the sandy soil added to the feeling of hallucination; a feeling that this was a dream, it could not really be happening.

"If this is what it's like to be rescued," Catherine commented angrily, "I'd just as soon stay a hostage."

"I'd feel a whole lot better if it was the Israelis coming in to rescue us," I replied.

Peter suggested dryly that when we got home we should write a new section for the guidebooks on Yemen—on how to deal with being taken hostage. As the bullets continued flying past, we joked about the advice we would give to other travelers. If you are going to be shot at for a couple of hours, I thought, it helps to do it with people who have a sense of humor.

I remembered Ruth's Arabic language phrasebook. "Does your book have any lines we could make use of right now?" I asked Ruth with a grin.

"Ach, no, Mary," she replied in her wonderful Scottish accent. "The book does na' seem to address this particular situation." At that moment, her canny humor was immensely reassuring. It was the last thing I would ever hear Ruth say.

Periodically, Gray Shirt would shout to us to move forward a few yards or to move back closer to him. Our arms became heavy with the effort of keeping them raised, and gradually we would drop one arm to give it a rest while holding the other up. If too many of us had our arms down at once, threatening shouts from the kidnappers behind the berm would force our arms back up in the air.

Earlier, the gunfire had seemed to come mostly from one direction, the direction we were facing while standing on the wall. Now it seemed to be coming from a widening arc surrounding our position. We sensed the attackers were gradually encircling the campsite, although they were still too far away for us to see them. My logic told me none of us would survive. Even if neither side intended to kill us, there were simply too many bullets flying and shells exploding for us not to be killed. Yet, at the same time, I felt certain I would survive. I could imagine myself back in

Rochester, back at work, telling family and friends about what had happened. The belief in my survival kept me thinking rationally, trying to figure out what else we could do.

Over by the vehicles, one of the kidnappers appeared to be emptying something from a container under the gang's own truck. The terrifying possibility that it was gasoline occurred to me. Did they plan to force us all into one of the Land Cruisers and set fire to it? It was an unlikely and terrible scenario, but the very idea panicked me more than the prospect of being shot to death. Maybe imagining something even worse than what was actually happening made it easier to cope with reality. In comparison with being set alight locked inside a vehicle, being killed by a bullet or grenade was relatively palatable. Others in the group realized it was water that the kidnappers were taking from a container under the pickup—they appeared to be washing themselves in some kind of ritual prebattle or predeath ablution rite. I turned to Brian and Eric who were standing on the edge of the group closest to the kidnappers.

"Have either of you been in the army?" I asked hopefully. They both shook their heads. There was no practical military experience to call upon in the group. We were college professors and managers, and this was definitely stuff they don't teach you at Harvard Business School.

Margaret Thompson was helping Sue Mattocks, who was hyperventilating. "Close your hands over your mouth, like this," Margaret demonstrated. "It cuts the oxygen you are breathing in."

Twenty yards from us, the kidnappers were shouting "Allahu Akbar! Allahu Akbar!" God is great. Every few minutes a puff of smoke, like a lonely, miniature cloud, would appear in the sky followed by the sound of an exploding shell. A bullet whizzed by my face so close I could feel the air move against my cheek as it went by. There had to be some alternatives to just standing in the crossfire waiting for one of us to be hit. What would the kidnappers do if we just lay flat on the ground? Chances were high that they might be willing to shoot one or two of us to force the rest to stay standing. We didn't want to take that chance. What if we just made a run for it, if we spread out and all ran in different directions until we reached cover? Some of us might get hit, but maybe the odds would be better than all of us just staying out in the open like sitting ducks. I tested this suggestion on the rest of the group. No one looked too keen on the idea.

"How about you run first, Mary?" Peter suggested back.

"You've got a point," I acknowledged. I wasn't prepared to test my theory alone. A shell exploded right overhead. We all jumped. I decided then that the instant any one of us got shot, all bets were off and I would immediately make a run for it. The odds of being accidentally shot could be no worse while running than standing. I didn't know much about guns, but I knew it must be harder to hit a moving target. I looked at my watch. We had been standing out in the middle of the field, in the crossfire of a raging gun battle, for forty-five minutes. Longer than the opening scene of *Saving Private Ryan*, I thought, as though that served as a benchmark for holding things together under fire. I thought of civilians all over the world who live in war zones and deal with this fear of violent death every day. I thought of soldiers going to war. How do you cope with the anticipation of a chunk of metal ripping you apart at any moment? How do you not go mad? I gained a whole new respect for war veterans.

It amazed me that none of us were dead yet. Whether that was because both sides were great shots and carefully avoided hitting us, or both sides were lousy shots and just kept missing, I couldn't be sure. I was also astonished by how calmly every one of us was dealing with this life-and-death situation. No one was screaming or panicking. Most of us being introverts, we were dealing with it internally rather than expressing our emotions. The calmness of the group helped immensely.

Gray Shirt and Purple Skirt shouted and motioned for us to come back. Time for a change of tactics. Leaving us as decoys in the middle of the field of battle wasn't working. Back at the dirt wall—Point 8—there were still four or five kidnappers firing their rifles from behind the shelter of the wall. Several others appeared to be noncombatants, staying over near the vehicles. There was no sign of the drivers; nor had we any idea where the group of five fellow tourists had gone after they were taken ahead of us in the ravine. Now the kidnappers wanted us standing back on the wall. None of us felt we had any choice—refusing to do so would get us shot. I stepped up on the wall. At that moment, a bullet whistled right over my head. I couldn't cope any longer. Instinctively, I took a step down and backward to escape the terrible vulnerability of being up on that wall. Purple Skirt grabbed my leg and pushed me back up, shouting and pointing his rifle at me. The momentary loss of control passed. It was the first time any of the kidnappers had actually touched me, and I was shocked by the physical contact, even though it was a painless push, not a blow. OK, I guess I can do this, I thought, regaining control. I sure didn't have many alternatives. Catherine stood to my immediate right and Eric next to her at the right-hand end of the line. Sue was on my left and I was aware of Margaret, Pat, and the others beyond her. The eleven of us were again lined up in the face of the incoming fire.

Two men came through the bushes beyond the open field and walked towards us. They were walking surprisingly casually, looking back over their shoulders from time to time as they approached our position. Now we began to see individuals approaching in the far distance, but the figures were too small to make out details. The persistent sound of gunfire had become so familiar that I hardly noticed it. It had become part of the audio wallpaper. The battle between my logical belief that we would all die and my intuitive belief in my survival continued to rage inside my head. In spite of all evidence to the contrary, I profoundly trusted my intuition.

Several kidnappers were lying against the dirt wall where we stood, resting their rifles on top of it as they fired between our legs. I turned to look at Catherine next to me. Tears were streaming down her face. I reached out and held her hand then turned and took Sue's hand as well. It was the only way to offer comfort, to communicate. At that moment, I knew that the one choice I was free to make, that human beings are always free to make in any circumstance, was about my own behavior.

I would not let these terrorists see that I was afraid. If I were going to die, I would die well. It was the one thing in my control. The simple act of taking Catherine's hand gave me a sense of still having choices. The gunfire continued. Time and again, I heard the whistle of a bullet, felt air move against my face as a bullet rammed its way through the space around me.

"You can do this," I told myself. "You are still alive. You can do this. Just one more minute. Just one more minute. You can stay alive for one more minute." I could not believe this was the day, the place, where my life would end. Dying here seemed such an incredible waste. In some deep place within me, I had a powerful sense that this was not the script for the end of my life. There was too much more I needed to do in the world. I found myself becoming more angry than afraid. I could not believe I would die like this, in some godforsaken desert, because of some cause I didn't even understand, let alone care about. I would not die here. I talked myself through a process of staying alive, one minute at a time.

The nearest of the attacking forces was now in shouting distance, just beyond the second of the two fields in front of us. Purple Skirt, standing just behind Eric, was shouting to them. Suddenly, he grabbed Eric and pulled him backward off the wall. Eric was bent over and Purple Skirt was holding a pistol to Eric's head. I watched over my shoulder in horror. An image flashed into my mind from the Vietnam War, that famous photo where a South Vietnamese officer is holding a gun to the head of a suspected Viet Cong. He's going to blow Eric's brains out, I thought. Three feet away from me and he's going to blow his brains out. The danger of our situation had instantly escalated. I did not doubt for a moment Purple Skirt would do it. He continued shouting to the advancing front line and one of the attackers shouted back. From the tone of their voices, and the ongoing shooting, it did not seem that the rescue team was there to negotiate. Still bent over, Eric suddenly pulled away from Purple Skirt. I felt certain Purple Skirt would shoot him but he let Eric go.

The stakes had been raised. Not only were we all at risk of being shot accidentally in the crossfire but now one of us had been directly and explicitly threatened with execution. In spite of the escalating terror, I found myself fascinated to see what would happen next, more annoyed than frightened by the prospect of getting killed. "If I die now, I won't get to see how it all ends," I thought. Not missing the outcome was a surprisingly powerful motivation to stay alive.

An instant later, Purple Skirt jumped up on the berm alongside Catherine and grabbed her hair, which was tied back in a ponytail. He had put his pistol away and he held the barrel of his Kalashnikov against her right side. He shouted again to the attackers and twice I heard him say

"American." He was threatening to kill the American woman if the rescue force did not back off. Catherine was sobbing.

"I'm not American. I'm Australian," she cried.

"I don't think he cares much at this stage," I said grimly. No one was checking passports anymore. Purple Skirt suddenly pushed Catherine forward onto the flat ground in front of us.

"Sleep, sleep!" he shouted. Catherine, in spite of the terror of the moment, understood his meaning and curled up in a fetal position, lying still on the hard-baked sand. Purple Skirt continued shouting. The shouts returning from behind the far wall did not sound like someone ready to back off. Purple Skirt raised his gun. I could not let her die. If he wanted to kill an American, it should be me. I considered jumping down in front of Catherine to distract Purple Skirt, to tell him I was the American, not Catherine. But any sudden action could make things worse, prompting Purple Skirt to kill us both reactively, and I was not certain that I was capable of taking a bullet for Catherine. In the instant that I hesitated, Purple Skirt fired several rounds of bullets. Small puffs of sand sprang up like little fountains in a circle around Catherine's curled-up body. He had deliberately missed her but wanted the approaching force to think he had killed her. Catherine lay on her side facing towards me, arms over her face, knees tucked up towards her chin, shaking. I never did find out if I could have sacrificed my life for someone else. There was no time to think about it. I was acutely aware of being next in the lineup. Purple Skirt had held a gun to Eric's head. He had fired bullets around Catherine. The attackers were not backing off. Now it was my turn, and now Purple Skirt might feel forced to make good his threats.

Purple Skirt grabbed the back of my shirt, just below my neck, and I felt the hard barrel of his Kalashnikov jammed against my spine. He continued shouting, the tension in his voice escalating. He pushed me forward with his gun and I thought he wanted me to lie down like Catherine. But he kept hold of my shirt and came down the dirt wall behind me. We walked forward across the open field toward the rescue force. The barrel of the gun, pressing hard on the vertebrae in my spine, became the center of my consciousness. I knew he could pull the trigger at any moment. I had an image of the bullet shattering my spine into a thousand pieces. I willed him to move the gun, just an inch either side, so when the gun went off it would be a clean shot, an instant death.

The universe now consisted only of Purple Skirt and me. My brain seemed to have compartmentalized, processing information on several levels simultaneously. One part was focused on willing the gun barrel to move, just an inch, just an inch. A second part was analyzing Purple Skirt's intentions. Obviously, he was using me as a shield to move closer to the rescue force, but what was he trying to achieve? Where were we going? What was the point? I needed to figure out Purple Skirt's strategy so I could come up with a countermove. If I knew his intent, I could figure out what I should do next. In a third place in my brain I was simply angry. I am not going to die here. I don't know who you bastards are or what you want but it's not my issue. I'm not going to die in this godforsaken desert for your pathetic little war. On yet another level, I seemed to be analyzing myself, amazed I could still think logically and strategically, surprised that the threat of dying didn't create the incapacitating terror I would have expected.

We approached the center berm separating the two fields. Suddenly, it occurred to me. He's on the offensive, just using me to get to this next wall so he can shoot at the attackers at closer range. He'll dispose of me once he's there. My anticipation of him pulling the trigger heightened as we reached the berm, and my heart pounded as he pushed me up and over it.

What's his point? What's the purpose? The need to figure out what Purple Skirt was doing took on an intense urgency in my mind, but I couldn't come up with a theory to explain his tactics. I went up and over the dirt wall, relieved to cross another milestone without that final squeeze on the trigger.

"Just one more minute. Just one more minute. You can do this," I continued to tell myself, and took two steps down the other side of the berm into the second field—Point 9. Suddenly, I could no longer feel the gun barrel against my spine. I turned to see what had happened. To my surprise, Purple Skirt was lying on his side on the ground right behind me. I was puzzled. What was I meant to do? Did I miss hearing him tell me something? Was I meant to lie down here too? Twenty-four hours of being ordered around at gunpoint had already programmed me to follow orders. Then I heard Purple Skirt groan and realized he had been shot. All my focus had been on the threat of being shot myself. The possibility that Purple Skirt would be shot simply hadn't occurred to me. I had to make an immediate decision. I looked back towards the ridge of dirt where my fellow hostages were still standing. Going back there sure didn't make any sense.

I looked down at Purple Skirt. He was struggling to get up, trying to prop himself onto his left elbow. I could see no blood and his AK-47 lay on the ground in front of him. I could just hunker down here and try to lie low, but the idea of being stuck out in the middle of a battlefield any longer, alongside my buddy Purple Skirt, had little appeal. I decided to make a run for it. This was my one chance to escape. I turned and took a couple of steps in the direction of the rescue force. A movie sequence flashed through my mind: where the good guy thinks he has vanquished the bad guy and is casually turning away, then the bad guy makes one last unobserved effort and fires off another round. Hollywood had taught me well. I turned back and made a grab for the gun. It was lying alongside Purple Skirt, and I didn't want to get close enough to him that he might grab my ankle and pull me off balance. I reached for the nearest end, the barrel, expecting to just pick it up and go. With a shock I found Purple Skirt had grabbed the other end.

"Oh, shit, how do you get yourself out of this little mess?"

At that instant I made the fight-versus-flight decision. The adrenaline rush was overwhelming and exciting.

"I want that gun, you little bastard." I wanted to put the barrel of it up against his head and see the fear in his eyes; I wanted him to know what it's like to have someone hold a gun against you and hold your life in their hands. The anger and hostility was intensely personal. Suddenly, to my surprise, I was enjoying myself.

"Hey, if you're gonna die here, you may as well do it on your own terms," I told myself out loud. No way was I going to run without a fight. I pulled as hard as I could on the barrel of the rifle trying to keep it pointed off to the side of me. Purple Skirt was holding tight to the stock, screaming at me, "No! No! No!" I cannot recall if he used Arabic or

English. Only the meaning came through to me. Hard as I pulled, I could not loosen his grip. I moved a couple of steps closer and kicked him in the face. It was a pathetic, girly kind of kick that at best knocked some dirt in his eyes. He still clung to the gun. He was stronger than I expected, in spite of his bullet wound, and it occurred to me that he could actually win this bizarre tug-of-war. The phrase "to have a tiger by the tail" suddenly took on real meaning. But it was also exciting and I was too far invested in this little fight to give in. In a moment of revelation, a thought occurred to me: so this is why men like war.

I inched closer to him and brought my right foot down hard on his head. I knew that pointing the soles of the feet towards someone is considered an insult in Arab cultures and I took perverse pleasure in how insulting it must be for this holy warrior to have his face under the sole of an infidel woman's foot. Symbolism aside, my purpose was much more pragmatic. By using his head for a leverage point, I gained enough extra force to rip the gun from his hands.

For a moment I considered killing him. I suddenly knew I was capable of killing another human being and enjoying it. The realization shocked me as though I had met some new person, someone inside me that I never knew existed, someone capable of evil. One problem—this evil one didn't know how to use an AK-47. I looked up, conscious again of where I was, of the immense danger of staying out in the crossfire. It would take me precious seconds or longer to figure out how to use the rifle. Purple Skirt was already wounded and disabled. Shooting an unarmed man on the ground was not self-defense. The fact that he still had a pistol and possibly a grenade on him did not occur to me.

I looked Purple Skirt in the eye one last time: "salaam alaikum, mother-fucker," then turned and began to run.

Crossing that second open field, a distance of perhaps 30 yards, was mesmerizing. It seemed as though everything around me was muted. The gunfire, all sound, was strangely remote. I ran across the desert carrying the Kalashnikov, incredulous at what was unfolding. I felt like a cross between Lawrence of Arabia and Rambo.

"This isn't what you are supposed to be doing, Mary. You're a business executive. You don't do this stuff." Crazy thoughts flew through my brain. It seemed that time had slowed down, that I ran in slow motion. I could see little of the landscape around me. The desert was shrouded in a pale blue-white veil that seemed always to part just a little in front of me. Perhaps this is dying, I thought. You just move through this veil into another realm and find some new level of existence behind it. Perhaps I've already been shot and this is how dying is. I was not afraid. I had taken back control, accountability for my actions. Now I could die on my terms, not as a victim.

As I came closer to the third dirt wall, I suddenly snapped out of the adrenaline-induced high and thought about what lay on the other side. I had assumed it was the Yemen army coming in to rescue us, but I didn't know for sure. What if it were a competing terrorist organization? Even if it were the army, did they know who I was? In trousers, a straw sunhat and sunglasses, could they tell I was a woman? Would they care? Instinctively, I knew it wasn't real smart to run up and over that wall carrying a Kalashnikov. I had a powerful urge to keep it. It represented a victory against our abductors and one hell of a souvenir. I wanted to take it home with me.

"You're crazy," I told myself, as I continued running. "Customs will never let you back into the U.S. with this gun."

Reluctantly, as I covered the last few yards towards the wall, I tossed the AK-47 off to my right, ran up over the wall in a few strides and threw myself flat on the ground on the other side—Point 10.

My heart was thumping and my breath coming in gasps. I could feel the desert sand hot and scratchy against my cheek. Slowly, barely raising my head, I turned and looked around. Within about five yards of me, three soldiers in desert-colored camouflage crouched among the bushes. One gave me a thumbs-up signal and another motioned with his hand for me to lie low. I didn't need any encouragement.

Lying against the dirt, I could hardly believe what had just happened. "So this is how I escape."

All along, my intuition had told me I would survive, but standing there in the crossfire, survival had seemed impossible. Never could I have imagined this sudden twist in the plot, a lucky break so amazing it seemed to have been pulled from the final chapter of a thriller. Then another thought overwhelmed me. "Where does my life go from here? Where can I possibly go from here?" At that moment, I knew that my life was forever changed, my future dislocated from my past. There was no way back, only the challenge of finding a path forward to some different life.

One of the three soldiers slowly approached me, crouching low. He spoke to me in Arabic. I recognized only one word, which sounded like "kam"—meaning "how many." I didn't know if he meant how many hostages or how many terrorists. Pointing to myself, I held up all ten fingers and thumbs. Pointing to him, meaning Yemenis, I held up my eight fingers and said the word for eight, glad I had learned how to count in Arabic.

He repeated the word—it sounded to me like te-mar-nee—looking surprised. I nodded, holding my hands up again with fingers out and thumbs tucked in.

"Temarnee, teesa," eight, maybe nine. Motioning me to stay where I was, he moved up and over the dirt wall protecting me. The two other soldiers followed him.

Left alone, my thoughts turned to my travel companions still held as human shields some 60 yards behind me. The gunfire continued.

"Oh God, I hope they're OK, I hope they're OK." I said it over and over to myself as though repetition would increase the odds.

I could see no sign of any other soldiers and another thought crossed my mind. "What if there are only these three soldiers? What if the kidnappers still win?" I knew I would not have favorite hostage status if the kidnappers recaptured me. Perhaps I should keep running and put more distance between myself and them, in case they come after me. As I thought about whether to run or stay, I noticed another soldier walking slowly towards me through the scrub, then another and several more behind him. The shooting had stopped.

5

MASH IN MUDIYAH

soldier approached me, gesturing that it was safe to stand up. I brushed the dirt off my shirtsleeves and pants and shook the man's hand. He seemed to be an officer and pointed to me to go with the soldier behind him. The soldier took me by the hand—a gesture that put an immediate dent in my new macho self-image—and led me beyond the bushes towards a military pickup truck waiting with its engine running. I climbed into the passenger seat and nodded to a grim-faced driver, who immediately crunched into gear and drove off. Several soldiers with a .50-caliber machine gun were riding in the back of the truck and my young escort rode the running board, clinging to the passenger door. After a few minutes, we approached the cluster of trees where our convoy vehicles were still parked. I searched anxiously for any sign of the other hostages. The only one I could see was Eric, who seemed to be looking for something among our luggage, still left strewn where we had slept the night before.

The truck stopped. On the spur of the moment, I offered my straw sunhat to the young soldier gripping the door, and pointed to his cap. He looked puzzled for a moment then smiled and we exchanged hats. If I couldn't take home an AK-47 as a souvenir, the cap would have to do. I needed some tangible proof that all this had really happened—that it wasn't a movie or a dream. As I took a few steps toward Eric, I heard someone call out. A soldier sitting in one of our Land Cruisers was beckoning to me. I quickly moved over to the vehicle and he pointed over his shoulder. Opening the rear passenger door, I was shocked to see Margaret, my roommate, stretched out in the back, her jeans covered in blood.

During the final minutes of the gun battle, after I had wrenched the assault rifle from Purple Skirt and escaped, the kidnappers had realized they would be overwhelmed by the Yemen security forces converging on their position. One of them grabbed Ruth and began pushing her forward at gunpoint, just as Purple Skirt had with me. Ruth fell to the ground, killed instantly by a bullet that struck the back of her chest on the right side and exited on her left side. Moments later, the kidnapper we called Gray Shirt, realizing the battle was lost, began executing the hostages from left to right. A high-velocity bullet struck Peter Rowe in the upper rear of his left arm and traveled through his chest, causing immediate death. His wife Claire, who was standing next to him, was shot in her right hip. A second bullet slammed through her right shoulder blade exiting in front of her upper arm, and a third clipped her fingertip.

The remaining hostages jumped down from the dirt wall to take shelter in front of it. Margaret felt she had been "hit by a truck" as a bullet screamed through her left thigh, shattering the bone. Pat spun around to see Gray Shirt leveling his rifle at her chest. She looked him straight in the eye and he hesitated, long enough for her to drop down and curl into a ball on the ground. He then aimed his gun at Eric, who also turned to face him and shouted, "No, no, no!" Gray Shirt, who had shot three hostages from the back, seemed unable to fire face-to-face. He hesitated again, then turned and ran after the other kidnappers who were fleeing into the desert. Much later, Pat described to me how she used her headscarf to stop the bleeding from Margaret's leg while Claire lay crying out for a doctor. The rescue force had apparently not thought to bring a medic with them.

I knew none of these last brutal, tragic details of the battle when I climbed into the Land Cruiser with Margaret—only that she was badly hurt. Two soldiers were crouching with their guns beside her. Thank God she was alive and conscious. One of our drivers, Abdul, was in the driver's seat.

"Quickly. Go. Go!" I shouted to him. "Doctor, hospital, quickly." Abdul looked over at the soldier next to him and exchanged a few words.

"Go! She needs a doctor. Mahib," I shouted again, remembering at last the Arabic word for doctor and wondering why on earth they were waiting. Abdul started up the engine and began to drive. I was totally focused on Margaret and did not notice what was happening in any of the other Land Cruisers. Her face was pale and beaded in sweat but she seemed quite coherent. I desperately wished I had taken a refresher on first aid but knew only the little I could remember from a college Red Cross course: check breathing and bleeding. Margaret was breathing all right and the wound seemed not to be bleeding. A rounded shape protruded from her thigh at a strange angle under her jeans. Margaret thought it was a broken bone and I did not know what, if anything, I should do about it. The only thing I could think to do was to keep her conscious by making her talk to me. I glanced toward the soldiers. One of them looked sadly at me and made a horizontal gesture across his throat. I shook my head angrily at him. The last thing Margaret needed was to see this guy's opinion that she was going to die. With the limited medical care available to a Yemeni soldier injured in battle, Margaret's bullet wound probably would have been fatal, but I had to believe we could reach a doctor fast enough to save her.

The journey across the rocky desert terrain seemed to last forever. Margaret was extraordinarily composed. The jolting of the vehicle must have been agonizing, but she never complained and even cracked a smile from time to time. I asked her every question I could think of—about her daughter, her job, her ex-husband, other trips she had taken. I kept telling her she was doing great even as her face became increasingly ashen in color. She began to have more difficulty breathing and wanted to have her head and shoulders raised up. One of the soldiers helped me shift her as gently as possible, but I could see the movement caused her tremendous pain. Half an hour had gone by and we seemed no closer to any village or even a paved road. Being unable to communicate with Abdul or any of the soldiers was frustrating: I could not find out how much further we had to go. Margaret began to fade, closing her eyes and responding more and more slowly to my questions. I felt her pulse, which still seemed strong, but I wasn't sure I could keep her conscious much longer. After driving for nearly an hour, with Margaret on the verge of losing consciousness, we finally saw the stone walls of houses in Mudiyah.

The Land Cruiser turned through a gate into a walled compound and came to a halt. I guessed it must be some kind of clinic but it seemed deserted and I could see no sign of medical personnel. As I opened the vehicle door, I realized the other Land Cruisers were behind us and had also pulled into the compound. Sue Mattocks came up to me and hugged me as I stepped from the vehicle. "Peter and Ruth have been hit," she said.

"You mean dead?" I stared at her. Sue nodded.

"Yes, Claire has been shot too, but she's alive." Sue pointed to where Claire was being lifted onto a stretcher.

I followed the soldiers carrying Margaret and Claire into the hospital. We passed through a long, windowless corridor until we arrived at a locked door. The stretchers were put down on the floor as the soldiers struggled to open a padlock and chain. In yet another surreal moment, one of the soldiers used a rock to try to break open the padlock. At that moment, a Yemeni man in a white jacket came running along the corridor. To my relief, he had a key and opened the door into a primitive operating theater. The soldiers put Claire on the only operating table and Margaret was left on her stretcher on the floor. Catherine came into the hospital with Claire, while the rest of the rescued hostages remained outside. I was greatly relieved to see Catherine. The last I had seen of her was when Purple Skirt fired the circle of bullets around her, pretending to kill her.

The operating room, with its whitewashed walls and bare concrete floor, was not a promising sight. There was an iron bed in the back left corner and a rusty autoclave on a counter against the far right wall. Other than that, the room had no equipment.

The man in the white jacket began examining Claire while two women, dressed entirely in black and with only their eyes visible, knelt next to Margaret. They began to cut at Margaret's jeans to expose the wound. As they pulled away the blood-soaked denim, the round edge of the protruding "bone" was exposed.

It was the end of a small flashlight Margaret had in her pocket. Margaret and I grinned at each other—we both felt pretty dumb that we had assumed it was a bone. I knelt on the floor with Margaret's head resting on my lap. She remained incredibly calm and still managed an occasional smile. Nearby, Catherine stood next to Claire as the doctor checked out her three bullet wounds. She was extraordinarily lucky to be alive. Suddenly the room was crowded with people. More soldiers arrived carrying a wounded comrade and laid him on the bed in the operating room. Another wounded soldier arrived in a wheelchair. Various civilians wandered in and out just looking around. No one spoke any English. The operating room had become a chaotic MASH unit.

The medical staff did the best they could, applying a clean dressing to Margaret's thigh and hooking her up to a saline drip. I saw the look of worry cross Margaret's face as the nurse went to insert the needle in her arm and knew what she was thinking. "It's OK," I reassured her. "It's a new needle. I saw the nurse take it out of a sealed packet."

The doctor—or paramedic—in the white jacket left Claire for a few minutes and came to look at Margaret, who by now was extremely thirsty. A soldier brought in some bottled water but the doctor shook his head. She could not drink anything because she might need an anesthetic. All I could do to relieve her thirst was put wet tissues against her lips.

Once both Margaret and Claire were somewhat stable and getting professional care, I left the operating room to find out where everyone else had gone. I walked back along the dark corridor toward where light spilled in through the entry door. Several Yemeni men were sitting on the floor against the walls. Before I reached them, I stopped. Just inside the door were Peter and Ruth, their lifeless bodies lying uncovered on blankets on the floor. Sue had told me they were dead but the reality had not sunk in until now. Sun from the open door spotlit their pale, still faces. Peter was next to the wall and Ruth beside him. I knelt down by Ruth's head and all I could think of was how desperately her mother would want to be here with her. I reached out and stroked her cheek, cold like marble in the sunlight. "That's from your mother, Ruth," I whispered.

An old man sat nearby. His knees, wrapped in a cotton futa, were tucked under his chin. As I looked up, I could see the sorrow and regret in his eyes. I quickly stepped outside and sat on a concrete bench in the compound. Several soldiers were leaning against the far wall and I could feel them watching me. After a few minutes, Catherine came and sat down beside me and we held each other, still trying to comprehend what had happened, what was still happening around us.

When we returned to the operating room, a gray-haired man in a uniform approached. He wanted to know the names of the two who were dead and the two who were wounded. Catherine and I realized neither of us knew Ruth's or Peter's last names. The police officer seemed skeptical that we could be touring with people without even knowing their names. He told us a helicopter was on its way to pick us up and would be here soon. Catherine then left with the police officer to make a formal identification of the bodies and I stayed with Margaret and Claire. I was surprised to see it was only about 2:30 PM.

Claire's anxious eyes, filled with fear and pain, looked up at me. "Peter?" she asked me. "Is Peter dead?" I did not know how to answer her. Of course I knew he was dead. I had seen his body only minutes before. Yet it still didn't seem real. Maybe I was mistaken. Maybe he wasn't dead, just unconscious. Confused about what to say, I told Claire I would go and find out for her. I did not want to tell her the wrong thing. I did not want to tell her terrible news and worsen her own serious condition, but I also knew she deserved to know the truth.

Catherine returned and I took her aside to discuss what we should tell Claire about her husband. There was no English-speaking medical expert to advise us on how the news would affect her. Catherine and I agreed that Claire was already fearing the worst and, in her situation, we would want someone to tell us the truth. Catherine had been with her almost constantly since the shooting and offered to break the news.

The wounded soldier still lay on the bed in the operating room. I went over to him and offered him my hand. "Shokran," I said using the Arabic word for thank you. "Shokran."

I had never expected someone to get shot and wounded trying to rescue us. I had never expected an armed rescue. As I stood beside him I deeply regretted that, by being in Yemen, I had somehow put these soldiers in danger. This man probably had a wife, perhaps more than one, and children. There might be no income for his family if he were injured and unable to work as a soldier. He nodded and turned his head away.

I realized it was probably embarrassing for him to have this unveiled female stranger standing beside his bed in a culture where even the nurses' faces were completely covered. Hoping he had understood my intentions, I moved away.

People continued to come and go in the operating room, most just curious spectators as far as I could tell. Claire and Margaret were now feeling a great deal of pain. The doctor returned and we tried to ask him to give them something for the pain. He did not understand what we wanted until Catherine hit on the right word. "Morphine," she said, pointing to the two wounded women.

"Ah, morphine—yes," the doctor's eyes lit up in comprehension. He was able to inject some kind of painkiller, then made us understand he wanted to take X-rays of the wounds to find out if the bullets were still embedded. Claire and Margaret were wheeled down the corridor to the X-ray room. Afterwards, they were made comfortable on beds in a quiet, pleasant room at one end of the building while we all awaited the helicopter. By now it was about 4:00 PM. A nurse, short and comfortably plump under her black chador, sat at a wooden table in the center of the room, her eyes smiling kindly at us. A soldier stopped by to say the helicopter would come soon and we should be ready to go when it arrived. Two more soldiers wandered in, smiling and shaking my hand. They began an animated conversation with the nurse. One pointed to me, then made kicking and pulling movements. The nurse looked back and forth between me and the soldier, her exclamations becoming more excited. She came over and hugged me. I suddenly realized the soldier was telling her the story of how I had taken the AK-47 from one of the kidnappers. I had gained some notoriety in the Yemen army. We all started laughing.

Several more soldiers came running into the room. "Come. Come." They lifted Margaret and Claire onto stretchers and took off at a virtual run down the corridor. Grabbing up the envelope of X-ray film given to me by the doctor, I followed close behind. I barely had time to say good-bye to the nurse.

In the courtyard, the stretchers were put in an ambulance and Catherine and I were directed into pickup trucks with mounted machine guns.

The drivers and soldiers were tense. They clearly didn't want to waste any time. The trucks roared out of the compound to a grassy field at the edge of the town. A huge crowd of people encircled the helicopter, clutching at their khafiyas and futas as its rotors whipped the air into a frenzy around them. The truck driver blasted angrily on his horn, but the crowd would not part to let us through. He was forced to drive across a ditch to get into the field. Once inside the circle of excited onlookers, Catherine and I made a run for the helicopter, followed by the stretcher-bearers. Inside the chopper's bare metal interior, I saw Pat, Sue, Eric, Brian and Gill sitting on the bench along the right side. Catherine and I scrambled in to sit alongside them. The remaining five hostages—Laurence and Margaret Whitehouse, Andrew, Chris and David—were not in the helicopter and no one knew where they were. Soldiers carried in Claire and Margaret and lay their stretchers down lengthwise on the floor. Two paramedics accompanied them, holding the saline drips. Moments later, more soldiers carried the blanket-wrapped bodies of Peter and Ruth inside and placed them in the remaining floor space just inside the door. I looked over at Claire, relieved that she was facing toward the rear of the helicopter and was not able to see Peter's body.

The chopper lifted off immediately. Through a porthole I could see the desert pulling away below us. When the shoreline appeared, I realized we were headed towards Aden—not Sana'a as I had expected. During the hour-long flight, the paramedics monitored Margaret's and Claire's vital signs and maintained the lifesaving saline supply. The rest of us sat in shock and silence, any attempt to speak drowned out by the blades thwacking the air above us. Ruth's shoes poked out the end of the blankets just a few inches away from my feet. I looked down at my own shoes, then back to Ruth's feet, visualizing my beige lace-up shoes jutting out the end of that blanket. The sheer random nature of our places in the firing line determined who had survived and who had died on the road to Aden.

6

GETTING OUT
OF YEMEN

Ambulances and private cars met the helicopter on the tarmac of Aden airport and rushed us all over to Republic Hospital. Unlike the deserted clinic in Mudiyah, the corridors of this hospital were congested with patients, visitors, and staff. Margaret and Claire were taken to a room for examination while everyone else waited in the corridor. When a doctor arrived I gave him the X-rays. He spoke a little English and, to my amazement, demanded to see proof of insurance before he would examine the two women.

"They have insurance," I explained. "We all had to have insurance to come on this trip. Our papers were taken by the kidnappers. We have nothing with us—no passports, no money, no papers." My patience was wearing dangerously thin.

"Need insurance papers for treatment." This guy must have trained in the U.S., I thought angrily. "These women have been shot. You will get paid. They have insurance. They need medical treatment—now." I was shouting at him, pointing to the bullet clearly visible in Claire's X-ray and ready to wring the guy's neck—except that we needed him. Whether he believed me or just wanted this crazed American woman in her grubby clothes out of his face I don't know, but at last he turned to take a look at Margaret's blood-soaked thigh. Intent on finding a way to contact either the American or British embassy, I left the room and made my way down the crowded corridor.

"English? Does anyone speak English? Telephone? English?" For several minutes I received only blank stares as I pushed my way through the throng, trying to find someone who could help me locate a phone number and place a call.

"British man here. From embassy. He come back soon," a voice came from somewhere in the crowd of puzzled faces. I searched among the faces staring at me, looking for the speaker. At that moment David Pearce, the British consul, came striding down the corridor to take charge.

While Claire and Margaret remained in the hospital, the rest of us were transferred to the Movenpick Hotel where a senior manager of Explore, Peter Crane, and various Yemeni officials waited to greet us in a private reception room. They expressed their sorrow at what had happened and told us that arrangements had been made for us to stay at the hotel while they sorted out flights home for us. Peter Crane's eyes filled with tears as he spoke to us. I felt badly for him, sensing he needed help as much as we did.

The fate of our five fellow travelers was still a mystery. They were not at the hotel and no one seemed to know where they were. Gill in particular was desperate for news of her partner Chris. Just as we were being given keys to our rooms, a member of the hotel staff told me I had a phone call at the reception desk. It was Margaret Scobey, deputy ambassador at the American embassy in Sana'a. To my great relief, she assured me the embassy had been in constant communication with my family in New Zealand and that they already knew I was unharmed. The moment Ms. Scobey mentioned my family, I began to cry. The hotel receptionist tactfully placed a box of tissues on the counter beside me and withdrew to a back office. Ms. Scobey explained that, although she was in Sana'a, the embassy doctor Chuck Rosenfarb was already on a flight to Aden and would contact me as soon as he reached the hotel.

It was after 9:00 PM when I finally escaped to the privacy of my hotel room. A flood of phone calls followed. Most important were calls from two of my five brothers, overjoyed I was alive and amazed to hear my story. I called my best friend Marilyn in Rochester and left her a voicemail message, then took a few calls from the news media in New Zealand

and the United States. By midnight, I desperately needed some sleep and asked reception not to forward any calls except from family members. I had nothing with me but the clothes I was wearing. One sleeve was stained with Margaret's blood and desert dirt grimed my shirt and pants. I washed everything I was wearing in the bathroom basin and hung my clothes to dry over the shower so they would be clean and a little more respectable to wear next day. At that moment, just as I realized there was no bathrobe in the hotel room, there was a knock at the door. It was Dr. Rosenfarb from the American embassy. I had completely forgotten he was coming to see me. Great. A personal visit from the American embassy and I'm stark naked with all my clothes soaking wet. I was consumed with a fit of laughter when the doctor knocked again, no doubt concerned about my state of mind.

With a towel around me, I opened the door a crack, explaining to the doctor and another embassy official with him that I very much appreciated their visit, but I was not exactly dressed for company. They probably wondered if my state of dress reflected post-traumatic stress disorder but, after I assured them I was fine and did not need anything to help me sleep, they agreed we should postpone further conversation until the morning.

Never have clean sheets and a bed felt so good as they did that night. Never has life seemed so fragile and time so precious. Exhaustion quickly overcame me. I fell asleep before I had time to reflect further on all that had happened, not waking until the call for early morning prayers.

Next morning, I learned that the remaining hostages had been returned to Aden very late the previous night. We gathered in a conference room after breakfast to hear their story. Only Laurence, Chris and David Holmes had survived to tell it. Margaret Whitehouse and Andrew Thirsk were dead.

When the security forces approached Abu Hassan's campsite on the morning of December 29, Hassan made the decision to resist. He instructed several of his followers to go to the wadi and bring back five of the hostages. Margaret, Laurence and Chris were chosen because they happened to be at the front as we began to file down the wadi, but Hassan had apparently asked for Andrew and David by name. Yellow Pants tried to send Margaret back to stay with the rest of us, but Purple Skirt insisted she go ahead. Once they reached the campsite, the five hostages were taken in one of the Land Cruisers to the defense post set up the previous day. It was about a half-mile further down the dirt track from where we had camped the night before. A small hill provided the kidnappers a lookout point and shelter. Hassan positioned himself there with five men, including the chubby one who had reminded me of a Mexican bandit. Hassan hoped that the presence of the hostages, forced to stand in front of the kidnappers, would stop the army advancing. Bandit opened fire with his shoulder-mounted grenade-launcher. The soldiers returned fire and the battle was on. A kidnapper operating the machine gun hammered out rounds from the Russian-made weapon on its bipod support. Hassan also began firing his rifle toward the troops. As the intensity of fighting increased, two younger men urged Hassan to retreat. He told them to go back to the rear line at the camp where Purple Skirt was in command. I realized, when I heard this part of the story, that it was these young men, in retreat from the front line of the battle, whom I had seen walking towards us as we stood on the berm.

Hassan, Bandit and the machine gun operator fell back toward the road behind the hill, forcing the hostages to carry ammunition belts and explosives. Noticing that Bandit had been wounded, Hassan pulled David Holmes aside and demanded he call the British embassy on the satellite phone. Of course, David had no idea of the embassy's number and telephone directories are not usually on hand in the middle of a desert shootout. David feigned a heart attack and fell to the ground near the gunner, who resumed firing the machine gun between the legs of the hostages.

"I've been hit," Andrew called out, falling on his back as a bullet struck him in his abdomen. Margaret Whitehouse instinctively stepped forward and knelt beside him, pulling out a handkerchief to try to stop the bleeding.

"Bless me," she cried as a bullet struck her in the heel. As she attempted to help Andrew, both of them were shot again, in the head and legs, by high-velocity bullets. As Margaret collapsed, a round of seven bullets from the machine gun blasted through her left groin. With only two hostages left standing and the troops almost on top of their position, Hassan retreated once more, intending to join Purple Skirt at the camp. He grabbed Chris as a shield and pulled him along while the machine gun operator grabbed hold of Laurence. As Hassan was pushing him, Chris accidentally stepped on his foot, causing Hassan to lose his balance. Chris ran for some nearby rocks, and Hassan pointed his gun towards him but did not fire.

Meanwhile, Laurence, enraged by his wife's death, turned on the machine gunner, who had by now abandoned his heavy weapon. "You've killed my wife. You've killed my wife," screamed the mild-mannered teacher, grappling with the younger man and trying to wrest a pistol from him. The pistol went off—leaving two neat holes through the front of Laurence's shirt, but just missing his chest. Chris bravely ran back to help Laurence overcome the gunner. Soldiers reached them moments later, capturing Hassan and pinning down Laurence's assailant. Laurence revealed to us that one of the soldiers offered him the pistol, as if to indicate he should shoot the machine gunner in revenge for the death of his wife. Only David, still lying on the ground nearby, noticed that the wounded Bandit was pulling out a hand grenade. David shouted to the soldiers. More shots rang out, killing Bandit before he could activate the grenade.

While the security forces had overrun the front line and captured Hassan, the kidnappers holding the remaining eleven of us at the campsite were still engaged in battle at the rear. The officer in charge demanded that Hassan tell his men to surrender. Taking Hassan with them, the soldiers pushed toward the camp where the eleven of us still stood in the crossfire.

Chris explained that they did not know what happened next in the gun battle because the five of them—including Margaret who was already dead and Andrew who was close to death—were taken in military trucks back to the main road and then on to a military base. Andrew died en route, and his and Margaret's bodies were removed for separate transport to Aden. The three survivors were driven to Aden.

At the end of the two-hour battle, four tourists, two kidnappers and possibly one soldier were dead. Two tourists and several soldiers were wounded. Three kidnappers were captured alive, but a dozen more, including the murderous Gray Shirt, had escaped into the wide open desert.

As controversy over the rescue grew in the outside world, we survivors cloistered ourselves in the Movenpick Hotel. We had a floor to ourselves to which other hotel guests and the press were denied access. Even in the public areas of the hotel, the press maintained a remarkably sensitive distance from us, a few reporters cautiously striking up low-key conversations with those who were ready to talk. Mostly, we just wanted to talk to each other, helping fill in pieces of the bizarre and terrifying events we had experienced together. Many people were wonderfully kind to us. An American missionary and his wife, a nurse, brought us clothing. Embassy staff anticipated the need for us to borrow some cash for personal items we might need. A friend in Rochester and a work colleague also took the initiative to wire a few hundred dollars to me.

In groups of twos or threes, we made trips over to the Republic Hospital to try to offer some consolation to the widowed and wounded Claire. Margaret and Claire shared a room that was reasonably private and quiet. Both faced uncertainty about when they could be evacuated to London for better medical care and what long-term damage the bullets had done. While Claire was understandably despondent, Margaret displayed the same calm good spirits that had impressed me throughout our trip.

On the second day after the rescue, an American approached me as I was leaving a conference room in the hotel. He introduced himself as Mark Sofia, an agent with the FBI. He explained that the FBI had immediately sent investigators to Yemen and he would appreciate it if I would be willing to answer a few questions. I sat down with Mark and a second agent, Brad Deardorff, in their hotel room. They were both courteous and acutely aware of the traumatic events I had been through. I explained as best I could everything that had happened during the kidnapping, and sketched out the rough map showing the key features of the terrain and where I thought we had been taken on the first and second days. My recognition of the constellations during the night allowed me to indicate a "due north" direction on the map and, thanks to frequent reference to my watch during the kidnapping, I was able to assign a fairly precise time to key events. Mark and Brad asked if I would approach the other non-American hostages to see if any of them would also be willing to provide information and I agreed to ask. Several were willing to do so.

The Yemen authorities also conducted interviews with each of us individually. In the conference room that had become a gathering place for us to meet and receive updates on our situation, the British consul David Pearce explained to us the procedure for the police interviews. We were asked to stop by a table at an unused end of the hotel's dining room during a certain time of day. Several police officers sat around a table.

A man with thinning reddish hair translated for several other police officers, who took down notes. All these formal inquiries were conducted professionally and with respect for our ragged nerves. One British newspaper claimed that Laurence Whitehouse was asked to revoke his statement expressing uncertainty whether his wife was killed by army or terrorist bullets. The paper went so far as to claim that Laurence was denied permission to leave Yemen unless he changed his statement. Laurence told me that the story was a lie and he was never pressured to change anything he had said.

During the kidnapping, it had not occurred to me that there would be any formal investigation, let alone a trial of the kidnappers. My expectation, while I was held hostage, was that we would be released as a result of negotiations between the Yemen authorities and the kidnappers. I assumed that any negotiated agreement would allow the kidnappers to go free.

Although David Pearce and the tour leader Dave Nott did their best to keep us informed about what was being done to get us home, stress began to show among some of the hostages. David Holmes complained bitterly that Yemen police had still not returned our luggage to us. Relations between Gill and Chris seemed tense, Gill perhaps feeling angry that Chris had gone off without her as we left the wadi, leaving her alone during the terrible ordeal. Laurence was devastated by Margaret's death and sat weeping, telling us how bravely she had put herself at risk to tend to Andrew, how she uttered the words "bless me!" when she was shot—the same words she used when she missed hitting a ball at tennis. All of us took turns sitting with him and tried to offer some comfort. During that time I found myself drawing closer to Pat, whose composure and attitude seemed most compatible with my own. Sharing quiet conversations and a few jokes with her was a wonderful source of support. Dave Nott was also under considerable strain as he tried to make arrangements to get us all home. At one point, I took Dave aside and bought him an ice cream from the hotel's coffee shop, giving him a chance to talk through his worries and feelings about what had happened. I'm a great believer in the therapeutic powers of ice cream.

After a second night in Aden, on New Year's Eve we were flown by Yemen's domestic airline to Sana'a and transferred to the Taj Sheba Hotel. From my room that evening, I could hear the music of a noisy New Year's Eve party in the hotel's ballroom. It seemed strange that life was still going on as normal for so many people when my own life had entered a twilight zone. I love to dance and felt tempted to join the party, just to reclaim some aspect of my normal life, but the possibility of being photographed by a reporter kept me in the privacy of my room. Gill felt the same way, wanting to use the hotel swimming pool but not doing so for fear of being photographed.

On New Year's morning, all the hostages except me and the two wounded women boarded a flight to London. As I waved goodbye to the minivan escorting them to the airport, I felt immensely relieved to be alone at last. As a certified introvert, I had found the constant group interaction of the last few days highly stressful. I needed time to myself. The bodies of Ruth, Peter, Margaret and Andrew were sealed in metal caskets and, accompanied by David Pearce, were returned to London via Amman by Jordanian Airlines. The last of our tour group to return home were Margaret Thompson and Claire Marston. Margaret described their medical evacuation flight from Aden back to London on January 3 as the flight from hell. Along with the pain of her injuries, she suffered from food poisoning, which made her sick through much of the journey.

My flight to the United States via Frankfurt was not scheduled to depart until close to midnight on January 1. Margaret Scobey would escort me to the airport in her private car. In the meantime, Dr. Rosenfarb, his wife and twelve-year-old daughter kindly met me for lunch and took me to visit the Old Quarter so that I could replace a few of the souvenir items stolen from my luggage. Surrounded by the noisy crowds of Yemenis in the markets, I found myself instinctively regarding every one of them as a potential threat. Every loud noise set me on edge and every face framed in a khafiya reminded me of the kidnappers. How different it seemed now from when I had been in the same markets just a week earlier, on the first day of the tour. In spite of feeling edgy in the crowds, I was glad to have this chance to be among the people of Yemen again; to go home with this last memory of the vibrant, colorful culture I had originally come to see.

7

FALLOUT—PERSONAL AND POLITICAL

My first few days back in the United States were a whirlwind of reunions with friends and phone calls from TV and radio stations. A crowd of friends and television cameras was waiting at the Rochester airport to greet me, even though my connecting flight from Newark had been delayed nearly ten hours. My voice-mail box was crammed with messages from the media. One call invited me to fly back to New York the next day to appear on NBC's Today Show. I loved the idea of meeting the show's co-hosts Katie Couric and Matt Lauer, but flights were still disrupted by weather all over the northeast. The prospect of spending more time stuck in airports had little appeal, so instead I agreed to be interviewed remotely by Katie Couric from a Rochester television studio. Much to my amusement, the local TV station sent a white limousine to pick me up at 5:00 AM. The limo was longer than my driveway and I was relieved it was still too early and dark for any of my neighbors to see me climb into it. There were many more requests for interviews that I simply did not have time to do.

Thirty hours after arriving home from Yemen I was back at work, showing up in my office on Monday morning, January 4, to meet my new management team and start running the color copier business unit. At Xerox, the story of my separating a terrorist from his Kalashnikov spread quickly and did wonders for my management image. There were plenty of "don't mess with Mary" jokes and suggestions that my management job was a cover and I had really been a CIA operative all along. A corporate officer in the company leaned confidentially towards me at a meeting and said, "You realize you are now the most famous person in the company, other than the CEO."

"Sure," I replied with a laugh. "It's my fifteen minutes of fame." There were also expressions of love and relief at my safe return from friends and colleagues, which overwhelmed me. Perhaps the greatest blessing of my experience as a hostage was discovering, and deeply appreciating, how many people cared about me. Even total strangers, recognizing my face from the newspaper stories, would approach me in the supermarket to welcome me back to Rochester.

The first weeks after the kidnapping were a strange time in which nothing seemed real and I operated on autopilot. People asked if the experience left me feeling anxious or fearful. On the contrary: I felt invincible. If I had survived the kidnapping and rescue, I could cope with and survive anything. I drove my Jeep much more aggressively than usual through the city's snowy streets and saw little need even to lock my front door at night. Life had a surreal quality to it, as if it was a parallel existence. I was experiencing a disturbing feeling of disconnection from the world. In my first post-Yemen journal entry, dated January 6, 1999, I wrote:

> There is some new and different Mary writing in this journal today. She is here with me but I do not know her yet. How could I ever have imagined what Yemen held in store—how it would change my life, change even the core of who I am? It has stripped away all meaning from my former life, left choices as stark and barren as that Yemen desert. There is only living and dying—two states divided by a line so fragile I felt I could be in either state and not know the difference.
>
> Where did it come from—that belief I would survive; that incredulity that I might actually die; my refusal to accept that ending to my life? It was a death without meaning—and I rejected the lack of meaning, of purpose, more than I rejected death itself.
>
> I found no God in those moments of expecting death. It was indeed "a lonely place to die." Perhaps whatever we already believe becomes our resource at such a time. Those who

believe in God will experience God. Those who believe only in the meaning we give to our own lives will reach for meaning from within. It seemed to me only my willpower existed—that the will to stay alive was the only force at my command.

Will it be possible to go back to my corporate career? I am going to work, attending meetings, but I wonder how it can ever seem relevant again. People are talking about the same business issues and the issues seem so trivial. Can I ever care about a new product introduction or quarterly sales results again? Can it ever seem important?

Everyone comments on how calm I seem to be. And, in a sense, I am. I can accept what happened, feel good about my own behavior. There are no nightmares. Yet I am tightly wired. There is a grip of tension inside me that even sleep does not relieve. I feel the need to break out of everything in my past life and begin an entirely new journey, stripped of all possessions and pretense. But where is the journey to? I am lost in space, adrift between lonely planets and cold chunks of asteroids. In free fall, my body is occupied by the mind and heart of a stranger.

The first weeks of the business year always involved huge kick-off training events with the Xerox sales force; one scheduled for Chicago and one in Seville, Spain. These highly people-intensive events were particularly stressful for me in 1999. I attended every activity where I was needed, including giving motivational speeches, but found myself needing to escape whenever possible to the quiet of my hotel room. My own staff, and Xerox employees I had never met before, were wonderfully supportive. One man who had seen active service in the military, and had experienced live combat, was particularly empathetic. From his words and the look in his eyes, I could tell he knew exactly what I was feeling.

I did my best to imitate life as usual during the day, but spent my evenings searching the Internet, seeking the latest news reports on the kidnapping. There was so much I wanted to know about what had really happened—who was responsible, and what the consequences might be. Between the time we were rescued and my return to Rochester, I had seen very little news, other than some CNN coverage during the three nights we spent in the Movenpick and Taj Sheba hotels.

As I searched the world's Web sites, it became clear the kidnapping had kicked off a major diplomatic storm between Yemen and Britain. At issue was why Yemen security forces had been dispatched so quickly to launch an armed rescue. As soon as he received word of an ambush involving British citizens, Victor Henderson, the British ambassador to Yemen, had urged the government not to use force to resolve the situation. American embassy staff had reinforced this view, and Australia had sent an envoy from its nearest embassy, in Saudi Arabia, to help negotiate a peaceful solution. Since New Zealand maintains no embassy in that part of the world, the Australian envoy had been asked by the New Zealand government to look out for me as well as the two Australian hostages. I felt honored, in retrospect, to discover that the governments of four different countries—the United States, New Zealand, Australia and Britain—had all gone to bat for me.

Their insistence on peaceful negotiation was well founded. I discovered that kidnapping experts worldwide, whether police or private agencies, recommend that a hostage situation is best resolved by negotiation, no matter how protracted. The Yemen government's decision to launch an armed rescue attempt, only twenty-four hours after the abductions, was perceived by the various embassies as displaying a gross error in judgment and blatant disregard for their wishes and advice. Many felt that the deaths of four hostages might have been avoided had a more cautious approach been taken.

In defense of their actions, Yemen political leaders claimed their security forces had no choice but to attack if any of the hostages were to be saved. In a communique to British prime minister Tony Blair, Yemen's prime minister Abdel Karim al-Iryani was reported to have said that "the western hostages would have been killed by their extremist kidnappers unless the security bodies had quickly taken action to rescue them." He went on to say that "the extremists did not give any chance to negotiations," and that "the Yemeni security forces intervened when the kidnappers began to kill their hostages." Yemen's interior minister Hussein Arab maintained that the kidnappers had given an ultimatum: Unless two jailed

Islamic Jihad leaders were released in one hour's time, the kidnappers would begin killing one hostage every two hours. The Yemen ambassador to Britain was summoned to the Foreign Office twice to explain his government's actions. He stated that the kidnappers had "planned a massacre of the whole group of tourists." However, the Yemen leaders' explanations were in conflict with the testimony of those of us who were directly involved. We hostages all knew that, at the time we first heard gunfire in the distance, all of us were still together and alive in the wadi, with no direct indication that any of us were about to be killed.

I too was increasingly puzzled by the decision to rescue us so quickly by force. Within a few days of the rescue, I learned that the kidnappers belonged to a militant Islamic organization called the Aden Abyan Islamic Army (AAIA) and that several kidnappers, including their leader Abu Hassan, had been captured. From reports by journalists who were in Yemen to investigate the story, I discovered that the AAIA was opposed to the Yemen government, which was apparently holding some of its members in prison. With that limited knowledge, it occurred to me that rescuing the hostages may have been a secondary factor in the attack. Perhaps the security forces saw this as a unique opportunity to eliminate the troublesome Abu Hassan and his AAIA once and for all. The kidnapping of tourists provided justification to attack the AAIA while many of its members were assembled together in a known location. Perhaps the risk of hostages dying in the attack was considered acceptable collateral damage.

Preliminary information about the kidnappers' identities and their demands had already made its way into the international press by the time I returned from Yemen on January 2. Early newspaper reports, some published within twenty-four hours of our evacuation from the battle scene, identified the kidnappers as part of the Islamic Jihad movement. Two motives for the kidnapping were reported in the first few days after the events: the release of an Islamic Jihad leader called Sheikh Salih Haidara al-Atwi, and retaliation for the bombing of Iraq. Reporters had apparently gleaned that information from officials familiar with the negotiations.

Relations between Yemen and Britain had further deteriorated on January 3 when the London-based *Daily Telegraph* printed a story in which an official at the Foreign Office suggested that Yemen's application to join the British Commonwealth might not be approved. Yemen immediately took a "we don't want to play with you anyway" attitude, announcing that it was a former British foreign minister who had pressed Yemen to apply for membership in the first place and that Yemen was no longer interested in pursuing the application, thank you very much. The political tit-for-tat struck me as absurd. I wanted to sit both governments down in a room and tell them to stop being so damned childish: "Innocent tourists are dead. Men capable of violent acts of terrorism are running free in both your countries. Get your acts together, cooperate on gathering evidence, make arrests and conduct fair trials. Focus on the real issues, guys, and stop bickering." I knew, of course, that the world just doesn't work this way.

Each night, as I surfed the Web in my home office, I gathered small scraps of new information about the kidnapping. One story in particular jumped out at me, a story that disclosed the identity of Purple Skirt. I stared at his name on the page, strangely shocked to discover that he had a real name. At 3:50 AM on January 7, I made the following note in my journal:

> The British press are covering the issues much more than the U.S. press. One article named the terrorist who held his gun to my back: Ali al-Khadar al-Haj.
>
> How strange it felt to see a name, to think that he has a family, a mother who named him. To think this human being, who did not know anything about me, was willing to kill me for his cause. Yet I think killing was not so easy for Ali al-Khadar al-Haj. He did not kill Eric or Catherine, only threatened. Perhaps there was some corner of his heart, his conscience, that held him back. I would so much like to know what his intentions were as he forced me across the desert at gunpoint. What did he hope to accomplish when we reached the soldiers?

The identity of Bandit, killed by soldiers during the rescue, was also revealed in news reports. Bandit turned out to be an Egyptian, known by the alias Osama al-Masri, who was affiliated with Egypt's Islamic Jihad and its founder Dr. Ayman al-Jawahiri. Bandit had apparently moved to Yemen to avoid arrest by authorities in Egypt for his involvement in terrorism there.

The mystery I most wanted to solve was the kidnappers' motives. It seemed to me that without information about the kidnappers themselves—their names, their backgrounds, their family relationships—I would not fully understand why they had abducted us. I saw motive as something much broader than a specific set of demands. To me, motive was the entire personal and political context of these men's lives that culminated in the kidnapping. Knowing Purple Skirt's real name, knowing he was only twenty-six years old, and that he worked as a taxi driver—these details were small but important pieces of the puzzle. What the kidnappers really wanted was impossible to separate from who they were and how they viewed the world.

About a week after I returned home to the United States, I first became aware that several British men had been arrested in Yemen just prior to the kidnapping. Apparently they had been accused of some kind of bombing conspiracy. I was immediately curious about these jailed Britons and began to follow their story on the Internet as closely as I followed news related to the kidnapping.

Slowly, details about the British detainees began to emerge. On December 30, British diplomats first heard hints that the Yemeni authorities had received information, five days before the kidnapping, about a bomb plot against British facilities in Aden. Apparently, the Yemenis had obtained this information from an Islamic militant who had been arrested. On January 5, the BBC quoted security forces in Sana'a as saying the kidnappers had wanted to exchange the hostages for suspected bomb plotters but there was still no indication these plotters were from Britain. Only on Wednesday, January 6 did the interior minister Hussein Arab announce that eight members of "a western sabotage group" had been arrested in Aden on December 24.

One version of the story suggested that even this announcement was only forthcoming after an uncle of one of the detainees, Yemen-born Malik Nasser Harhara, became concerned about his nephew and went looking for him. When the uncle discovered that his nephew, along with some British and Algerian associates, was in jail, he turned to the British embassy for help. Yemen authorities claimed they had not informed the embassy about the arrests because they were not convinced of the authenticity of their detainees' British passports. When I read this, I immediately felt skeptical. Surely verifying the authenticity of the passports would have been best achieved by going straight to the British embassy. I concluded that the delay was most likely for another reason: to extract as much information from the prisoners as possible before any diplomatic intervention constrained the investigation. Once aware of the arrests, British diplomats immediately demanded consular access to the five men. On January 9, after the British foreign secretary had phoned the Yemen prime minister, the British consul David Pearce was able to visit the arrested men. He reported that the prisoners were looking "reasonably well."

Once the British authorities validated the detainees' passports, Yemen accused Britain of harboring terrorists. To prevent more terrorists arriving in Yemen, the Yemen government decreed that British citizens, unlike other members of the European Union, would no longer be allowed to apply for visas upon entering the country and must obtain visas at Yemeni embassies overseas. Britain, miffed at its demotion in status by a former colony, retaliated by banning all travel to Yemen by British citizens—for their own safety, of course. British Council centers in Sana'a and Aden were closed and their employees repatriated. It wouldn't be until the end of April 1999 that both countries would agree to reconsider these measures.

Few Britons, or any other nationalities, were likely to want to go to Yemen anyway. Concerned by the lack of security for travelers, British Airways cancelled all its flights between London and Yemen. A manager in the Taj Sheba Hotel told me before I left Yemen that within forty-eight hours of the deadly rescue, virtually every foreign tour group had canceled their reservations for his hotel. By mid-January, the chairman of the Association of Independent Tour Operators commented that he would be "amazed if there is a single UK tourist still in Yemen." The sudden drop in tourists forced Yemen Airways to cancel a quarter of its flights to and from Europe. As hotels struggled to stay afloat by offering 50 percent discounts and local tour companies went out of business in the first few months of 1999, Yemen lost an estimated $250 million in tourism revenues and thousands of tourism-related jobs disappeared. In a country with an unemployment level of about 30 percent, AAIA leader Abu Hassan won few admirers among his countrymen and the families they supported.

The political climate created a difficult international environment in which to investigate the kidnapping and deaths of the tourists. The Scotland Yard detectives and FBI agents discovered that Yemen authorities were simply not going to give them a free hand to conduct interviews and gather evidence.

On January 5, Abdel Majid Zendani, a senior figure in Yemen's major opposition party al-Islah, was quoted as telling a Dubai newspaper, "We refuse any interference by foreigners in our legal system." Zendani labeled such interference as an attack on Yemen sovereignty, and cautioned that British or United States investigations into the kidnapping would imply that Yemen "does not have people competent to do the job." Zendani's objections may well have reflected his own background as a veteran Afghan-Arab (an Arab who had joined the mujahiddin in the fight against the Soviets in Afghanistan) who was acquainted with Osama bin Laden, but his views were clearly shared by authorities in Aden. After four days in Yemen, the Scotland Yard detectives had still not been allowed to interrogate the captured kidnappers or visit the site of the kidnapping and rescue. Two of the detectives flew from Sana'a to Aden but, in spite of promises of full cooperation from the governor of Aden, were suddenly ordered by the province's security chief General Mohammed Salih Turaik to leave on the next available flight. A *London Times* reporter, Michael Binyon, suggested the position taken in Aden reflected not just a Yemen-Britain conflict but the ongoing rift between provincial authorities in the south and the national government in Sana'a. The official position from Yemen's interior ministry was one of full cooperation with the British investigators, yet neither Scotland Yard nor the FBI representatives gained access to the kidnappers. They were forced to rely instead on reports of interrogations conducted by Yemeni investigators.

From what I learned in the press, and from comments by FBI and Scotland Yard agents who interviewed me, relations between the

American investigators and Yemen authorities appeared to have gone somewhat more smoothly—perhaps because Yemen felt it had much more to lose by alienating the United States. On my December 31 flight from Aden back to Sana'a, I happened to sit next to Mark Sofia, one of the FBI agents who had interviewed me earlier that day. He confirmed that while the criminal aspect of kidnapping and shooting American citizens was certainly part of their investigation, the FBI agents sent to Yemen were mostly focused on possible links between the kidnappers and other known terrorists, including Osama bin Laden.

I found myself not only searching the Internet for clues about the kidnapping but trying to learn more about terrorism and Islam in general. In a Rochester bookstore I located *Inside Terrorism* by Bruce Hoffman. Hoffman's chapter on religion and terrorism points out that "terrorism and religion share a long history" dating back to the Jewish Zealots of the first century AD, the Hindu thugs of seventh-century India, and the Muslim assassins who used "treacherous violence" against Christian crusaders in the eleventh century. Hoffman notes that "for the religious terrorist, violence is first and foremost a sacramental act or divine duty executed in direct response to some theological demand or imperative . . . its perpetrators are consequently unconstrained by the political, moral or practical constraints that may affect other [secular] terrorists." Terrorist events based on religious ideology apparently result in far more deaths than those driven by ethnic, separatist or nationalist causes. How convenient for the militants, I thought, that acting on God's behalf justifies any extremes of violence.

My evenings—focused on the world of terrorism—contrasted strangely with my days, spent fighting the copier wars. The major responsibilities of my job as a business unit general manager were to ensure that we launched new color copier products on time and we achieved planned sales revenues and profits. A color copier is a perfectly good and useful thing, of course, and involves some impressive technology, but somehow it was hard to feel a better copier was going to make much difference in a world threatened by terrorism; a world where a lot of people think it's OK to kill you just because you don't adhere to the rules set down by their choice of religious beliefs. It was also hard to feel inspired by the prospect of having "launched the Xerox DocuColor digital color copier" as the noteworthy event in my eventual obituary. In journal entries during the week of January 7 I wrote:

> Today felt ominously normal. I now sense how easy it will be to slip back into the corporate career and live on the surface of life—never testing my real limits and possibilities. The idea of failing to really live scares me much more than death. Going from meeting to meeting, business trip to business trip. The months will rush by and what will I have accomplished? Does everyone feel like this? Is it part of middle age to see options closing off and get a kind of cabin fever? My friends don't talk about feeling this way. Perhaps I haven't asked . . . Somehow I can't see the rest of my life as limited to the climb to be CEO. How extraordinary that being a CEO should now seem rather mundane.

Disoriented as I felt about the course of my own life and my prospects at Xerox, I knew I was extremely lucky to have a life at all. I had come back alive and had the luxury of returning to my job. Margaret Thompson and Claire Marston had not been so lucky and, of all the survivors, they were most often in my thoughts. I called Margaret at her London hospital room on January 7, the day she was to have major surgery on her shattered left thigh. She sounded as calm and positive as ever, happy to have her daughter Carrie visiting her from Texas and buoyed up by the tremendous support she was receiving from well-wishers. My efforts to reach Claire were less successful. Her family had asked that no calls be put through to her room, and I learned only that she was doing as well as could be expected following surgery on her wounds earlier in the week. The pain of her injuries, combined with the emotional pain of Peter's violent death, prompted her family to shelter her as much as possible from any further distress.

A brief business trip to Europe later in January allowed me to stop overnight in London and visit Margaret. Pat Morris met me at a tube station and we drove to Wellington Hospital together. Margaret was sitting up in bed in a private room and looked much better than I was expecting. She proudly showed us how she was now able to swing both legs over the side of the bed, although she couldn't fully bend her "bad" leg yet. Doctors insisted on keeping her hospitalized because of the risk of infection. If a bullet misses vital organs and isn't immediately fatal, Margaret explained, the greatest cause of death is infection from the wound. Her doctors had already removed some dead tissue and would administer two weeks of intravenous antibiotics to keep gangrene at bay. I remembered the soldier in the Land Cruiser who had tried to tell me Margaret would die. No doubt he understood much better than I the risk of bullet-wound infection and the odds of survival for a gunshot victim who has no access to high-quality medical care.

It was good to talk with Margaret and Pat, comparing reactions and feelings with these two women who had shared the same experience. We talked about Ruth. Margaret distinctly remembered saying to Pat, "Ruth's been shot," moments before a bullet slammed into Margaret's leg. Yet Pat had no memory of hearing Margaret or seeing Ruth die. Pat feared that the images were buried deep in her subconscious and would suddenly return, reminding her of a scene she would just as soon forget. The way Ruth was shot led us to speculate that she had taken a bullet from an army sniper, a bullet intended for the kidnapper holding a gun to her back. However, inquest results would later show she was against a hard surface, probably already lying on the ground, when shot.

Margaret and Pat filled me in on meetings they and the other British-based hostages had had with Scotland Yard and the little news they had of Claire. We talked about counseling help and discovered none of us had felt much need for it. What was most valuable was simply to have time to ourselves, in the peace of our own homes—something Margaret had not yet been able to enjoy. When Pat and I left the hospital, I felt greatly relieved to know that Margaret was on the path to recovery and impressed as always at her amazingly positive attitude. Never once did she complain about the pain or the long weeks in the hospital, or express fear over how she would cope with the stairs when she resumed living alone in her upper-floor London apartment. She and Pat were already talking of doing a trip together in the future, perhaps to India.

Back at Pat's home, we sat on her living-room floor with a bottle of red wine. Like me, Pat does not believe in God. Faced with the prospect of immediate and violent death, she agreed that she did not suddenly "find God" either. Unlike me, though, Pat said she did believe she would die that day in the desert. "I have had a good life," she told me, "and I felt quite accepting of it. I thought that once I was dead there would simply be nothing—so dying didn't really matter after the fact."

On January 28, a tall, elegant black woman rang the doorbell at my home in Rochester. It was Detective Constable Beverly Mills from Scotland Yard, who had arranged to interview me as part of the Yard's investigation of the kidnapping. A few minutes later, we were joined by Brad Deardorff from the FBI. He explained that the FBI and Scotland Yard were working together on the kidnapping investigation and that Scotland Yard had agreed to let him sit in on Beverly's interview. I suggested we sit at my dining-room table where I served coffee and tea and a plate of cookies. Beverly asked if she could record the conversation. I had no objection, and was interested to learn from Brad that the FBI rules did not allow him to use a tape recorder. Their questions started from the very beginning: why I had decided to go to Yemen, and how and when I had booked my trip. No detail was overlooked. We began the interview at 3:30 PM and it was two hours before we had even reached the start of the ambush. By now, Brad had single-handedly consumed the entire plate of cookies.

By the time I had described the shoot-out, I realized I was twisting a paper napkin into knots in my hands. To my surprise, there were tears in Beverly's eyes. I was impressed that a professional detective, who has probably heard and seen variations on every form of violent crime, could still feel such empathy for the victims.

At one point, I described Purple Skirt (Ali al-Khadar al-Haj) aiming his handgun at Eric's head. "Was it a pistol or a revolver?" Brad asked.

"What's the difference?" I was embarrassed about my total ignorance of weaponry.

Brad lifted his sweater to reveal a gun in a holster on his hip. He apologized for bringing a gun into my home. "This is a pistol. A revolver has a cylinder."

"Ah, so revolvers are like the guns in westerns?" It had never occurred to me before that the name revolver comes from the bullets being loaded in a revolving cylinder. Seems obvious once you think of it.

"The gun Purple Skirt used was like yours," I told Brad. "It was a pistol."

Brad asked me if I remembered a low wall, like the one we stood on during the shoot-out, running perpendicular to the three parallel berms I had drawn on my map. He pulled out the map I had drawn for him in Yemen. I did not remember such a wall—Point 11 in Figure 3. Brad explained that the bullet that killed Ali al-Khadar al-Haj when he was pushing me forward at gunpoint was fired from behind that wall, striking him on his left side. I then understood why I had not immediately realized that Purple Skirt had been shot. He had fallen on his left side and the wound was not visible.

At the conclusion of the interview, about 9:00 PM, Brad commented that I probably didn't realize how lucky I was to have survived. "In most hostage situations where force is used for a rescue," he said, "the hostages are all dead within ninety seconds." Brad, a former Marine, had visited the scene of the shoot-out and noticed that the ground was covered in spent cartridges.

"It looked much more like a war zone than a crime scene," he told me. I commented that I probably owed my life to the soldier who shot al-Haj.

"You did quite a few things right yourself to save your own life," Brad replied.

8

A NETWORKING OPPORTUNITY

My close call with death had shaken up another special group of people: my family in New Zealand. I had had a number of phone calls with my brothers and sister, speaking to several of them within a couple of hours of our evacuation to the hotel in Aden. Even knowing I was safely back in Rochester, they were still concerned about me. My mother's advanced Alzheimer's disease made it impossible to communicate with her by phone. Staff at the nursing home where she lived later told me my mother had shown visible excitement when I appeared on a television news report. She had some awareness of events, but it was hard to know how much she understood of what had happened. By chance, a reunion of my high school was scheduled to take place in my home town of Palmerston North in February 1999. I decided to take the opportunity to visit my family and participate in the reunion. It was a rare chance to reconnect with friends and teachers from my childhood and teenage years. My boss at Xerox fully supported my request for time off and encouraged me to take as much time as I needed.

A week before I was due to leave for New Zealand, I discovered an unusual e-mail among the stack of messages my secretary Linda had left on my desk. It was dated January 27.

Hello Mary,
I concede this is an unusual sort of introduction, but it has the advantages of being expedient, direct and relatively

confidential. Besides, it's the only idea I could come up with.

I read with interest of your recent adventure in Yemen. You were lucky. Also pretty impressive under the circumstances. . . . Finding interesting people is difficult, particularly in Rochester. Meeting interesting women has been next to impossible. Therein lies the motive for this communication. I know nothing of your personal status, although from having read the local news stories it appears you are not married. This is not meant as a "come-on"; I'm much too shy for that. Rather, something like a networking opportunity, although I would like to meet you and/or talk with you.

The writer went on to explain that he was a finance executive at Bausch & Lomb, a Rochester-based company well known for manufacturing contact lenses and eye care products. He provided the names of two Xerox managers who were friends of his and could provide personal references for him. He concluded:

Again, I know this communication is a little unconventional. But you are an adventuress, and must be something of a risk-taker, so perhaps it will pique your curiosity. I hope so.
Regards,
Ray

I read the e-mail again with a chuckle. "Who is he kidding, claiming this isn't a 'come-on?' I bet Linda got a laugh out of this one." Then I noticed the e-mail was addressed not to me but to Mary L. Quinn, another Xerox employee who often received and forwarded e-mails intended for me. So much for the confidentiality Ray had intended. I set the e-mail aside but it had triggered an instinctive reaction. Intuition told me that this stranger, Ray Kaufman, was appearing in my life right now for a reason. I didn't know what the reason might be but I knew it was important I should meet him.

That evening, using my home computer, I replied:

Dear Ray,
I was intrigued to receive your e-mail today, and Mary L. Quinn who forwarded it to me was no doubt equally intrigued . . .

I explained that I was leaving for an overseas trip shortly but, if he would like to send me his home phone number, I would call him when I returned in several weeks' time. I also suggested he use my home e-mail address, rather than my Xerox address, for further correspondence.

Busy with all the work I needed to complete before my trip, I gave no further thought to the mysterious Ray Kaufman or his unexpected e-mail. I hoped that the trip to my native land and to my family might offer some relief from the underlying sense of tension I continued to experience, and provide some new perspective on the career uncertainty that continued to gnaw at me.

"I feel I've outgrown the corporate America thing," I wrote in my journal on the eve of my flight. "I am ready for a new growth path, a new mountain to climb . . . I walk nearer the unknown than ever before, pulled towards something I cannot see or touch but know is in my future . . ."

Families are never more important to any of us than when we face danger. It is often only when we come close to the possibility of never seeing them again that we appreciate how unique and precious a force they are in our lives, even when we live far apart. On the second day of the kidnapping, it was a photo of my five brothers and sister that I took from my suitcase and carried with me into captivity in the wadi. The photo had been taken a year earlier at my younger sister's wedding. My two oldest siblings were not in the photo. A stroke had cut Owen's life unexpectedly short when he was only fifty and Angela had died at the age of forty-three after a long battle with cancer. I find it strange when people regret getting older. The alternative to getting old is not living long enough to become old. After my own close encounter with dying, each year of being alive seems even more precious.

My ten days in New Zealand passed by all too quickly: noisy, joyous gatherings with my brothers and younger sister and their families; quiet times sitting with my mother in the garden of the nursing home; the fun of reuniting with so many schoolfriends from my childhood; interviews with television and radio stations. A New Zealand television channel was producing a show called *Coming Home* about expatriate New Zealanders and had asked to include me as one of the profiles. As a result, the *Coming Home* crew followed me around for much of my trip, much to the amusement of my family. With my brother Frank and sister Gabrielle and several nieces and nephews, I visited Waitarere Beach, where I had spent most of the summers of my childhood. The beach house my parents had once owned was still there, although we had some difficulty locating it. Sand dunes had built up substantially over the years, obscuring the house from the seashore. Other than the movement of the sand and the addition of more holiday homes, the tiny beach town of Waitarere had changed little in thirty years. There are still only two shops there, the same ones where we used to buy ice cream and milk shakes and the huge, boiled sweets we called gobstoppers. The tiny Catholic church where we attended Mass every Sunday morning still stands among the marram grass, adjacent to the church hall where we played bingo with a regular crowd of friends and neighbors every Wednesday evening. Cars can still drive along the broad expanse of hard-packed, silver-gray sand that stretches for miles along the North Island's southwestern coastline. The same breakers roll in relentlessly from the Tasman Sea, where I learned to body surf. Waitarere Beach represents my best memories of a New Zealand childhood.

I spent one particularly eventful day in Wellington, the capital city. The day included a morning appearance on a national radio talk show; lunch with an old boyfriend followed by a tryst, for old times' sake, back in my hotel room; afternoon tea with three nuns; and dinner at the beach-front home of a lesbian couple, one of whom I especially wanted to meet because she was a recipient of the 100 Heroines Award. As I noted in my journal that evening, Not a bad day's work!

It was difficult to return to winter in Rochester. Auckland in particular had become increasingly attractive to me. The city is situated on the beautiful Waitemata harbor. Its downtown bustles with outdoor cafes where young executives in designer suits talk on mobile phones and silver-haired sponsors of the America's Cup yacht race sample wine and mussels. On Queen Street, throngs of Asian college students wearing the latest grunge elbow their way past sunburnt tourists and office workers. With the largest Polynesian population of any city in the world, Auckland combines the casual warmth of the South Pacific with the technology and energy of the United States and the elegance of Europe. Could I find a way to live in both Auckland and America, to have the best of both worlds? I had hoped my trip to New Zealand would help resolve my doubts and uncertainty about my future, but it only created more complexity in the equation of life—more desires to fulfill and less willingness to compromise.

On my flight back to the United States, I watched New Zealand's coastline slip away from view into the vast Pacific Ocean. I knew I had to find a way to spend part of my life in these beautiful islands, yet not give up everything I had worked to achieve in the United States. Inevitably, my future would be something different from what it would have been had the kidnapping not occurred. Knowing I could just as easily be dead, I had the option to reinvent my life. The next thirty or forty years could be designed from scratch, as if my "first life" had never happened. It was an intriguing idea: starting life again with the benefit of all I had learned in my first life, but unconstrained by any former choices I had made. I could be anyone I wanted to be. I also knew I could not ignore my many unanswered questions about the kidnapping. Before I could leave the past behind, I had to understand it. Only then could my life go forward.

9

"I ONLY GAVE ORDERS TO KILL THE MEN"

In those early weeks of 1999, the trial of the kidnappers seemed my best prospect for finding out why the kidnapping had happened. By following news reports I knew that from the day of the rescue on December 29, Yemen's security forces had continued their search for the remaining kidnappers. Local tribal groups were asked to assist in identifying and reporting the whereabouts of those who had escaped. At the same time, prosecution lawyers prepared to bring charges against the three kidnappers already in custody as well as eleven more men who had been identified as participants in the crime but who were still at large. Including the three who died during the rescue, the number of kidnappers identified by name in news reports was seventeen. That correlated closely with my personal count of about eighteen men during the ambush, and reassured me the Yemeni police were more or less on track with their investigation.

Some details about Abu Hassan and his background began to emerge in the press. Newspapers published photographs of him, taken in his jail cell or being dragged into the courthouse by armed guards. I stared at the pictures of Abu Hassan, trying to link his face to my own memories of the man who had demanded our passports, who had come up to me asking, "Mary? Who is Mary?" and questioned my real nationality. I was surprised that his face did not seem more familiar to me. Of course, while we were held hostage, many of the kidnappers kept their faces at least partially covered with their headscarves and we did not really know which of them was the leader. Abu

Hassan was no more significant to us than Purple Skirt or Bandit, who had also appeared to be giving orders. "It's just as well I'm not being called upon to pick him out in a lineup," I thought to myself, as I filed away the photographs. My detective dad would not have been impressed.

According to press reports, Abu Hassan—or Zein al-Abidin abu Bakr al-Mehdar—was born in 1970 in the Markha district of Shabwah, where his family belonged to an important tribal group. When Hassan was only a young boy, his family, like many others, was expelled from the country by the communist regime controlling what was then the People's Democratic Republic of Yemen. He received his education in Saudi Arabia, graduating in 1987 from a general secondary school. During his teenage years, Hassan was also exposed to the teachings of the highly conservative Salafi sect of Islam and embraced its philosophy. I tracked down some articles about the Salafis and discovered they are a minority religious group who believe in returning to the roots of Islam as it was practiced in the time of the Prophet Mohammed. Salafism is a spin-off of Wahhabism, the predominant form of Islam practiced in Saudi Arabia.

With Hassan's inclination towards fundamentalism, it is not surprising that, soon after leaving high school, he was recruited to join the mujahiddin (or holy warriors) who fought to expel the Soviets from Afghanistan during the 1980s. In mosques all over the world, Muslim leaders exhorted young men to join their Afghan brothers in jihad against the Soviet occupation. Tens of thousands were recruited, particularly from Arab countries, to train and fight in Afghanistan. These non-Afghan mujahiddin became known as the Afghan-Arabs. Many of them were Yemenis, and Abu Hassan was among them.

With only this broad-brush picture of the lead kidnapper available to me, I looked forward to further press coverage of the trial, anticipating it would reveal more about Abu Hassan and his motives.

The trial began a mere two weeks after the rescue, at the courthouse in Zinjibar—the capital of the province of Abyan. I gave serious thought to whether I should try to attend the trial. It seemed important that one of the hostages should be there as a face in the courtroom to remind the judge, the defendants, the lawyers, and onlookers about the impact of the crime on real people: tourists who had simply been interested enough in their country and culture to visit. However, there was no possibility of my returning to Yemen without abandoning my job responsibilities and that did not seem fair to Xerox and the people who worked in my business unit. I also realized my presence would create yet another security problem for the Yemen government since I would be an easily recognized target for AAIA supporters who might seek to finish what Hassan had started.

British journalists covered the trial and I avidly followed the details they reported. Hassan and the two others who had been captured during the rescue arrived, handcuffed, in an armored police van accompanied by several pickup trucks carrying machine guns and troops. About two hundred soldiers took up positions on the courthouse balconies and the surrounding streets as a precaution against militants or tribal supporters who might try to free Hassan. Dressed in a clean shirt, a plaid futa and the empty leather case for his jambiya, he was dragged shouting into the courtroom.

"I did everything in the name of God, so I am sorry for nothing," Hassan yelled. "I am very famous now, but let everyone know I only gave orders to kill the men not the women." The waist-high dock wall, closed with a simple bolt, was all that separated the three defendants from the throng of lawyers, journalists, and diplomatic representatives crowding the courtroom. Reporters for al-Jazeera television, the BBC, and *The Times* of London jostled to question Hassan before the arrival of the judge and prosecutors. Asked how he felt about his victims—including Margaret Whitehouse, whose funeral was taking place that same day—Hassan showed only contempt and spat on the floor. "If my gun had not jammed I would have killed more," he sneered.

Pleading innocence was clearly not on Hassan's agenda. Nor was he concerned with endearing himself to his courtroom audience: "May God strike you all," he cursed to the crowded room.

When Judge Najib Mohammed al-Qaderi arrived, a member of the prosecution team read out the charges: abduction of sixteen foreigners, killing four of them, highway robbery, sabotage, and forming an armed militant group called the Aden Abyan Islamic Army to destabilize the government. Hassan then announced that he was rejecting representation by his appointed lawyer, Mohammed Thabet, and intended to represent himself. He was clearly more intent on using the courtroom and the trial publicity as a soapbox for his opinions than on defending himself against the charges—charges for which the prosecution demanded the death penalty.

The names of the hostages were also read out to the court, with a moment's silence after the names of those who died. Hassan paid no attention, using the time to joke with the co-defendants in the dock beside him. Asked his occupation, Hassan stood upright and announced grandly that he was a "mujahid working in the cause of God." His co-defendants were two brothers, Ahmed and Saad Atef, who claimed more earthly professions as a teacher and a soldier respectively.

To a number of observers, it seemed that Hassan rather than the judge was in charge of the proceedings. Hassan embarked upon an hour-long diatribe, which included lecturing the audience on the Koran and proclaiming his prowess as leader of the Aden Abyan Islamic Army. "Young people answered my call for jihad and have a blind obedience to me," Hassan boasted. Claiming to be "the managing mind" of the AAIA, he asserted that his organization was formed to "hoist the banner of jihad and fight secularism in Yemen and Arab countries. . . . We are launching jihad for the sake of Allah," he told the court. "Do you call that sabotage?" His impassioned monologue included further abuse of his hostages, calling us "the grandchildren of pigs and monkeys." When I read this quote in the newspapers, I found it humorous rather than insulting: the kind of petty name-calling I would expect from a schoolchild rather than a terrorist leader. Hassan's observation that "God sent [the hostages] to me so I took them," also amused me. I rather fancied the idea of being selected by God—I had never considered my life in quite such portentous terms. Other Marys, like the virgin I was named after, might receive such appointments from on high, but not me. Of course, believers of all religions tend to credit God for their lucky breaks. "I know Jesus was watching over us," a tearful woman will say to reporters after her family survives a tornado that demolished her home. Was Jesus not looking out for the three children killed in an auto accident the same day or the innocent bystander shot by a sniper? Did Hassan ever consider whether it was also God who sent the Yemen army to him? I have noticed that gods are rarely blamed for the things that go badly.

When the judge tried to interrupt him, Hassan merely dismissed the man in the black robes and green sash, telling him, "We are doing this my way, not yours." Hassan denied the court had any right to try him since it was not a true Islamic court. The judge seemed willing to let Hassan have his way, perhaps through weakness or perhaps because he was happy to let Hassan condemn himself. At one point during the first session, Hassan gave money to onlookers and sent them out to buy bottled water for everyone in the courtroom. Later, Hassan insisted that proceedings stop for half an hour so everyone could pray.

Of the two defendants initially on trial with Hassan, the elder brother Ahmed claimed he was innocent of the charges. He had not been present during the ambush, he said, and had been drawn into the battle when he arrived later to look for his brother. Ahmed explained to the judge that he had once been a member of AAIA but had left the organization some time ago. His younger brother Saad also pleaded not guilty. When Hassan took him from his village, Saad explained, he had only agreed to go along out of duty to try to free the Islamic Jihad leader Sheikh Haidara al-Atwi. According to courtroom observers, the eighteen-year-old looked terrified when Hassan lunged towards him in the dock, shouting, "He had to listen to me because I am the emir [leader] of the group and he had to obey me."

During the trial, Hassan described in some detail the ambush of our tour vehicles and the subsequent rescue by the government forces. He related how Osama al-Masri (Bandit) was wounded early on in the attack. Hassan described to the court how he then gave orders for the rest of the kidnappers to withdraw from the front line and, if they themselves were about to be killed, to shoot the rest of the hostages. His egomania and posturing aside, much of what Hassan claimed in court was consistent with the actual events I and my fellow hostages experienced.

Hassan continued his courtroom theatrics, appearing in a smart red turban and fingering his prayer beads as he insisted on representing himself. At one point in the trial, a female lawyer was added to the defense team. Hassan was not impressed. "I would rather die than be represented by a woman," he shouted, much to the amusement of his audience.

At times ranting to the court and at other times mumbling to himself or joking with his fellow defendants, Hassan took every opportunity to revile the United States, Britain, and the Yemen government. He accused President Clinton of bombing Iraq simply to distract attention from the Lewinsky scandal, and criticized the Yemen government for making military facilities available to the Americans. As for Britain, Hassan raged, this once great empire had become a mere puppet of America, its former colony.

I was greatly disappointed when, after the preliminary sessions, the judge closed the trial to outside observers, including journalists, and I was unable to follow its subsequent progress. Not only had I hoped to learn more about why the kidnapping had occurred but I was troubled about the likely outcome. Yemen had introduced the death penalty for kidnapping just four months before we were taken hostage, in an effort to control the country's epidemic of tribal kidnappings. Morally opposed to the death penalty for any crime, I found myself in an ethical dilemma over the possibility that the kidnappers would be executed. I debated whether I should contact the Yemen government, perhaps even its president, Ali Abdullah Salih himself, and request that the prosecution not seek the death penalty. I called the American embassy in Sana'a for advice on how to do this and was advised that my input would be unlikely to have any impact.

My views on the death penalty aside, I was not confident that Hassan would stay behind bars indefinitely if he were not executed. The pragmatism of Yemen's legal system and politics suggested that he might well be set free if future circumstances made it expedient to release him. How would I feel if my appeal for clemency resulted in Hassan's escape or release, and allowed him to kidnap and murder others? I also found myself on weak moral ground pleading with Yemen not to use the death penalty when a man had just been sentenced to death for the murder of a child in my own home city of Rochester, New York. It had not occurred to me to become active in protesting that death sentence. Could I be so ethically opposed to the death penalty that I would appeal the execution of Abu

Hassan in Yemen, yet remain passive about the same issue in the state of New York? Was there a greater moral responsibility to act in a situation in which I was personally involved as a victim, or in the community where I lived and had the power to vote? In spite of my belief that the death penalty is never morally justified, I chose not to become an activist in the matter, either in New York or in Yemen. I would leave the fate of Abu Hassan and his followers to the people, the procedures and the president of Yemen.

10

THE BRITISH BOYS

The kidnappers' trial was not the only high-profile court case going on in Yemen during the early months of 1999. By the time I returned from New Zealand, the British men arrested in Aden were also facing trial in Yemen, charged with "forming an armed gang to carry out a criminal plan to threaten the security of Yemen and carry out terrorist acts of killing, sabotage and bombings." The trials of the Britons and of the kidnappers took place almost simultaneously, but in different cities—Aden and Zinjibar respectively. I was curious to know more about why these British men were in Yemen in the first place. Their own families probably felt the same way.

News that their sons, brothers and husbands were imprisoned in Yemen for plotting terrorist acts came as quite a shock to the detainees' families in Britain. Many found it impossible to believe their loved ones could be associating with terrorists, let alone engaged in terrorism themselves. Relatives stressed that several of these "boys" were not even particularly religious and had shown no interest in Islamic fundamentalism. Having just returned from a reunion with my own family, I could sympathize with their distress. Even so, I was not convinced by the families' explanations for the men's presence in Yemen. One of the detainees, Shahid Butt, was described as a shop worker from Birmingham. Butt had a wife and four children and, according to news reports, had been active in Muslim humanitarian programs. He helped set up a youth club at Birmingham Central Mosque and volunteered in a drug prevention program. With his imposing height (over six feet) and outspoken views, Shahid Butt was highly visible in Birmingham's Islamic community and well known for his devotion, both to his religion and to serving fellow Muslims in need.

His brother Rachad was quoted as saying that Shahid had gone on holiday six or seven weeks earlier. They understood he was enjoying himself and studying Arabic. It seemed unlikely to me that a shopworker with a wife and four children to support would have the financial luxury of taking off on his own for a vacation lasting a couple of months. Did Shahid Butt's family really believe that explanation? I also discovered that Shahid Butt had been convicted in 1995 of fraudulently claiming over $25,000 in government welfare benefits, using stolen National Insurance numbers (the British equivalent of social security numbers), and had served an eighteen month jail term. His criminal record did little to enhance his credibility but may well have explained his ability to afford extended foreign trips. Monica Davis, the English wife of another detainee, Ghulaim Hussein, had a slightly more plausible explanation for why her husband was in Yemen. They were planning a family seaside vacation in Yemen, she said, and her husband had gone ahead to check if the country's climate was suitable for their little daughter, who suffered from asthma. Hussein had apparently given Yemen's fresh air the thumbs up because she and her daughter were to join him as soon as Monica finished her university exams. I was willing to believe the family vacation plans, but did Ghulaim Hussein really go to Yemen just to check the suitability of the climate? After all, some phone calls to the British consulate or to a doctor in Yemen could have addressed those concerns at considerably less expense.

I also noticed that, in all references to the detainees, their relatives and supporters called them "boys," implying an image of youth, innocence and vulnerability. I found the references to these "scared young boys" amusing, given three of the five detainees were in their twenties and a fourth was aged thirty-three. The persistent effort to represent them all as innocent youths discredited the families' message in my eyes. I did not doubt that their fears for their loved ones were genuine, but I did doubt whether they really believed their menfolk were in Yemen purely to study or take vacations.

Although skeptical of the families' arguments in defense of their arrested relatives, I was impressed at the speed with which they mobilized. Just one day after receiving news of the arrests, the families retained Gareth Peirce, an attorney well known in Britain for her defense role in other high-profile terrorism trials. They issued a public statement on January 7 saying, "We believe [the detained Britons] are being made a scapegoat by the Yemeni authorities for their bungled operation of the hostage fiasco." The statement went on, "It is also a fact that they were arrested a week before the kidnapping event occurred, which indicates that the Yemen government had already planned its scapegoats as a safety net in the likelihood of the rescue attempt going wrong."

Whether the Britons were guilty of a bomb plot or not, I found it hard to imagine the Yemen government, or any government, was capable of preparing contingency plans for a crime even before the perpetrators had planned it. Were the detained men's families suggesting that the Yemen government knew in advance that Abu Hassan was planning a kidnapping, that there would be a high-risk rescue and that scapegoats would be needed in the event the rescue went wrong? That seemed highly improbable. The scapegoat claims suggested to me that the families and their lawyers already perceived a connection between the arrest of the British men and the kidnapping, which had happened four days later.

I became increasingly curious to find out more about what that connection might be. Abu Hassan had said he wanted to exchange us for friends of his who had been arrested by the Yemen authorities and were in prison. Could these Britons be the men Hassan described as his friends? Could their arrest have been the event that triggered the kidnapping? Unable to get much information about how the kidnappers' trial was progressing, I followed reports about the trial of the Britons, which, I thought, might shed more light on the kidnapping.

On January 27, immediately after the Eid-al-Fitr holiday that marks the end of Ramadan, the first session of the Britons' trial began in Aden's Preliminary Court under Judge Jamal Mohammed Omar. A prominent Yemen lawyer, Badr Basunaid, agreed to represent the accused, although he was given only one business day to prepare the case before the trial started. According to observers, proceedings were chaotic from the beginning. The imposing colonial courthouse building was surrounded by several hundred soldiers, while other soldiers escorted the defendants into a courtroom packed with journalists, consular staff, human-rights observers, and relatives from Britain. The defendants immediately began shouting that they had been tortured in prison and forced to make false confessions. They removed their shirts, attempting to show marks on their backs and arms that they attributed to beatings and electric shocks. Soldiers hurriedly insisted that television cameras be turned off. Wives and sisters burst into tears at this first sight of their loved ones.

After some semblance of order was restored, the prosecution stated the bombing conspiracy charges against the defendants. Chaos broke out again when the Arabic-English interpreter mistakenly stated that the charges carried the death penalty. Even when the error was corrected, the observers and panicked relatives had little reason to feel confident in Yemen's legal process. One relative later exclaimed she was terrified that "the boys, at least some of them, were heading straight for the firing squad."

The prosecuting lawyer went on to assert that "the conspiracy started in Finsbury Park in London in the offices of Abu Hamza, who exports terrorism to other countries."

"Abu Hamza? Who is he?" I asked myself.

A significant new character had been introduced into the plot. And a singularly colorful character he turned out to be. Directing my online research towards Abu Hamza, I discovered that he was an Egyptian-born Islamic cleric who operated out of a mosque in the north London suburb of Finsbury Park. His real name was Mustafa Mohammed Kamel. Judging by the published photographs, Abu Hamza was an easy man to recognize. Not only was he heavily set and over six feet tall, but he had lost both hands and one eye, reportedly as the result of a land mine in Afghanistan. Photographs typically showed the mullah dressed in a shalwar kameez— the traditional loose-fitting shirt and cotton trousers worn in Pakistan— brandishing his hook prostheses, and glaring from his one good eye.

As one reporter aptly said, "Hollywood could not have created a more menacing-looking villain." Abu Hamza, it seems, had taken over what was once a family-oriented neighborhood mosque and turned it into the head-quarters of his aggressively fundamentalist organization, the Supporters of Sharia, or SOS.

On its Web site, I discovered that the SOS was committed to restoring rule by Islamic law in traditionally Muslim lands: "Muslims and non-Muslims are being oppressed throughout the world. SOS is one of the organizations struggling to remove the oppression created by man-made laws. So that the whole of mankind can enjoy the freedom, purity and justice of living under Allah's laws—The Shari'ah." The Web site described the mission of SOS members as: "support of mujahiddin and refugees in Afghanistan, Bosnia, Kashmir, etc; participation in these countries as frontline soldiers; Islamic education, reconstruction and countering anti-Islamic propaganda, and studies to learn from past mistakes."

I uncovered a number of newspaper articles about Abu Hamza and the Supporters of Sharia, some of which addressed the dissension within the Muslim community. Many Muslims who prayed regularly at the Finsbury Park mosque were not happy about the arrival of Abu Hamza. His radical preaching encouraged a following of militant young men and disrupted the family focus that the local community valued in the mosque. Disputes developed with the mosque's governing committee over Abu Hamza's use of cash donations and his habit of housing refugees at the mosque. In spite of this dissent, Abu Hamza continued to preach on a regular basis and the Supporters of Sharia continued to grow, attracting new members from Muslim communities throughout Britain and from overseas, including a few from the United States.

Abu Hamza was not only a fiery recruiter of young Muslims intent on jihad. He also turned out to be the stepfather of the youngest of the five Britons on trial in Yemen, an eighteen-year-old by the name of Mohsin Ghalain.

The Yemen government's anger that Britain appeared to be harboring organizations intent on carrying out terrorist attacks against Yemen was fanned by the one-eyed mullah, who gave interviews and press releases advocating jihad in Yemen. As early as January 15, Prime Minister al-Iryani had contacted the Foreign Secretary in London to demand "clarification" of Abu Hamza's "dangerous statements" to the British press and to al-Jazeera television. On the streets of Aden and Sana'a, Yemenis could not understand why Britain tolerated the likes of Abu Hamza and allowed his organization to operate freely. Just before the trial began, the British press reported that Yemen was seeking to extradite Abu Hamza. Hamza announced he would fight extradition, although the British government denied Yemen had made any formal request. Since no extradition treaty exists between Yemen and Britain, it is unlikely a formal request would have been made—but very likely Yemen communicated its strong desire to lay its hands on the handless Hamza, one way or another.

On the day the Britons' trial started, Yemen's security forces announced they had successfully tracked down and apprehended four more foreigners who were hiding on al-Batan mountain, about 250 miles northeast of Aden. Apparently, security forces had been tipped off by a local sheikh and had shelled the campsite. Of the six men who gave themselves up without a fight, two were British citizens of Pakistani origin named Shazad Nabi and Ayaz Hussein. Another was an Algerian, Ali Merksen. The fourth captured foreigner was also British. He turned out to be seventeen-year-old Mohammed Mustafa Kamel, the son of Abu Hamza. Clearly, Abu Hamza's connection to the arrested Britons was more than casual. Either he was just another parent—as distraught as any of the families who had protested the arrest of their loved ones—or he was well aware of why his son and stepson had gone to Yemen. As the four new foreigners joined the Britons in the dock at Aden's courthouse, Abu Hamza claimed he had no knowledge that his sons were even in Yemen. The last he had heard of young Kamel Junior, Daddy claimed, was that his son had planned a religious visit to Saudi Arabia.

Two local men were arrested with the four foreigners on al-Batan mountain. I stared in amazement at their online photographs. They were none other than the interpreter we called Yellow Pants and the wild-eyed Grenade. Yellow Pants admitted to being present at the kidnapping, but claimed his role was purely to translate between Arabic and English. A Tunisian who operated under the *nom de guerre* of Abu Haraira, he gave his occupation as schoolteacher, which explained his interest in improving his English and engaging in conversation with the hostages. Grenade's real name was revealed as Abdullah Salah al-Junaidi. The look in his eyes was instantly familiar to me, that same intense stare I had seen as he guarded us in the wadi, fondling his hand grenade.

The discovery and capture of three more Britons in the company of two of our kidnappers removed any doubts in my mind that they were indeed involved with Abu Hassan and the Aden Abyan Islamic Army. But how and why, I asked myself, had the British men become involved with the AAIA? And were the kidnappers also involved in the bombing conspiracy? The kidnappers' trial was still off-limits to outside observers, including the press, so I had no access to the answers it might have provided. I could only wait and see what clues about the kidnapping might emerge as the Britons' trial continued.

11

ARROW FROM
CUPID'S BOW

While the two trials were lurching along in Yemen, I had a more appealing matter to investigate at home in Rochester. Ray Kaufman had sent me another e-mail. About a week after my return from New Zealand, I dialed his number. We arranged to meet at a small café overlooking the Erie Canal. Ray was there right on time. Among the many things I would discover about him was his passion for punctuality. The man in neatly pressed khakis and a Gore-Tex parka who came forward to meet me was unexpectedly handsome and looked much younger than his fifty-two years. His brown hair, cut to military precision, showed no trace of gray and his lean frame no sign of middle-age spread. I had the same instinctive reaction as I'd had when I received his first e-mail. This man was going to be important in my life—plus he was cute.

The following weekend Ray invited me to a performance of the Rochester Philharmonic Orchestra followed by coffee and dessert at a nearby brasserie. Our conversation ranged from his days in the Marine Corps and his hunting safaris in Africa to my women's rights projects and travels around the world. We compared notes on our respective big company careers, discovering both of us dreamed of something different, something more than the executive ladder. Ray spoke of his two college-age daughters and his dream of retiring in Alaska. I told him of the beauty of New Zealand and my dream of spending more time in the country of my birth. When we eventually looked up, not only had every other customer left the restaurant but also the staff had moved all the tables and chairs to an adjoining room in preparation for a reception the next day. Ray and I were sitting alone at our table in the middle of a completely empty room and neither of us had even noticed.

The winter snows gave way to spring, and Ray and I were spending time together every week. The first time I had dinner at his home his love of hunting was immediately evident. A zebra skin adorned the foyer and a full-size African lion had pride of place in his library. A gun rack held several hunting rifles, although Ray assured me these were usually kept locked in a safe and displayed in the library only for special occasions. My presence for dinner apparently qualified. To my consternation, Ray suddenly thrust a rifle towards me. "Here, see how this feels."

I had not touched a gun since disposing of the AK-47 and wasn't at all sure I cared to handle this one, in spite of the gorgeous walnut stock and elegant engraving. Ray showed me how to position the rifle against my shoulder and lean my cheek against the stock. The weight of the gun made it impossible for me to hold it up for more than a minute, and I handed it back to Ray.

He suggested I might like to go and try some target practice at a cabin owned by one of his friends. "Thanks, but no thanks," I said. I wasn't interested in being anywhere near the sound of gunfire. However, I was interested in spending more time near Ray.

As the days lengthened and the feeling of constant inner tension eased, I regained more day-to-day involvement in my job. The possibility that my future might lie in some direction outside Xerox, and even outside corporate America, felt less disturbing to me, although I still could not imagine what that alternative life might be. On Good Friday I wrote in my journal:

> Finally I'm enjoying work again. At least I'm getting engaged in the business issues. But it still isn't the same as it once was. The sense of importance of what I'm doing in business has been lost—forever, I think. The idea of staying on this career path only another eighteen months or so seems comfortable to me but what lies beyond is as much a question as ever.

The arrival of my brother Frank with his wife and two daughters for a ten-day visit over Easter also inspired me to be open to new directions in life. Frank had left a successful career as a partner in a prestigious New Zealand law firm, and was on his way to live semipermanently in Europe in pursuit of his own dream. His fascination with eastern Europe's emergence from communism led him to take the risky step of moving his family to England and setting up a business base in Bulgaria. If Frank—two years my senior and with a family to support—could make such a dramatic change in his life, then surely I too could pursue anything I wanted.

One of the things I wanted happened to be a certain former Marine. I noted in my journal on April 9:

> Ray on my mind! Could it be I'm actually at risk of falling for this man? I've been thinking about him—a lot—this past week, since having dinner at his home. It would not have taken much for me to have stayed the night but Ray didn't make a move. He has the patience of a hunter, I think.
>
> It seems remarkable to me that this man has come into my life at this time. He is here for a reason, to teach me something. And he needs something from me. His candor and vulnerability about being a parent, about being alone on weekends, took me by surprise. I would not have trusted someone else so easily with those fears. There are different sides to Ray that I did not expect to find in one man. That is what fascinates me about him.

A month later I did agree to visit the cabin with Ray and his friends Gerry and Charlie, who owned the property. The cabin was situated in rural hills near the town of Naples, an hour's drive south of Rochester. Charlie and Gerry use their 100 acres of land to hunt deer and fish for bass. I liked both of them immediately and, like Ray, they dispelled some of my former prejudices about the kind of men who own guns and hunt. They used an open field across the road from the cabin as their rifle range. Targets were stapled to wooden frames set up about 50 yards from an old picnic table they used as a shooting bench. Ray was careful to check everyone was using ear protectors before showing me how to load and fire a .22 Ruger. Thanks to Brad from the FBI, at least now I knew the difference between a pistol and a revolver. I turned out to be a pretty good shot with the pistol at 25 to 30 yards, and with a .22 caliber rifle managed to consistently hit a clay pigeon attached to the target. I'm not sure who was more surprised at my accuracy, Ray or me. Although I felt very safe with Ray and his friends, the sound of gunfire, especially from the high-powered hunting rifles, brought the knot of tension back in my chest. Gunfire was the one thing that triggered immediate flashbacks to the kidnapping and rescue.

A short time after we spent our first night together, Ray left for a week to take his younger daughter to London as her high-school graduation gift. It was the longest week I could remember. From the moment he left, I was counting the hours until he would be back. That's when I knew that while I might have escaped bullets from the kidnappers and the Yemen army, I had not escaped the arrow from Cupid's bow. I was surprised to receive a letter postmarked from West London a few days after Ray left and suddenly was afraid to open it. Perhaps, with the perspective of distance, he had decided to end the relationship and didn't want to see me again. I opened the letter with trepidation.

> . . . I am astonished to now find you entering my life and hopefully allowing me a place in yours. You have come at a time when I was certain I would never find a woman who could interest me, let alone inspire me. How long do you suppose it will be before I can again focus on a subject without my mind wandering to you? I know I would like to become a part of your life and to find what level we can go to together . . . I would love to see this coming Sunday morning sun from your bedroom window.
>
> Will call as soon as we land.

Falling in love with Ray proved the perfect antidote to being kidnapped. The irony was that if I had not been kidnapped, I would never have met him. I still had many doubts about the new directions in which my life might go, but no doubts at all that I would go there with Ray.

My work focus and energy were, in many ways, back to normal but there were no other rungs on the Xerox ladder that held much appeal for me. At no other time in my life could I recall not knowing exactly what I wanted to do next. The loss of direction worried me, but I felt confident the right alternative would suddenly become blindingly obvious. Perhaps, I told myself, I still needed to resolve unanswered questions about the kidnapping before I could put the whole thing behind me.

There was much I still did not understand about the kidnappers themselves and their motives. Certain questions still nagged at me. What was Abu Hassan's connection with the Islamic world in Britain? Were the arrested British men the "friends" Hassan had told us about, the "friends" whose freedom he would win in exchange for our lives? I knew these Britons were accused of participation in Abu Hassan's training camps, but I did not know why they would have been trying to bomb British facilities in Yemen or how they came to be involved with the Aden Abyan Islamic Army in the first place. Early reports after the kidnapping had not mentioned the Britons as part of Hassan's demands. Rather, the newspapers mentioned the Yemeni sheikh, Salih Haidara al-Atwi. One report also referred to a Syrian militant called Nankly. Who were these two men and what was their connection to Hassan or to the Britons? There were still many pieces missing from the puzzle.

12

VERDICTS IN ADEN

The trial of the British men in Aden provided my best source of new clues. Fortunately, the trial and the political impact it was having in Britain continued to be covered in depth by the British press, whose reports I tracked on various Web sites.

In the second session of the trial, the prosecution brought forward its witnesses. The first was the owner of a rental-car agency in Aden, who confirmed that Mohsin Ghalain (Abu Hamza's stepson) had rented a white Daewoo from him. Police witnesses then testified that at midnight on December 23, 1998, Malik Harhara was driving the Daewoo from the direction of Abyan and, as he approached a traffic island on the outskirts of Aden, was apprehended by a police officer, ostensibly for driving the wrong way around the roundabout. In the car with Harhara were Mohsin Ghalain and Sarmad Ahmed, whose name and cell phone number were provided as the contact on the Supporters of Sharia Web site. When the police officer asked for the men's identity papers and began to question them, Harhara suddenly drove off. Fleeing the police checkpoint, the three Britons raced towards Aden with the police in pursuit. After taking a wrong turn, they became lost in Aden's back streets and eventually became trapped in a busy night market. The men abandoned the car and ran off into the night.

According to the police officers, the trunk of the car was found to be full of weapons and explosives, which were displayed in court. Observers noted that the evidence was not enclosed in any protective plastic nor were the exhibit items numbered. Court officials and even witnesses were allowed to handle the exhibits freely. There was no hard evidence that the weapons and bomb-making equipment displayed in the courtroom had come from the defendants' rental car—no fingerprints to prove the defendants had ever handled the goods.

Several aspects of the story about how the Britons were apprehended did not ring true. Having spent a week on Yemen roads myself, it seemed highly unlikely to me that a police officer would bother to pull over a vehicle at midnight for something as mundane as going the wrong way around a traffic island. In a typical Yemeni town, locals showed little regard for traffic rules and I couldn't imagine a policeman would pay the slightest attention to such a minor infringement. The fact that the car happened to be stashed with weapons and explosives seemed too much of a coincidence.

I was also suspicious of the reported speed with which the police located the two hotels where the defendants were staying. Apparently, three of them were found in their hotel and arrested in a little more than two hours after the rental car was abandoned. Three more were located in another hotel fewer than twenty-four hours later. Were Yemen police really that efficient? There had to be more to the story than was coming out in the press reports of the trial.

Through March and April, the trial continued in erratically scheduled sessions. The prosecution introduced a videotape showing three of the defendants handling weapons and demonstrating booby traps. The tape was apparently recorded in Albania, a predominantly Muslim country bordering the conflict in Kosovo. The tape suggested that Butt, Ghalain and Abu Hamza's son, Kamel Jr., had engaged in weapons training. Although it hardly proved the defendants guilty of a bomb plot in Yemen, it did make at least three of them look not quite the innocent, fun-loving students of Islam they claimed to be. Mohsin Ghalain explained the tape was simply a souvenir of a trip to Albania. Most tourists would have settled for T-shirts and coffee mugs emblazoned with "Albania." Of course, most tourists would not have been in Albania in the first place, but I am hardly in a position to criticize another person's choice of holiday destination.

More damaging to the defendants were their signed confessions. I located an English translation of these on the *Yemen Times* Web site. Essentially, the defendants admitted participating in training at camps operated by Abu Hassan and that they were paid by Hassan to conduct attacks on facilities in Aden during the Christians' Christmas and New Year holidays. Even one of their defense attorneys described the admissions as "pretty damning." The defendants formally retracted the confessions on the grounds they were forced to write and sign them through torture. Although the Yemen authorities had repeatedly denied British government requests that its own doctors examine the men, the judge authorized a new medical committee to investigate the torture allegations. This committee, made up of a Dutch doctor and two Yemenis, informed the court that it could find no evidence of torture. Of course, this was now several months after the confessions were obtained and any physical injuries may well have healed.

With long, unpredictable adjournments in the ongoing trial of the Britons, the British press coverage of events in Yemen declined and public interest in the fate of the defendants waned. Even the Muslim community in Britain was less convinced that these "poor boys" were quite as innocent as it had first assumed. Muslim businesses and charities gradually discontinued their financial support of a "Justice for Britons in Yemen" initiative and distanced themselves from the case. Only close family members continued the fight by maintaining their demands on the Foreign Office and urging the British government to intercede with authorities in Yemen.

On August 8, 1999, the judge who had presided over the six-month trial of the eight British and two Algerian defendants announced his verdict. All ten were found guilty as charged. Sentences varied in accordance with degree of complicity. Malik Harhara and Mohsin Ghalain, judged to be the ringleaders, received sentences of seven years. Shahid Butt, Sarmad Ahmed and the two Algerians were sentenced to five years each. Mohammed Mustafa Kamel received a three-year sentence, which in part reflected his age. The remaining defendants—Ghulaim Hussein, Ayaz Hussein, and Shazad Nabi—were considered to have played minor roles and were sentenced to time already served.

The guilty verdicts and the sentences produced a renewed outcry from relatives and supporters in Britain. According to Shahid Butt's brother, the trial was "a complete joke. They never had a chance. They are innocent." But, while a small core of relatives, human rights activists, and Muslim leaders continued to express their belief in the men's innocence, public opinion had shifted.

Unlike the original arrests, the guilty verdict did not generate heated press conferences. There were no rallies or marches on the Yemen embassy or the Foreign Office. However, British prime minister Tony Blair did send a letter to Yemen's President Salih, expressing his concern over the use of torture and its apparent role in producing a guilty verdict. The Foreign Office offered to propose to Yemen authorities that the men serve their sentences in a British prison, but the families rejected that on the basis it implied the men were indeed guilty and deserving of time in prison. Appeals of the verdicts and sentences were filed by the defense attorneys, but to no avail. The three defendants who had already served their time were free to leave Yemen. The remaining five Britons and their two Algerian companions remained in Aden's al-Mansoor prison, the place where I would later meet them.

Abu Hamza, the mullah of Finsbury Park, London

Abu Hassan, leader of the Aden Abyan Islamic Army, in his prison cell in Zinjibar. Hassan was captured during the gun battle to rescue the hostages, and was tried and executed in 1999.

The ill-fated tour group stops for refreshments at a roadside restaurant in the Hadramawt region.

Left: Ruins at Marib in Yemen are believed to be the ancient capital of the Queen of Sheba.

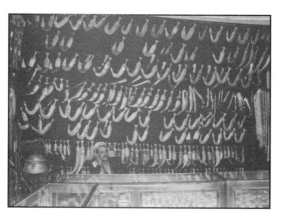

A merchant offers a wide selection of jambiyas, the ornamental curved daggers worn by most Yemeni men.

A spice vendor in the Old Quarter of Sana'a.

The British and Algerian defendants appearing in court during their trial in Aden, 1999.

The convoy of Toyota Land Cruisers stops for a photo opportunity on its tour of Yemen.

The Aden villa rented by some of the Britons prior to their arrest.

A view from Point 10 in Figure 3 looking back towards the berm (Point 9) where Quin wrested the AK-47 from Purple Skirt, one of the kidnappers.

A view from above the drop-off (Point 2 in Figure 3), looking towards the open valley (Point 3) and the mountain range (Points 4 and 6).

A view of the field (Point 5 in Figure 3) where the hostages were used as human shields. The berm (Point 8) where the hostages stood runs below the trees (Point 1).

In Afghanistan, Quin and others watch as commander Shah Ahmed Masood (second from left), signs his support for the Declaration on the Essential Rights of Afghan Women. He was assassinated on September 9, 2001.

Quin discusses issues confronting Yemen with the then Prime Minister, Dr. Abdel Karim al-Iryani.

Quin reflects on the deaths of four of her fellow travelers after laying a wreath at the site where Ruth and Peter died (Point 8 in Figure 3).

13

JUSTICE IN ZINJIBAR

In spite of the judge's decision to close the kidnappers' trial to the public, over time I was able to track down various documents that allowed me to piece together how the trial had progressed. A translated transcript of the interrogations of Abu Hassan by Yemen authorities and of the testimonies given by our drivers was particularly revealing. From time to time, I also received a phone call from someone at Scotland Yard or a representative of the American embassy in Sana'a providing me with an update on developments, particularly as the trial drew to a close. Additional information came to light months later, when I had articles from Arabic newspapers and Web sites translated into English.

Although Hassan's ideological raving appears to have continued unabated, the trial did follow some semblance of order. During several sessions in February, the prosecution presented a number of witnesses to support their charges. The four tour drivers, who had been captured along with us, testified to the events of the initial ambush and were able to describe some of the satellite phone calls Hassan had made. Mohammed with Glasses and Abdul testified that in one call Hassan was heard to say, "We've got the goods that were ordered—sixteen cartons marked British and American." I noted another key statement in the drivers' testimony: "I heard Abu Hassan saying that the demands are eight youths who are detained in Aden and the Algerians who are wanted because of the explosion." According to the drivers, Hassan then directed one of his men to take Mad Mohammed's Land Cruiser. Apparently, it was to visit the local

ATM since the kidnapper returned half an hour later with a supply of money for Hassan.

Soon afterwards, Osama al-Masri (Bandit) arrived in Hassan's vehicle, having finished setting up the defense post. He and Hassan then made their way on foot in the direction the hostages had been taken. The drivers testified that we had been used as human shields, but none of them witnessed the killings of four hostages. One driver noted that he had heard Hassan say all the hostages would be shot if things got bad. When one of the drivers referred to the kidnappers as a "gang" in court, Hassan strongly objected, insisting again that they were not a gang but "fighters for an Islamic state." A soldier testified that he had seen the kidnappers open fire on the security forces, but he too was unable to say who had actually shot the hostages.

Hassan commented to the judge that, in his opinion, the witnesses' accounts were mostly accurate.

The prosecution team then brought forward what they called scientific evidence, to prove the hostages were shot and killed by their captors and not by crossfire from the troops. Markings on the bullets recovered from the bodies, they explained, showed that the bullets could only have come from the kidnappers' guns. I remain curious about the quality of this evidence since the autopsy work performed by British authorities as part of their inquest was less definitive. The British inquest, however, was intended only to distinguish between death by natural causes and death by misadventure, not to provide proof of guilt in a court of law. The prosecution seemed confident of its own forensic evidence and the chief prosecutor made a point of showing the evidence file to a BBC reporter following the court session.

The demonstration of a link between the kidnappers and the Britons accused of a bombing conspiracy was an important element in both trials. Badr Basunaid, the defense lawyer for the British men, had recognized that evidence used in the kidnappers' trial in Zinjibar could prove highly prejudicial to his clients. As he had feared, the team prosecuting the kidnappers introduced cassette tapes and training manuals from the Supporters of Sharia that the police had found in Hassan's possession. At this stage, Hassan retracted earlier admissions he had made about directing three of the Britons to conduct bomb attacks. Instead he claimed that he alone was responsible for the bombing conspiracy. His purpose, he said, was to cleanse Aden of Americans and Christianity. The satellite phone used by Hassan to make calls during the kidnapping was also introduced as evidence, the prosecution showing that it had been purchased by Abu Hamza in London and brought to Yemen by his stepson, who had trained Hassan how to use it. Although the link between the AAIA and the Supporters of Sharia was not particularly crucial to proving guilt in the kidnapping and murder charges, it did have importance for the additional charges of forming an armed gang to destabilize the government. Yemen hoped to establish compelling evidence that would persuade the British government to turn Abu Hamza over to them.

I found relatively little information about the defense arguments used in Hassan's trial. Hassan's self-incriminating tirades left little room for defending him against the charges of kidnapping and forming an armed gang. The lawyers who attempted to provide a defense were limited to raising doubts about how the four hostages had died, arguing that they had not been deliberately executed, but had been killed in the crossfire by army bullets. Their deaths could therefore be blamed on an ill-advised and poorly executed rescue effort. However, the defense did little to refute prosecution evidence that at least some of the bullets that hit the hostages who died had come from the kidnappers' weapons.

In the case of Ahmed Atef, defense witnesses established that he had indeed been in another town when the ambush took place. That said, apparently he had joined in with gusto once he arrived at the kidnappers' campsite, and was willing to man the machine gun at the defense post as the soldiers approached. He was believed to be responsible for the seven machine-gun rounds that struck Margaret Whitehouse in the groin, causing wounds that would certainly have killed her even if other bullets from the crossfire had not.

During Hassan's trial, the AAIA continued to make threats against Yemeni authorities and foreigners, in particular urging the British and American ambassadors to leave Yemen or be killed. In London, Abu Hamza assisted the AAIA by communicating these threats to the western press. He knew there was little action British authorities could take against him. He was, after all, just exercising his right to free speech.

The final session of the kidnappers' trial took place on March 17, just eight weeks after the kidnapping. In closing, the prosecution called the AAIA a "Nazi" organization whose members deserved to be executed. The one defendant for whom the prosecution did not seek the death penalty was Salim al-Badawi, an absentee whose only role was to reconnoiter the ambush area in advance. Still representing himself, Hassan acknowledged that he kidnapped the tourists to bargain for the release of the arrested British men and, without a trace of remorse, informed the court that he was ready to take up arms once more against "the enemies of God." He urged others to continue striking against the hegemony of the West and scorned any possibility of a dialogue between civilizations. "The only dialogue is the dialogue of bullets," he said. In spite of these confessions and threats, Hassan urged the judge not to pass the death sentence on him or his followers since it would be a contradiction of Sharia law to kill a Muslim for murdering a Christian.

In the absence of a jury, it was now up to Judge al-Qaderi to reach a verdict. He took several weeks to consider his decision—a decision he knew would be closely scrutinized in Yemen and all over the world.

On May 6, the defendants were brought back to the courthouse to hear the verdicts. Security was again very heavy in anticipation of demonstrations by family members and tribal supporters, and possibly even an attempt by the AAIA to release Hassan by force. Surprisingly, no representatives of the foreign press or any of the embassies attended, although Yemen newspapers such as *Al-Ayyam* sent journalists to cover the event. For once, Hassan did not interrupt as the judge issued the verdicts.

Abu Hassan, al-Junaidi (Grenade), and Abu Haraira (Yellow Pants) were found guilty on all charges and sentenced to death. The elder Atef brother, Ahmed, was sentenced to twenty years in prison, his lighter sentence presumably reflecting the fact he had not participated in the kidnapping but had played a role in killing two of the hostages. His brother Saad was acquitted—apparently because the judge recognized the eighteen-year-old was terrified of Hassan and had become involved against his will.

I was not surprised by these outcomes.

What stunned me was the judge's decision to acquit all the defendants tried in absentia. The trick to being found innocent under Yemen law, it seemed, was to avoid showing up at your trial. One of those missing suspects must have been the man we called Gray Shirt: the one whom my fellow hostages saw murder Peter Rowe; the one who wounded Margaret Thompson and Claire Marston; the one who aimed his rifle at Pat and Eric and who might have killed them, too, if he had not hesitated then turned to run from the approaching troops. Gray Shirt had escaped capture and now, apparently, would never be held accountable for his crimes.

This was Yemen's first court case in which the death penalty option for kidnapping was used. As I pieced together the developments of the trial and the verdicts, I sensed that Hassan and his colleagues had not been anticipating the death sentences. Hassan's initial response was bravado: "Far beyond all of this, all that I did, I did for Islam." He went on to warn the court, "Have no doubt that Islam will triumph over the West and Muslims will one day possess nuclear weapons and the military power which will make military victory possible. It will be possible for us to create an Islamic nation and prevent the American warships from crossing the Bab al-Mandab [the strait that links the Gulf of Aden and the Red Sea]." "This court is against Islamic law, and therefore the verdict of death is against Islamic law. The verdict on me of death is considered martyrdom in the eyes of God. The judges of Yemen are not independent and this verdict was issued for predetermined political reasons." Judge al-Qaderi advised the defendants that they had fifteen days within which to file an appeal. Hassan retorted that he would appeal to no one, only to God.

An *Al-Ayyam* reporter managed to speak to the defendants before they were taken from the court. Hassan took the opportunity to send a message to his followers: "I urge all westerners to pack their bags and leave within twenty days for I order all the Aden Abyan Islamic Army and all the mujahiddin to kill them after twenty days and drive them from this country. It is not a crime for us to establish an Islamic nation and for us to try to rescue our Muslim brothers from the deterioration in which this land lives." Hassan added, "We were not in contact with any foreign front, in

London or elsewhere. Tell westerners to pack their bags and leave Yemen or there will be very severe revenge."

Grenade echoed his leader's retaliatory tone: "God willing, our brothers will rise up and drive the westerners from Yemen and we have hope all the people will join them." But the former teacher Yellow Pants seemed more puzzled by the logic of the verdicts, saying to the reporter, "Why is there one law for tourists and another law for all other people? If we kidnapped Egyptians, would the same law apply?" The verdicts made headline news throughout Yemen. So great was local interest in the outcome of the trial that *Al-Ayyam* had to print a second run of its newspaper for the first time ever.

Curiously, I could find no mention of two of the kidnappers, Salim and Said al-Maqab, in news reports or diplomats' notes about the trial. Reportedly, they had turned themselves in on February 6 and were included in a list of the arrested kidnappers published online by *Yemen Gateway* on February 22. However, there is no mention of how they responded to charges or any testimony they may have given. They were also not mentioned in later press reports about the verdicts and sentencing. It is not clear whether they were among the defendants at Hassan's trial, tried separately later, or simply released.

Reactions to the death sentences were mixed. Laurence Whitehouse told the press that both he and his murdered wife, Margaret, were personally opposed to the death sentence, and he would have preferred to see a lengthy prison sentence. Australian foreign minister Alexander Downer noted that he was pleased with the outcome, adding that Australia did not support the death penalty but respected Yemen's laws. David Pearce, the British consul to Yemen, pointed out that neither Britain nor any member of the European Union could support the death penalty, and he hoped the sentences would be commuted to life in prison.

In London, Abu Hamza informed the western press that anyone who contributed to carrying out the executions would become a legitimate target for the AAIA. The Yemen government must be brought down, he said, because it executes Muslims for having killed infidels.

In contrast, many Yemenis were more than happy with the verdict and sentences. The editor of the *Yemen Observer* noted, "These [kidnappers] represent nothing, absolutely nothing, in the psychology of the Yemeni people, and nothing that has anything to do with the gospel of Islam." The leader of Yemen's Islah party, Abdullah bin Husayn al-Ahmar, hoped the president would authorize the execution of Hassan. "If you ask whether people like Abu Hassan have any future in Yemen the answer is no, no, a thousand times no."

In light of the death sentences and the potential threat from AAIA retaliation, Britain's Foreign Office again advised all British citizens to leave Yemen if their presence in the country was not absolutely essential. Some legal and diplomatic observers in Yemen commented privately that they thought it unlikely any of the kidnappers would in fact be executed. It would just make a hero out of Hassan and trigger further retaliation by the tribes or by the AAIA militants. Some people even felt the Yemen government would let the matter fade from international interest, then quietly release the condemned men.

The death sentence was evidently quite a wake-up call to Abu Hassan, who suddenly became much more amenable to working with his defense attorney. In spite of his contemptuous response to the idea of an appeal, the court-appointed defense team went ahead on behalf of all those found guilty. "This is a false, false verdict," lead defense lawyer Mohammed Thabet commented to *Al-Hayat,* a London-based Arabic paper. "It is not based on reality or the statements of the witnesses. This verdict for all of them is based on the confession and evidence against one of them [Hassan]. How can this be applied to all of them?"

The case came before the Appeals Court in Zinjibar in the first week of July 1999. The British consulate in Aden gave me a summary of the appeals process provided to it by Thabet, and I had the documents translated from Arabic to English. The prosecution again presented its case and Thabet demanded to see their evidence. Apparently, the Appeals Court immediately repealed the "not guilty" verdicts on the absent defendants. Presumably, this was at the request of the prosecution, which has the right to appeal a judge's decision in Yemen. I was pleased to know that the door was open once again for bringing Gray Shirt and the other missing kidnappers to justice.

In subsequent sessions, the court allowed the defense attorneys to question the defendants, giving them an opportunity to prove they had not been involved in the kidnapping or deaths. Hassan read his own statement. He emphasized that the AAIA was a political party, which had had a number of conversations with government representatives in the past, and again admitted to having carried out several explosions to force the government to stop apprehending and deporting members of his organization. Hassan took upon himself all responsibility and asked that the rest of the defendants be acquitted. He offered the court a deal: "The Aden Abyan Islamic Army will halt all its activities unconditionally in return for [the government] releasing all its members and issuing a collective pardon for our colleagues, as well as considering our Muslim brothers in Yemen who fled the oppression of rulers in Algeria, Egypt and Libya."

On August 4 the court, presided over by three judges, announced its decision to uphold the death sentences against both Abu Hassan and al-Junaidi (Grenade); commute the death sentence against Hassan's interpreter Abu Haraira (Yellow Pants) to eight years in prison, due to lack of evidence; and uphold Ahmed Atef's sentence of twenty years. Hassan's willingness to compromise quickly disappeared. He told the court that his group would continue to attack foreign targets and Yemeni officials and would work to establish an Islamic state in Yemen. "Don't start a fire because you will not be able to put it out," he threatened.

Within hours of the appeal decision, a grenade exploded in a Sana'a market, killing seven people. Members of AAIA, and Abu Hamza in London, claimed it was a retaliation for the court decision, but government authorities insisted the grenade was set off in a dispute over a shopkeeper refusing to sell a cheap watch and that there was no connection to the kidnappers' verdicts. Certainly, this explosion did not fit the AAIA's modus operandi of targeting government- and foreign-owned buildings and avoiding harm to Muslim civilians.

Thabet pursued the next option for his clients: an appeal to Yemen's Supreme Court, to which relatives of Abu Hassan also made clemency appeals. A committee of five sheikhs, from tribal groups in Hassan's home province of Shabwah, was formed with the purpose of meeting with President Salih and requesting that he not sign the order of execution. During a presidential visit to the Shabwah area, a further three hundred tribesmen gathered in an attempt to meet the president and plea for clemency, but they were turned back by security forces. According to one Yemen newspaper, Hassan himself tried to flatter his way into the president's good graces, sending Salih a letter of congratulations on being re-elected to another term in the September 1999 elections. These last desperate efforts did not pay off for Hassan. In October, the Supreme Court commuted al-Junaidi's (Grenade's) death sentence to twenty years in prison but upheld Hassan's death sentence. The execution was authorized by President Salih.

On October 18, I arrived at my office at Xerox and poured myself a cup of coffee. I had a few minutes to spare before my first meeting of the day and casually scanned the front page of the *Wall Street Journal*. Toward the bottom of the international news column, a brief paragraph caught my eye. The execution had taken place. On October 17, 1999, Abu Hassan had been put to death by firing squad in the grounds of the prison. I felt no satisfaction at the news. The death of Zein al-Abidin abu Bakr al-Mehdar would not bring back Ruth or Margaret, Peter or Andrew. Perhaps some of their relatives would be glad of the outcome, although I knew Laurence Whitehouse would not. Strangely enough, I felt a sense of regret that now I would never have the chance to speak to Abu Hassan in person, to find out face to face what he hoped for at the fateful moment that he planned the ambush and what he really expected the outcome to be. His outbursts in the trial were conflicting and theatrical, containing only seeds of the truth. The rest of his story had died with him.

The execution of Abu Hassan and the imprisonment of three other kidnappers did not eliminate the Aden Abyan Islamic Army, much as the Yemen government liked to claim it no longer existed. During the time of Hassan's trial and appeal, there were several bombing events in Yemen, some of which were attributed to the AAIA by Abu Hamza in London. The acting leader of the AAIA was a man known as Abu Muhsin. I recalled that Hamza's son Kamel had stated in his confession that he was sent by Hassan to stay at the home of someone with that name, immediately after the first Britons were arrested at their Aden hotels. It seemed likely that this was the same Abu Muhsin who had reportedly stepped in to take Hassan's place. Abu Muhsin had sheltered Abu Hamza's son and now, as the AAIA's new leader, continued to use Hamza as a spokesperson.

Several more groups of suspected AAIA members were arrested during and after Hassan's trial. In May 1999, about fifteen men were detained and charged with plotting to kidnap Americans who worked at the Baptist hospital in Jibla and then demand the release of Abu Hassan in exchange for the hostages. In August, a bomb exploded at the British embassy in Sana'a, resulting in sixteen more arrests. Again, the attack was attributed to pressure to release Hassan. Many of the men charged received short sentences or were released for lack of evidence.

Abu Muhsin's leadership of AAIA was short-lived. He was arrested, along with several others, two weeks after Hassan's execution. I discovered, in a report translated for me from an Arabic Web site, that Abu Muhsin's real name was Hetam bin Farid. In their confessions, some of the Britons had mentioned being met at the airport in Yemen by Hetam bin Farid. That made sense: Hassan had arranged for a trusted member of AAIA to ensure his recruits' safe passage into the country.

Interestingly enough, during his subsequent trial, Abu Muhsin claimed that he was operating within the AAIA as a spy on the payroll of police investigators. Was it possible, I asked myself, that the man who alerted the police to the Britons' carload of explosives was the very man who had helped recruit them? Could it have been Abu Muhsin who, a month later, disclosed to police the whereabouts of Hamza's teenage son? Was Muhsin a double agent? Or did he disclose the fugitive's whereabouts in the hope of cutting a deal for his own freedom? This plot had more twists than a tangled line on a fly rod. My speculations aside, Abu Muhsin's spy argument was not accepted by the judge, who sentenced him to seven years in prison. I can only hope that Gray Shirt was among all these AAIA members arrested and tried during 1999 and 2000. I'd like to think that he received some measure of justice for the murder of Peter Rowe, and the attempted murders of Claire Marston and Margaret Thompson.

14

FIGHTING BACK
WITH FEMINISM

In November 1999, my mother died. Her long decline into the clouded confusion of Alzheimer's disease was over. Thankful for Ray's emotional support, I flew to New Zealand immediately to help my brothers, sister and sisters-in-law arrange her funeral. All of us felt the strange conflict of sorrow at losing our mother and relief that she was now at peace. On the morning of the funeral, the weather was damp and overcast in my home town, cooler than it should have been for the southern springtime. As we gathered in the cemetery around the gravesite my mother would now share with my father, the clouds parted and a bright beam of sunlight shone down on us, just as the casket was lowered into the earth. I like to think it was my mother's way of saying goodbye and reassuring us that she was happy. I may not believe in the various human definitions of God but I'll be surprised, and more than a little annoyed, if there isn't an afterlife. I tend to view death as setting out into completely uncharted territory on the greatest journey of all.

I regretted that Ray never had an opportunity to meet my mother, and I looked forward to the time when I could introduce him to the rest of my family. That opportunity came up sooner than I expected. As an avid fly fisherman, Ray had often talked about wanting to fish for trout in New Zealand's renowned lakes and rivers. With an English friend, Gordon, he had tentatively been planning such a trip even before we met. No way, of course, was I going to let him do a fishing trip to my home country without me. In February 2000, Ray and I met up with Gordon in the South Island and the three of us spent a week fishing in the Rakaia River area.

Partway through that week, I left the two men fishing and flew to Auckland for a couple of days. I had decided to buy an apartment. The America's Cup yacht races were in full swing on Auckland's Waitemata harbor, with an intense battle taking place between the defending New Zealand boat and the Italian challenger. New apartment buildings were under construction in the waterfront area of Auckland's downtown, known as the Viaduct Basin. I chose a one-bedroom apartment in an unfinished building overlooking the harbor and the America's Cup marina. A water view was an absolute requirement for me—and this was a view that could not be built out by future construction. I did not know how often I would get to spend time here, but I trusted my instincts that having a place of my own in Auckland was the right thing to do. During the second week of our trip, Ray and I traveled around the North Island, visiting my family and sightseeing together. We went to Waitarere Beach and also managed a day of fishing at Lake Taupo and the Tongariro River.

Soon after our return from New Zealand, Ray received word that a forthcoming addition to his "family" had been born. A few weeks later, we drove two hours west of Rochester to pick up Ray's new hunting dog, a German short-haired pointer he named Rakaia. It was impossible not to fall in love with Rakaia at first sight. With silky ears far too big for his head and sprawling paws too big for his chocolate-brown body, he alternately slept and squirmed in my arms all the way back to Rochester.

Ray had owned hunting dogs all his life but his most recent, a ten-year-old Brittany spaniel named Mac, had died from cancer just before we first met. I knew Ray had mourned the loss of Mac, and nearly a year had elapsed before he felt ready to take on the care and training of another dog. Growing up in New Zealand I was used to having dogs around, but my career and travel commitments in the United States had never allowed me to consider owning a dog of my own. I was delighted at the arrival of Rakaia in our lives and touched that Ray had chosen a New Zealand name for the puppy.

By the summer of 2000, Ray and I had both made up our minds to leave our jobs with Bausch & Lomb and Xerox respectively. We wanted to move west. Ray hoped to find another corporate job in a community that offered easy access to great hunting and fishing. I wanted to explore the possibility of creating a company of my own, a business that would allow me to spend time in New Zealand as well as with Ray in the United States. We decided we would target several western cities and move to whichever one resulted in a good job for Ray. I figured that, once I knew what business I wanted to start, I could run it from any city, although I had a preference for somewhere with frequent short flights in and out of Los Angeles Airport. High on our list was Portland, Oregon, but we were also open to Phoenix, Reno, Sacramento, or Boulder.

My decision to leave Xerox coincided with the offer of a more senior strategy role in the company. Perhaps if I had been offered the company's top strategy job I would have stayed, but Anne Mulcahy, whom I liked tremendously and who would soon become Xerox's first female CEO, could not guarantee when that position would become open. My intuition told me that it was time to move on with my life, and I advised Xerox I would resign in June of that year.

Leaving my job freed up my time to become more involved with global women's rights issues. I continued my participation on the board of CEDPA in Washington DC, and was able to travel to Egypt with other board members to visit the organization's field operations there. In Egypt, CEDPA works in villages and towns to promote general hygiene and health, especially reproductive health. Through culturally sensitive programs, CEDPA's staff and partner organizations work with families to encourage girls to attend school, to postpone their daughters' marriages until adulthood and to discontinue the dangerous practice of female circumcision. I was particularly intrigued with CEDPA's "positive deviants" approach to change. This innovative program identifies women who have already rejected circumcision for themselves or for their daughters, and then recruits these "positive deviants" to help other families in their communities make the same choice. Such women fully understand the cultural norms and the pressures to conform to tradition. This makes them able to offer much more credible encouragement and influence than an outsider could.

During the early months of 2000, I also became more actively involved in trying to support Afghan women in their fight against repression by the Taliban. My awareness of this had been triggered by the 100 Heroines Project. One of the recipients of the Heroines Award was Dr. Siwa Samar, an Afghan physician who was organizing medical care for women at refugee camps in Pakistan and who was putting herself at great risk to provide health care for women in Afghanistan.

The situation for women in Afghanistan was beyond belief. I could not understand why so few Americans, especially women, showed any real interest or concern about it. Even among some of my women friends in Rochester there was a mistaken belief that the repression of Afghan women was part of that country's traditions and culture. Few people had any awareness of the origins of the Taliban and its ongoing political support from Pakistan. The Feminist Majority was one of the few women's organizations in the U.S. that seemed to be paying attention to Afghan women. Through lobbying efforts, it had persuaded President Clinton to stop American oil companies from doing business with the Taliban and was influential in the United States' refusal to recognize the Taliban as Afghanistan's lawful government.

Through an Internet link, I discovered that NEGAR, an organization of women based in France, was planning a conference of Afghan women to be held in Dushanbe, the capital of Tajikistan, at the end of June 2000. I contacted NEGAR and offered to help with the conference. Thanks to the generosity of my friends and neighbors, I raised enough money to send two Afghan-American women to Dushanbe and—using my own funds—attended the conference myself.

It was a remarkable gathering of Afghan women from Europe and the United States, as well as many Afghan refugees living in Tajikistan. A few women were also able to travel secretly across the border out of Afghanistan itself. In addition to about 250 Afghan participants, thirty non-Afghan women (including several Americans) also attended. We wanted to help in any way we could and to demonstrate our support. A highlight of the conference was a speech by Halida Massaoudin, an Algerian feminist and member of parliament, who attended under tight security. Her courageous battle against fundamentalist forces in Algeria prompted many death threats against her. Massaoudin's brilliant oratory and her heartfelt words of encouragement and support electrified the audience—myself included.

In many ways, it was probably one of the worst-organized conferences I have ever attended. Yet, in spite of the enormous barriers to pulling it off, the organizers achieved their objective. The Afghan delegates created a powerful document, the *Declaration of the Essential Rights of Afghan Women*, written in the Pashto and Dari languages. Working closely with Nasrine Gross, an Afghan from Washington DC, I assisted in translating a French version of the document into English. The wording was based on existing documents such as the United Nations Declaration on Human Rights and the Platform for Action, which came out of the 1995 UN Conference on Women in Beijing. Sitting on some steps in the dimly lit hotel lobby, Nasrine and I worked until long after midnight on getting an English translation ready for distribution to the press the next day. Fortunately, I can read French better than I can write or speak it. In the course of translating, I also contributed an extra couple of phrases to the original document and the Afghans agreed to those additions. It seemed a tiny contribution, but I felt privileged to be able to assist these women in their efforts to take back control of their rights and their country.

Following the conference, I traveled with eight other delegates—four Afghan women who had not seen their homeland for twenty years and four journalists, one of whom was a man—into the Northern Alliance-controlled area of Afghanistan by helicopter. I anticipated a military helicopter similar to the one that had evacuated me in Yemen. When we reached the military airport in Dushanbe and I laid eyes on the Northern Alliance helicopter awaiting us, it was all I could do not to turn around and get back in the car. The rotary-wing aircraft sitting on the tarmac was the most dilapidated, patched-up, sorry-looking excuse for a vehicle I had ever seen. It didn't help to know the Northern Alliance had originally had five helicopters but was now down to two because the other three had all either crashed or been shot down in the past two years. The odds were not good, but I knew the Afghan women were counting on having an American in the delegation. I followed the foreign correspondents and Afghan women toward a mini-skirted woman in uniform who checked our passports and visas. My visa for Afghanistan had been issued by the Northern Alliance diplomatic representation in Washington DC. As with all but three countries in the world, the United States did not recognize the Taliban government and there was no official Afghan embassy in America.

Taking a deep breath, I climbed the half-dozen metal steps into the helicopter. Half the interior was occupied by a huge yellow fuel tank painted with a skull and crossbones. The floor was covered with several well-worn oriental rugs. I suspected their purpose was not so much decorative as to insulate us from the wind penetrating holes in the fuselage. A single parachute—of World War II vintage—hung on the rear wall. A battery, wired to God knows what, rested on the floor next to the fuel tank. The only faintly reassuring factor was that the only man in our group had been a parachutist in the French military and he seemed willing to get on board. In addition to the nine of us from the NEGAR conference, several Afghan families and dozens of boxes of cargo were crammed on board. The door closed and the helicopter lifted into the air. My fate was sealed. Feeling apprehensive rather than truly afraid, I decided to rely on Muslim philosophy. Insh'allah—as Allah wills.

The dry, golden-brown fields and river valleys of southern Tajikistan soon gave way to the dramatic mountains of Afghanistan. Between the harsh jagged peaks of the Hindu Kush mountain range were streaks of lush green valleys. I could understand how small communities might remain completely isolated within each of these valleys, developing their own customs and even distinct dialects, rarely encountering any stranger—even from the adjacent valley. At one point, we suddenly lost altitude. A tense conversation between Afghan passengers and a crew member was translated for me. "Don't worry," one of the Afghan women told me. "They are just dropping below the mountain ridge on our left because the Taliban have Stinger missiles in the next valley over." "Great," I thought. "I survive Yemen only to get shot down by American technology we supplied to the Taliban." Halfway through the two-hour trip, the helicopter made a scheduled stop at the town of Taloqan. We landed in a football field, scattering children and goats to the sidelines, and I caught my first glimpse of women shrouded in bright blue burkas. The two family groups disembarked and several men in military uniforms boarded in their place. As we took flight again, I noticed that one of these soldiers kept his face turned away from us. He was crying. I guessed that he was leaving his family behind to go and fight with the Northern Alliance, or perhaps someone close to him had just died. Later in the flight, I noticed one of the Afghan women speaking to him and he seemed glad of the consolation.

I was amazed by the beauty of the Panjshir Valley. A powerful river flowed between the steep mountains, a life-giving force for the fertile fields lining its banks. For the Afghan women, it was an emotional moment to set foot on home soil for the first time since they had fled the Russian invasion. A welcoming committee of men in traditional Afghan dress escorted us in four-wheel-drive vehicles to a nearby village. We stayed for three days in the family home of Shah Ahmed Masood, the Northern Alliance military commander. Masood himself was at the front lines 30 miles away in anticipation of renewed summer fighting against the Taliban troops. The house was large with a number of spacious, although sparsely furnished bedrooms. I knew I was not at the Hilton when I opened a closet in my assigned room and found it stashed with about twenty Kalashnikovs and old Lee Enfield rifles. I only needed a coat hanger.

Each day we visited as many villages and schools as we could, meeting with women and girls and sharing news of the conference. Copies of the *Declaration of the Essential Rights of Afghan Women* were shared with teachers and village women. We visited the refugee camps, located on the most barren land in the valley. It was heartbreaking to see families protected only by simple tents formed from sheets of blue plastic and held in place with rocks. Many of them would still be living in the same conditions when winter arrived and buried the camps under three feet of snow. A few larger tents were used as classrooms. The children, separated into tents by age and gender, sat on the dirt floors reciting their lessons. They had no books; not even paper or pencils. Their teachers were grateful for the writing materials one of the Afghan women had been able to bring. I walked through the camp accompanied by an interpreter.

Whenever I stopped to speak to women and men, they asked me the same questions: why has the world forgotten about us? Why does America not do something about the Taliban? Why does America not stop Pakistan from attacking us? I told them part of the truth: Newspapers in America are full of many crises in the world. Millions of people are displaced by wars in Kosovo, Sierra Leone, Indonesia, Kashmir, and the Congo. Afghanistan is just one disaster among many competing for the world's attention and assistance. Should I have told them the rest of it—that most Americans hadn't a clue where Afghanistan is or why there had been a war going on there for twenty years? Should I have told them that, while their situation was desperate, most of the international aid to Afghanistan was going to the Taliban-controlled south where people were starting to starve to death from the drought? Should I have told them that America would not care as long as the situation in Afghanistan did not directly affect them, that America becomes involved in any country's problems only when American interests are at stake? I did not say these things. What good is truth when it destroys hope? On the second day of our visit, the summer offensive broke out on the plains separating the Panjshir Valley from Kabul. The fighting was about 30 miles from us. We had planned to visit some schools in the Northern Alliance territory outside the valley but, as we drove toward the narrow canyon separating the valley from the Shomali Plains beyond, the stream of new refugees turned into a flood. Listening to the journalists interviewing some of the exhausted and terrified women, I learned their villages had been bombed the night before. They had fled in the darkness with the few belongings they could carry, walking with their children and babies to seek refuge inside the Panjshir Valley. There was no possibility of us venturing further that day and our vehicles turned back, joining the slow convoy of refugee-laden trucks making their way laboriously through the valley.

Under such circumstances, it did not surprise me that these Afghan women were more concerned for their immediate safety and finding food for their children than with their human rights. Even inside the Northern Alliance-controlled Panjshir Valley, free from the edicts of the Taliban, I noticed that the women all wore burkas when outside their family compounds. Women did freely raise their burkas to reveal their faces when they needed to tend a child or select vegetables from a market stall—a gesture that would have earned them a severe beating, if not arrest, under Taliban rule. When strong winds scoured our faces with sand and grit, it occurred to me that the idea of the burka, with its mesh to look through, might have originated as a practical way to protect faces and eyes from blowing sand. Without sunglasses and a scarf to protect my eyes and face, I might have been tempted to borrow a burka myself. Only when it became a garment forced on all women to control them and obliterate their public identities did it become a symbol of oppression.

I later expressed this view to some of the European women who attended the conference and was taken aback by their hostile reaction. My suggestion was deemed politically incorrect by certain feminists. One of them commented that we could not afford the slightest public admission of the burka having a legitimate role. Such a comment would be quoted out of context by Taliban supporters. Perhaps that concern was justified, but I always feel disappointment when those who fight for freedom suppress any views but their own. It reminded me of how certain American politicians advocated punitive trade measures against New Zealand when that country, seeking to be nuclear-free, denied entry to any nuclear-powered ships. The whole point of freedom is to ensure nations and individuals can make their own choices about how they want to live. Being free to choose only what suits the advocates of freedom is hardly freedom at all.

Seeing the day-to-day struggle Afghan women faced to stay alive made me wonder if our western concepts of women's rights were an absurd luxury in this context. Was it a waste of time to fight for women's rights when even the most basic human needs of food, clean water and shelter from the cold were not being satisfied? Then I realized that the war that left them hungry and cold was their only possible resistance to a regime that denied them education, employment, and the right to vote. The *Declaration of the Essential Rights of Afghan Women* was not irrelevant to these women: it expressed the underlying reason they continued in their struggle to survive, even if many of them could not read it for themselves. The declaration did not tell Afghan women not to wear a burka or a scarf. It claimed their right to make that choice for themselves. My small efforts in support of rights for women in Muslim lands were my own counter-terrorism efforts. They were my way of striking back against men like Abu Hassan and Osama bin Laden, whose philosophies deny women any roles beyond caring for homes and children. Such men are a persistent threat to American women also––not only because we are American but because we are women.

Late on the afternoon of our third day, our delegation was taken to a small jail in the Panjshir Valley where the Northern Alliance held a few dozen captured Taliban prisoners. The Northern Alliance was keen for the journalists in our group to speak to these prisoners because most of them were Pakistanis. The role of Pakistan in funding and arming the Taliban was not widely understood by the rest of the world. In the eyes of anti-Taliban Afghans, their struggle against the Taliban was essentially a struggle against an invasion of their country by Pakistan.

We arrived at a walled compound and were shown into a large reception room lined with sofas. Tea and cookies were brought in and placed on several low tables. After about twenty minutes, a dozen men shuffled into the room accompanied by several armed guards. They sat down on the floor in front of us looking resentful and suspicious. Only one guard remained in the room with the prisoners. The security seemed minimal and I looked around at the open windows, making a mental note of my escape options. In the crowded room, it seemed one of the Taliban could easily have grabbed the lone sentry's rifle and held one of us at gunpoint. I find I consider these possibilities, and think about contingency plans, more readily now that I have "hostage" on my curriculum vitae.

In a somewhat chaotic process, the journalists and Afghan women plied the prisoners with questions. Some of the dialogue was translated into English but much of it remained in Pashto or Dari. I followed what I could, fascinated to be within arms' reach of actual Taliban. Their stories were typical enough. They had been recruited from various madrassas and training camps in Pakistan, and had signed up because they believed in creating and defending pure Islamic states where Muslims could live according to Sharia law. The conversation was not limited so much by language as by the apparent inability or unwillingness of the prisoners to express any original thoughts. Their reply to any question was that they were fighting to make the whole world a true Islamic state because this was what Allah wanted and what Allah expected of them. When asked why women should be forced to wear burkas and stay at home, the Taliban men replied that it was for the women's own protection and it was required by Islamic law. Our delegation pointed out to them that the Koran does not forbid women to go to school or to work, but they refused to consider any view other than the indoctrination they had received in schools and training camps in Pakistan.

It was all very familiar stuff—the same story I had heard from Abu Hassan and his followers in the Aden Abyan Islamic Army. I find the belief that their god needs them to restore his rules on earth to be breathtaking in its arrogance. It's an extraordinarily egotistical position, after all, to believe that an all-powerful God needs your help. Not that Muslim extremists have any monopoly on such arrogance: some Christians feel the same duty to help their God impose his rules on entire societies. It seems to me that if a god—of the Christian or the Islamic variety—had even a fraction of the powers attributed to him, he would hardly need human help.

I have met many fundamentally good people who believe they are called to do God's work and I admire them for what they do. Yet, I suspect such people are humanitarians at heart and would do good in the world regardless of their religious convictions. Those who use religion to justify acts of violence are a different breed. I remain skeptical of whether any of these men, Yemen kidnappers or Taliban prisoners, really believe what they are saying. Do they truly think that this is what their god wants, or does religion simply provide the angry and ignorant man with an excuse to wage war and the cunning leader with a pitch to recruit him? I felt nothing but contempt for these Taliban prisoners. I wanted to spit on them.

The morning after that meeting we were to fly back to Dushanbe. The Afghan women had been very hopeful of meeting Shah Ahmed Masood, but the outbreak of fighting made that seem unlikely. Then, as we were packing up, we received word to gather in the living room. Masood was here to meet with us. The moment he entered the room I sensed his enormous charisma. Tall, dark and handsome, he was impeccably dressed in a pressed khaki jacket with his trademark wool cap worn at a jaunty angle. He listened attentively as the Afghan women explained the conference they had organized in Dushanbe and presented him with the declaration. He asked some questions and showed real empathy for our concerns. I watched him closely and could readily see why he had become so revered by his troops and civilian supporters. Masood then signed the declaration to express his commitment to restoring the rights of women in Afghanistan. We were each presented with a small Afghan rug before Masood departed as quickly as he had come. I had met the Lion of Panjshir, perhaps Afghanistan's greatest hero. During the meeting all of us had taken numerous photographs of him. Masood would die in just such a meeting the following year when two suicide bombers, in the guise of journalists, triggered a bomb hidden inside a camera on September 9, 2001—two days before Americans would finally begin paying attention to Afghanistan and, by default, recognizing the plight of Afghan women.

I was relieved to return to Dushanbe, not so much because I wanted to leave Afghanistan but because I had promised Ray I would be back in Rochester in time to accompany him to a family reunion his mother had organized in Hawaii over the week of July 4. Not wanting him to worry, I had not mentioned that I might travel into Afghanistan after the conference. As it was, my flight from Dushanbe to Moscow arrived early enough for me to connect with an American-bound plane that same day, and I arrived back in Rochester a day earlier than I had expected.

"So, how was Afghanistan?" Ray asked me slyly, as we drove away from the airport. It turned out that he had tried to call my hotel in Dushanbe a few days earlier and was told I had just left with a group going into Afghanistan.

"Are you annoyed that I didn't tell you beforehand?"

"I wasn't surprised. I think I half expected you would go there. What's important is that you are home safe." I showed Ray the photos of the helicopter that had transported us into the Panjshir Valley. He just shook his head, giving me one of those "you must be crazy" looks.

15

PURSUING THE PROMISED LANDS

I t struck me as strangely ironic that my philanthropic concerns with justice for women should have taken me to Afghanistan, the very country that had nurtured and inspired my kidnappers. Although both the trials were over and Abu Hassan had been executed, I still had a strong sense that I did not understand the events that had led up to the kidnapping. Hassan's motives, as expressed in court, provided a clear indication of his anger toward President Salih and the evils of western society. He clearly had a beef about the bombing of Iraq. Was the kidnapping just a spontaneous escalation of his anger at the world, triggered by the arrests of the Britons? If so, then who was Sheikh Haidara al-Atwi and why did early reports immediately after the kidnapping indicate that he was the man Hassan wished to free? How did the British guys even become involved with the AAIA in the first place, and why? I must have inherited too much of my detective Dad's inquiring mind.

I started to do more research into the recent histories of both Afghanistan and Yemen, seeking a context for the AAIA and its activities. I bought books about the Russian occupation of Afghanistan and the rise of the mujahiddin, about the emergence of the Taliban and the history of Yemen. I prowled the Internet for increasingly obscure articles describing the return of mujahiddin to Yemen. One pertinent clue at the time came from a wide range of Web-based resources and from books such as Paul Dresch's *A History of Modern Yemen.* I also contacted a couple of Middle

East scholars in Washington DC who had expertise on Yemen. None of these sources provided the full story, of course, but each supplied a few more pieces of the puzzle, which allowed me to understand the environment Abu Hassan encountered when he returned to Yemen from Afghanistan.

After serving with the mujahiddin between 1988 and 1990, Abu Hassan was now an "Afghan-Arab," a term used to refer to non-Afghans who fought against the Soviets in Afghanistan. He returned to Yemen at a time when the formerly separate states of the Yemen Arab Republic in the north and the People's Democratic Republic of Yemen in the south were unifying into a single nation-state. Under political leaders who adhered to the Arab socialist movement, south Yemen had evolved into a Marxist state after achieving independence from British colonial rule in 1967. By 1990, this regime had become too unstable to survive, and the stage was set for unification of the north and south under the leadership of the northern president, Ali Abdullah Salih. Afghan-Arabs from south Yemen, who had just succeeded in eliminating communism in Afghanistan rejoiced to see the end of the Marxist era in their home country as well. Abu Hassan was among those who anticipated that the rulers of the new unified Yemen would adhere to the Islamic principles they had been fighting for in Afghanistan.

Between 1990 and 1993, the new Republic of Yemen was beset with economic problems and the fallout from the Iraqi invasion of Kuwait. President Salih had made the decision to support Iraq in the Gulf War, earning the intense displeasure of the United States and Saudi Arabia. The subsequent eviction of more than half a million Yemenis from their jobs in Saudi Arabia, combined with the return of the militant Afghan-Arabs, created a huge unemployment problem and social instability.

It also added to the growing conflict among the country's many newly formed political parties.

In addition to the three thousand Yemenis who returned home from Afghanistan, as many as double that number of non-Yemeni Afghan-Arabs made their way there. Algerians, Egyptians, Syrians, Jordanians, Iraqis, Somalis, and Sudanese joined the Yemeni militants who disappeared into Islamic Jihad terrorist training camps in the mountains and deserts of south Yemen. The country was an attractive choice for them, particularly for those who could not return to their homelands without fear of arrest. The harsh, mountainous terrain of Yemen was not unlike Afghanistan, and it provided remote sites where the government exerted little presence and even less control. Yemen's long southern coastline on the Indian Ocean and its ill-defined border with Saudi Arabia to the north allowed easy and undocumented entry into the country. The non-Yemeni Afghan-Arabs could also be assured of hospitality from their Yemeni fellow veterans. To help settle the Afghan-Arabs in Yemen, Osama bin Laden is believed to have supplied an estimated $20 million in funds that were—according to some sources—administered by Ali Mohsen al-Ahmar, a powerful general in the Yemen army and a half-brother of President Salih.

An important influence on Abu Hassan was Sheikh Tariq al-Fadhli, the son of a formerly powerful sultan in Yemen's southern province of Abyan. Al-Fadhli's family had lost its extensive lands in Abyan during the Marxist regime: sultanates did not fit well with a communist manifesto. Like Abu Hassan, al-Fadhli had personal as well as religious reasons to hate the communists. He not only recruited fellow Yemenis for the war against the Russians in Afghanistan but fought there himself. In Afghanistan, al-Fadhli developed his connections with another man whose family originated from Yemen and who shared his passion for fighting the communists: Osama bin Laden.

Al-Fadhli was intent on recovering his family lands and aristocratic title in Abyan. He saw the opportunity to exploit the fundamentalist passions of men like Hassan, and to use this religious rationale to take revenge on those who had denied him his inheritance. Capitalizing on a prediction by the Prophet Mohammed that "twelve thousand men will come out of Aden's Abyan to aid the cause of God and His Messenger," al-Fadhli created a Yemeni version of the Egyptian fundamentalist movement known as Islamic Jihad. His homegrown terrorist organization shared the same name and philosophies as the organizations in Lebanon and Egypt, but operated independently of them and focused on its own priorities. In Yemen, Islamic Jihad's stated mission was to help save

Muslims in Bosnia and to wage war on all non-Islamic regimes in Muslim lands. No doubt al-Fadhli found it much easier to recruit followers to these high-minded causes than to rally them around his personal agenda of reclaiming the family farm.

Islamic Jihad probably conducted several sporadic bombing attacks in the south of Yemen, most notably the 1992 bombing of the Aden Hotel, where they believed U.S. troops would bivouac en route to Somalia. As it turned out, the troops were absent when the bomb exploded, but an Austrian tourist and a hotel worker were killed. In response, the Yemen army sent its Third Armored Brigade to attack al-Fadhli's home in the Maraqisha mountains in Abyan. However, the wily sheikh had sited his fortified camp within the boundaries of a village, and the army was reluctant to carry out an air attack, which could result in death and destruction for the villagers. Al-Fadhli escaped and later reappeared in Sana'a after negotiating a deal with the government. In 1994, he volunteered his jihad followers to fight alongside President Salih in the continuing conflict with the Marxist secessionists in the south. Among these followers was Abu Hassan.

After Abu Hassan had helped to defeat the communists occupying Afghanistan, he was angry to see his home province still under the influence of godless Marxists. A despised beer factory was producing alcohol in Aden. Women, often unveiled, were engaged in jobs where they worked openly alongside men. And after years of communist control, agricultural land produced only a fraction of the bounty achieved under private ownership. It was not surprising, then, that Hassan would join al-Fadhli's Islamic Jihad and, in 1994, also align himself with Salih. In a brief but bloody civil war in 1994, Salih consolidated his control over the unified republic of Yemen, finally putting down the socialist resurgence.

President Salih's subsequent success in maintaining control in Yemen was partly due to his strategy of keeping friends close, but enemies even closer. Former opponents were offered key roles in the new government and many of their followers were absorbed into jobs in the military, police or other government departments. As a reward for his services, Sheikh Tariq al-Fadhli was offered a place on Salih's personal advisory council and the restoration of his family lands in Abyan. Since the recovery of his inheritance was al-Fadhli's real objective, he did not hesitate to convert from jihad terrorist to card-carrying member of the establishment, and he encouraged his followers to do the same. Many Islamic Jihad members took advantage of the chance to build a more peaceful life for themselves, but Abu Hassan was not among them.

This second conquest over communism did not bring the results the fundamentalists expected. Abu Hassan became increasingly angry at the refusal of President Salih to govern Yemen according to pure Islamic law. The newly reunified republic appeared to be taking a more moderate path and, although basing its law on the Sharia, it did not adhere to Sharia alone. Salih's government even supported greater educational, employment and political opportunities for women. This did not satisfy the strict Salafi principles to which Hassan adhered. He admired the Taliban and its uncompromising imposition of what he perceived as traditional Islamic law in Afghanistan. He was determined to continue fighting for a true Muslim state in Yemen as well—a state where Sharia alone determined law, behavior, and beliefs. Abu Hassan envisioned a state where there was no alcohol, no usury, and women were fully veiled. There would be no western cultural influence and certainly no American military presence.

Between 1994 and 1998 Abu Hassan split his time between Saudi Arabia and Yemen, developing his own sources of funds and gathering a few dozen like-minded followers around him. A volatile personality, given to passionate outbursts and deep concern for the well-being of his friends, Hassan had sufficient charisma to establish himself as a leader. He described his supporters as "ordinary youths who were with us in Afghanistan." One supporter, known as Abu Hani, lived in the Saudi city of Mecca and sent him funds. The amounts were typically 10,000 to 15,000 Saudi riyals, delivered in person by young Yemeni men returning home from Saudi Arabia.

Apparently, various levels of government made repeated attempts to negotiate with Hassan and incorporate him into the mainstream—as they had with al-Fadhli—but he was not willing to settle for the middle ground. He had reached the conclusion that Yemen must once again be split into two countries but—unlike the People's Democratic Republic of

Yemen in the 1970s—the new southern state would be Muslim according to Mohammed, not Muslim according to Marx.

This historical background helped me better understand the political, social and personal conflicts that had spawned a man like Abu Hassan. He had been trained in violence as a mujahid; he had participated in the successful overthrow of the communist regime in Afghanistan; he had been strongly influenced by fundamentalist Salafi beliefs as a teenager in Saudi Arabia, and he felt he had been sold out by the promises of men like Salih and al-Fadhli in his homeland of Yemen. He was also, judging by his courtroom appearances, a borderline psychotic, obsessed with control and convinced he was being called by God to fulfill an ancient prophecy. The odds were never good that he would settle down with a wife or two and pursue life as a law-abiding, upright member of society. Now, by virtue of his execution, he was unavailable for further comment.

My next-best option was to contact someone who knew him. I located an address on the Supporters of Sharia Web site and sent an e-mail to Abu Hamza.

16

THE MULLAH OF
FINSBURY PARK

No longer constrained to Rochester by my corporate career, I made plans to go to London. I wanted to see what new insights I could obtain from Scotland Yard detectives about their investigation of the kidnapping. I planned to visit Margaret Thompson and Pat Morris again and, if possible, get in touch with some of the other hostages. There was someone else I wanted to meet in London. Although Abu Hamza had not responded to my e-mails, I felt sure I could find a way to get in touch with him once I arrived.

One week before my flight to London, terrorists in Yemen struck again. On October 12, 2000, a massive bomb was detonated on a small dinghy that pulled up alongside the American warship USS *Cole* as it refueled in the harbor at Aden. Seventeen sailors were killed and thirty-eight wounded. The two men on board the dinghy were also killed in the apparent suicide bombing. Once again, the United States sent investigators to Yemen. The country was becoming all too well known to the FBI antiterrorist branch. As I read the front-page news stories of this latest terrorist attack, I wondered if the Aden Abyan Islamic Army was involved. The date of the USS *Cole* attack was close to the first anniversary of Abu Hassan's execution on October 17, 1999. Was this a coincidence? New developments in Yemen seemed to be expanding the story faster than I could find answers.

I arrived at London's Gatwick Airport early on the morning of October 20 and took the train to my hotel on Jermyn Street, near Piccadilly

Circus. Pat had kindly invited me to stay with her, but she was out of town for a couple of days and I decided to use a hotel until her return. In addition to trying to get in touch with Abu Hamza directly, in advance of my trip, I had contacted several lawyers involved with the British men's trial. One of them, the Amnesty International volunteer Rashad Yaqoob, offered to try to arrange a meeting for me with Hamza, but then I had heard nothing more from him. After a shower and a traditional English breakfast at the hotel, I decided I would go to Hamza's Finsbury Park mosque. It happened to be a Friday so I figured the mosque would be busy. Perhaps there would be someone there who could put me in touch with Abu Hamza.

The mosque was a short walk from the tube station and the grimy commercial strip of the Seven Sisters Road. The neighborhood of Finsbury Park was once home to working-class Irish but, over time, new waves of immigrants had settled in the area, bringing with them the cuisines, dress, customs, beliefs, and languages of Bangladesh, Egypt, Morocco, and Pakistan. By 1990, the newcomers had built themselves a mosque with millions of pounds donated by a Saudi prince. They set up their shops and restaurants along the Seven Sisters Road and worked hard, creating new lives and new identities for themselves and their children.

I turned into St. Thomas Road anticipating a white building with delicate arches and a soaring minaret. The curving residential street of Edwardian terrace-houses seemed an unlikely location for any mosque, and the building I found bore little resemblance to the elegant architecture of Arabia. North London's mosque was built of brick and its square-edged minaret reminded me of a factory chimney stack. Its front door, accessed through a gate in a tall, wrought-iron fence, was at the top of half-a-dozen steep steps leading up from the pavement. A group of young men stood talking together at the bottom of the steps. One of them wore camouflage fatigues and a wool hat like the one given to me in Afghanistan. The others had on white cotton shalwar kameez, better suited to the heat of Pakistan than the chill of a London winter. I suspected these men were not standing on the sidewalk as a welcoming committee. I crossed the street and walked by casually, uncertain what to do next.

Two blocks along St. Thomas Road was The Auld Triangle pub. It was only 10:00 AM, but the pub was open so I walked in and ordered a beer. It did not take long to strike up a conversation with the only other patron, an Irishman in his late sixties with thinning hair and a deeply lined face.

"Aye, they're a funny lot over there," he replied in response to my casual comment about the neighborhood mosque. "They're all Turks and the like, you know." He leaned towards me confidentially, a trickle of beer spilling on to his once-white cable-stitched sweater. "My brother did some plumbing there once. Terrible conditions they live in, you know. No proper bathrooms, not even for the women." I was well into hearing the man's life story of how he had immigrated to England and fallen on hard times when I suddenly had an overwhelming feeling that I should leave. A strange certainty came over me that I was about to meet the mullah. Excusing myself from the Irishman's Dickensian saga, I grabbed my coat and left the pub. Halfway back towards the mosque, I stopped to photograph the building. As I put my camera away, I looked up to see a battered blue Mercedes attempting to maneuver into a parking space directly across the street from me. Instantly, my eyes glanced at the steering wheel. The driver had no hands.

"Well, well," I said to myself and smiled, "as Abu Hassan would have said, God has sent him to me." I watched for several minutes as Abu Hamza attempted to park the car, amazed that a man with his disabilities could drive at all. Several of the young men from the mosque were approaching his car. As they gathered around the driver's door, talking to him, I crossed the street and approached one of the men who stood a little apart from the rest.

"Excuse me, but is that Abu Hamza?" I asked, pointing to the Mercedes.

A brilliant smile lit up the man's heavily bearded face. "Yes. How do you know about Abu Hamza?" His English was fluent and educated but heavily accented; probably a Pakistani.

"He is a famous man," I replied. "I have read about him in America and have come here to meet him." After some friendly conversation about my interest in Islam and how Muslims are perceived in America, the young man agreed to let Abu Hamza know I wanted to speak to him. He pushed his way through the throng of devotees still clustered around the car door. Hamza glanced toward me with disinterest. When the mullah finally heaved himself from the vehicle, I approached him. He wore a brown wool overcoat covering a gray cotton shalwar kameez. A black turban-like hat and wispy beard framed his mottled red face. The milky left eye stared sightlessly toward me.

"My name is Mary Quin. I arrived here from America this morning in the hope of speaking with you. Did you receive the e-mails I sent?" Abu Hamza seemed distracted, only half listening to me as he made his way toward the mosque's front door followed by his retinue. "No," he replied. "E-mails are not easy for me." He glanced down towards the stumps of his forearms thrust into the pockets of his coat. "Come inside. There are some books that will tell you everything you need to know." I followed him up the steep steps into the mosque. The left side of a corridor was lined with shelves already filling up with the shoes of the faithful. On the right were several tables draped in cheap cotton fabric where plastic knick-knacks and items of clothing were offered for sale. Abu Hamza turned into a small room off this corridor. It appeared to be a bookshop with publications in Arabic as well as English. Gesturing with the stump of his arm, Abu Hamza pointed out to me a couple of paperback volumes. "Read these. They will explain my teachings. Here, this one covers what really happened in Algeria." Another man entered the shop and Abu Hamza instructed him to sell me the books. Hamza began to leave the room.

"Wait," I said, stepping quickly between him and the door. "I will read your books but I need to talk to you. I'm writing a book myself and have come all the way from the United States to talk to you. Is there any time over the weekend you could spare me fifteen minutes?"

Hamza explained he was too busy. He had a sermon to prepare for this afternoon's service and a protest rally to attend outside the Egyptian embassy. I assured him I would show up wherever and whenever it was convenient for him. Hamza paused, "Come back here at six o'clock on Sunday evening and I'll give you fifteen minutes." I stepped aside as his bulky frame pushed past me and disappeared down the corridor.

My next appointment was with Rashad Yaqoob, who had made himself less than popular with judge and journalists while serving as an

Amnesty International volunteer at the Britons' trial. I found my way to the cramped office he shared with another lawyer at a Muslim financial services business. There was barely room to put a guest chair in the space between the two men's desks. Yaqoob had explained to me on the phone that morning that his wife had just given birth to identical twin daughters, so I was not surprised when he arrived late and harried. I offered him two chocolate cigars I had purchased on my way to his office.

Yaqoob was a small man, about 5 feet 6 inches tall, and his body seemed lost inside his ill-fitting suit. His eyes were huge and flashed with the nervous energy he exuded as he moved piles of papers round his disorganized desk, trying to create space for my notebook. Once we were settled, Yaqoob explained that he belonged to Amnesty International's network of pro-bono lawyers. He became involved in the case of the British men in Yemen when he received an "urgent action" release from Amnesty, warning that the men might soon be executed without trial. He immediately tracked down the men's families in Birmingham, Luton, and London to offer assistance and got in touch with the well-known barrister Gareth Peirce to seek advice. Discovering that Yemen law did not allow non-Yemeni attorneys to represent the defendants, Peirce and Yaqoob started to alert the media at once. Their intent was to create enough publicity about the "boys" to prevent any possibility of execution without trial. At that stage, Yaqoob told me, the Foreign Office was still denying that any Britons were under arrest. The families heard about the arrests through a Yemeni relative of Malik Harhara, one of the defendants. The Foreign Office did not confirm the men had been detained in Yemen nor contact their families until two-and-a-half weeks after the arrests.

Yaqoob was adamant that the British men were completely innocent of the bombing conspiracy charges. He told me he was unaware of any link between the arrest of the Britons and the kidnapping until "stories started in the Middle East." The evidence in the trial, he assured me, confirmed that the "boys" were not Hassan's purpose. Hassan's kidnapping demands had to do with objections to the refueling of U.S. military vessels in Aden and reported plans for American installations on Yemen territory such as the island of Socotra. When I questioned whether Yaqoob really believed the Britons were only in Yemen to study Islam and learn Arabic, he assured me they were and described how Shahid Butt was a model of charitable good works both in Birmingham and overseas. I have been a member of Amnesty International for many years myself, and fully recognize the horrifying human rights violations that the organization struggles against all over the world, but I decided that if Yaqoob really believed what he was telling me, then he was well-meaning but naïve. I asked him if he would be willing to put me in contact with the British defendants who had already been released.

"They are not in England," Yaqoob told me. "For their own protection, they are staying in a third country."

"In Pakistan, perhaps?" I asked.

"In a third country," the civil rights lawyer replied.

His wife was still in the hospital and Yaqoob was anxious to get back to her and his new babies. When I asked if he would be willing to introduce me to any of the Britons' relatives, he put me in touch with Shahid Butt's brother Rachad. I made arrangements to meet Rachad Butt, but he cancelled the meeting at the last minute, explaining he had been called out of town to a business meeting. Apparently, Rachad was a manager working for that ultimate symbol of American global domination, McDonald's.

I moved over to Pat's charming home in a quiet suburb of London. She urged me not to disclose her address, or reveal that I was staying with her, to anyone associated with the kidnapping. Pat had largely kept her name out of the newspapers, and even some of the people she worked with had no idea she had been taken hostage. She preferred to keep it that way and I respected her need for privacy. I assured Pat that if I felt anyone might be following me after my meeting with Abu Hamza, I would not return to the house but would call her from a hotel or restaurant. She was performing with the orchestra that Sunday evening, but assured me she would contact the police if I had not returned from my meeting with the mullah by the time she got home. I did not really have any concerns about returning to the mosque but was glad someone knew where I was going and when I should be back. Grabbing a shawl for appropriate mosque attire, I headed out to catch a bus that would drop me at the Finsbury Park train station.

On my way I reviewed what I knew about Abu Hamza. According to an in-depth interview published by the British newspaper the *Guardian*, Abu Hamza was born Mustafa Mohammed Kamel in Alexandria, Egypt. His family was neither wealthy nor particularly religious, but they did belong to Egypt's growing urban middle class and they valued education as a means to prosperity. His father was a naval officer and had enough money to send his son to university to study civil engineering. Before completing his degree, Kamel traveled in 1979 to Britain, a country many of his friends had visited. What was supposed to be a vacation evolved into immigration. Kamel adapted easily to his new life. His English improved quickly and he took advantage of his good looks and friendly, outgoing nature to date local girls. One of them, Valerie Fleming, became his wife. Valerie's parents liked Kamel and welcomed him into their family. There was no reason for him to return to Egypt in spite of the disappointment of his own family, who had hoped for his return.

Without a degree, Kamel's employment opportunities were limited. He got work in the nightclubs of Soho as a bouncer. With his powerful physique, he would have been an intimidating presence, and had no trouble getting work. The job gave him a first-hand look at a world of drinking, dancing, and sexual freedom that he had never been exposed to in Egypt. At first, the casual relationships between men and women shocked him. The provocative way the women dressed and their shameless behavior in the clubs were unlike anything he could have imagined back home. But the money was good and the hours suited him. He had free time during the day to finish his engineering degree part time at Brighton Polytechnic.

Valerie became increasingly curious about Islam and plied her Muslim husband with questions. As he tried to explain his religion to his wife, Kamel could not help but see the conflict between the life he was living and the teachings of the holy Koran. He continued to read and to educate himself, as well as Valerie, about Islam—and concluded he could no longer work in the clubs. Religious study consumed more and more of his life, leading him to examine the beliefs of the faith he had been born into and to seek answers to his questions from Islamic scholars.

Over the next five years, Kamel progressed from a personal study of Islam to sharing his new knowledge and beliefs by preaching to others. His great dream became the formation of a single Muslim state ruled according to Sharia, the Islamic law. The struggle of Muslims against oppression and corrupt secular governments in Islamic lands became his primary cause. He began helping some of the young men who had gone to fight in Afghanistan and had returned to Britain injured and in need of shelter. His own home country, Egypt, was among the Muslim lands under the control of a government that did not rule according to Sharia. Perhaps he should join the growing fundamentalist movement in Egypt. No, his family told him. He would be arrested and tortured there and he would put his entire family at risk of retribution by the government.

Instead, Kamel decided to support the effort in Afghanistan. The war against the Soviets was already over, but the country needed to rebuild its infrastructure and provide basic services for its people. Afghanistan had the real possibility of establishing a perfect Islamic state. When his marriage to Valerie ended, he emigrated—first to Pakistan then, in 1992, to Afghanistan.

A year later, according to the *Guardian* interview, Kamel was using his civil engineering training to help reconstruct roads in Nangarhar province. As he drew a line in the ground with a stick, to illustrate a technical point, he activated one of the millions of landmines that lie in wait to maim and kill indiscriminately all over the war-ravaged country. Kamel was rushed back to Pakistan, and eventually to Britain, for treatment. Both hands and his left eye were destroyed but he had survived. (The landmine story is Abu Hamza's official version of what happened. American antiterrorism investigators later commented to me that his injuries were more consistent with a chemical explosion than a landmine, suggesting he may have been hurt while constructing a bomb.) From Kamel's perspective, the loss of his hands meant only that Allah intended for him to serve in a different role. He would stay in Britain, where his freedom of speech was assured, and use his voice rather than his hands to do the work of Allah. And so Kamel, taking the name Abu Hamza, created the Supporters of Sharia.

Abu Hamza had a gift for preaching. I saw him in action on the videotape he had sold me. His physical presence was as imposing in the pulpit as it must have been at the doorways to nightclubs. He began his sermons slowly, quietly, his eyes downcast and the stumps of his arms shoved deep in the pockets of his long, loose-fitting shirt. As he warmed to his theme, his fervor increased and his one good eye scanned the upturned faces of the kneeling men and boys, who watched him intently. His right arm could no longer be contained in his pocket and the stump gesticulated wildly, punctuating the air as he made his points. His sermons often started with a genuine message about right behavior drawn from the Koran, but frequently evolved into impassioned denunciations of Israel or the United States or the latest antiterrorism efforts in Britain. The message to the young men in his congregation was clear: They had a religious responsibility to prepare themselves for jihad. And where better to train for jihad than in Afghanistan or Yemen? The term jihad has come to be associated with waging war or terrorist acts against enemies of Islam. But I learned from my reading about Islam that the true religious meaning of jihad is "striving or struggling in the way of God." The greatest jihad is the struggle to do what is right in spite of your own human failings of greed, pride, and selfishness. At a secondary level, jihad involves defending Islam— a meaning that has proven to be a clever recruitment tool in the hands of those with personal and political agendas. For a man like Abu Hamza, jihad was the perfect pretext and London the perfect place from which to wage his private war.

It was dark when I approached the mosque's front door. Men leading small boys by the hand were making their way into the building for an evening service. As I walked up the steps, a man appeared in the doorway and asked what I wanted. I waited on the steps while he went to verify my appointment with the mullah. After a half-hour wait in an empty basement-level prayer room, I was escorted to Abu Hamza's office.

I removed my shoes and draped the black shawl over my head and shoulders before I continued along the corridor to an office door hidden behind a heavy curtain under a stairwell. Abu Hamza was sitting behind a desk talking to the man who had sold me the books on Friday. Several youths in their late teens sat on the floor against one wall and looked at me curiously. To my surprise, four young children were playing on the floor around Abu Hamza's feet. I took a seat across the desk from the mullah.

"Salaam alaikum," I said in greeting. He returned the traditional expression of peace and immediately launched into a commentary about Algeria.

"I have not come to talk about Algeria," I cut him off. "I have come to talk about Yemen. I am one of the tourists who was taken hostage by Abu Hassan."

Abu Hamza was momentarily speechless. He looked closely at me, then leaned back in his chair and slowly smiled.

"So. I am surprised that you would come here—very surprised."

"May I record our conversation?" I placed a small tape recorder on the desk between us.

"Yes, you can record it. Well . . . I will answer your questions and there are probably some things that you can explain to me." The mullah spoke a few curt words to the children and they instantly stopped talking and sat quietly.

My fifteen-minute conversation with Abu Hamza lasted nearly an hour. He told me that he had never actually met Abu Hassan. Contrary to various news reports, which claimed the two men had met while fighting the Russians in Afghanistan, Hamza told me Hassan had first contacted him by phone about a year before the kidnapping. "Abu Hassan needed a mouthpiece for the Aden Abyan Islamic Army. At first, I was not willing to help him. I did not think he was really committed to restoring Sharia law in Yemen." The two men remained in communication, however, and after several months Hamza became satisfied that the leader of the AAIA did share the same goals as the Supporters of Sharia. I asked Hamza about the phone call Hassan had reportedly made to him immediately after we were captured.

"Hassan made many phone calls," Hamza acknowledged. "One of them was to me. The kidnapping was not planned. Hassan didn't even know what he had in his hands. He wanted to force the government to let his people go. He just knew he had some foreigners and it would embarrass the government."

"Who were the people Hassan wanted to free?" I asked. "What were his demands?"

"He wanted to free al-Atwi, a mujahid who has killed seventeen Yemeni soldiers. [Al-Atwi] has his own group, not part of the Aden Abyan Islamic Army. There was also a Spanish guy, an Arab with a Spanish passport. The [Yemen] government gave his children to the Spanish government and accused him of plotting bombings for the Saudis. And eight others—members of the Aden Army. Iraq was not the main issue."

I asked if Hassan had also demanded the release of the Britons who had been arrested.

"I think . . . I'm not sure if he mentioned the British guys."

I knew Hamza was not being honest with me. One of those arrested was his wife's son, and he must have known his own son was on the run in Yemen at the time. How could he "not be sure" whether Abu Hassan was including the Britons in his ransom demands? For the moment, I changed the topic and asked Hamza if he thought the kidnapping was a good thing.

"Islamically, the kidnapping was a good thing," he replied. "It denounced an un-Islamic government and showed the government cannot protect tourists. It stops the use of tourists' money against Islam. You do not understand this, but tourism is the reason the government gives for allowing gambling, alcohol, and usury banks. The government looks after [the needs of] tourists not their own people. Tourists are being used by the government.

"Politically," Hamza continued, "the kidnapping was not a very good move. Technically, it was not a good move. It resulted in the destruction of the AAIA leadership. People inside the army and supporters who used to give them aid now find the war too big. The U.S. government is involved. [AAIA and its supporters] have to hide."

When I asked Abu Hamza if he had supplied Hassan with a satellite telephone, the mullah shrugged. "Perhaps. [The Supporters of Sharia] issue a news magazine. Hassan needed a secure phone line to send us news. He could not take the risk of using a normal phone." As if to justify his own role during the kidnapping, Hamza assured me he had urged Hassan not to harm any of the hostages. Negotiation was the key to a successful outcome.

From his London home, Hamza had advised Hassan to stay to the rear of his men and negotiate by phone. According to Hamza, Hassan had tried to call government contacts to demand an immediate exchange of prisoners, but the government refused any dialogue. "That was a mistake," Hamza commented, "because it led to the collapse of the tourist industry. [President] Salih is a Bedouin—he has no sense." From his tone, I inferred that calling someone a Bedouin was no compliment.

"Why, do you think, did the Yemen security forces attack so quickly?"

"Because of the satellite telephone. The government was afraid that Hassan would use the phone to reach the press. The government wanted to keep him quiet."

Unsure how much more time the mullah would give me, I returned to the subject of the arrested British men, particularly his sons. He confirmed that his former wife Valerie Fleming was the mother of Mohammed, but would not provide any information about his current wife, the mother of his stepson Mohsin Ghalain. With the long-suffering air of any parent, Abu Hamza expressed his frustration over his sons' behavior. "They didn't tell me where they were going. They were green, inexperienced. They don't realize there is no freedom of speech in those countries. If I had known I would have told them to change their names in their passports . . . You can't control a teenager, you know."

"Do you object to people like me visiting Muslim countries?"

"No, I don't object if people visit respectfully. Like you," he nodded towards my head-covering. "You come here to the mosque dressed respectfully. I object to tourists who abuse Muslim hospitality, and I object to the use made of tourism dollars."

"What is your ultimate goal?" I asked. "Do you realistically think every country will eventually become Muslim, even England?"

"I don't intend everyone should be converted to Islam," the cleric replied, "but the image of Islam has been distorted. Western countries want Muslim countries to be poor and weak. I want peace for those who love peace, war for those who love war."

Curious to know more about Abu Hassan, I asked Hamza his impressions of the militant leader. "He is a soft-hearted man, very loyal to his people. He was worried that the men captured by the government would not survive. Hassan knew they would be tortured." Then he dropped a bombshell. "Abu Hassan is still alive."

"Why do you think that?" I asked carefully. "I read he had been executed."

"His family did not receive the body. In Islamic custom, the body is always turned over to the family for burial."

"Does Abu Hassan have a family?"

"Oh, yes, he has a big family."

"If he is still alive, where is he? In prison still—or has he left the country?"

"I believe he is in prison, under tight security. If he were free he would have contacted me."

"Why would the government have claimed to execute him?"

The mullah expanded on his theory. "The government has little control of the south, the tribal areas. If the tribes thought Hassan was still alive in the prison, they would have stormed the prison to set him free. The government made a deal with the AAIA, then let everyone else think Hassan was dead." The story seemed shaky and I attributed it to wishful thinking on Hamza's part—or his egotistical need to embellish the situation and appear to have inside knowledge. Nonetheless, the possibility that Hassan was alive intrigued me.

Hamza asked me about my own impressions of Islam and whether I would go back to a Muslim country after what had happened in Yemen. I told him there were good and bad aspects to all religions, and I hoped one day to return to Yemen and see those parts of the country I had missed on my original trip. He was also interested to know which other Muslim countries I had been to. I mentioned Egypt and Uzbekistan but chose not to disclose my visit to the Northern Alliance-controlled part of Afghanistan. Somehow, I did not think Abu Hamza and I would see eye to eye on the subject of the Taliban and Afghan women's rights.

Suddenly Abu Hamza leaned forward. "Do not go back to the south of Yemen. They will not bother with kidnapping foreigners next time," he warned. "Rocket attacks on tourists will be next. From the top of a hill, they can fire a rocket at a car. You will not see it coming . . ."

The interview was over. Hamza said he could spare no more time, and called on one of the youths sitting behind me on the floor to escort me from the mosque. I thanked him for his time and asked if I could follow up with him in future if I had more questions. He gave me his cell phone number.

The young man who escorted me to the lobby of the mosque was Caucasian. I struck up a brief conversation with him and discovered he was an American, a student at the University of Illinois. He would not tell me his name, but confirmed he had come to the mosque to study Islam with Abu Hamza. His goal, he told me, was eventually to go to Afghanistan and live in the Islamic state created by the Taliban. He seemed a polite, soft-spoken young man, hardly a militant. I wondered if he had any idea of what life under the Taliban was really like. I wonder now what became of him and how many more Americans there were like him, seeking a Taliban version of the Promised Land.

During the remainder of my time in London, I met two of the detectives who had conducted Scotland Yard's investigation of the kidnapping and provided evidence for the inquest into the deaths of the tourists. They were now actively involved in other terrorism cases, but provided me with a copy of one of their reports. Pat was also a great source of information, since she had saved a number of newspaper articles about the kidnapping and the trial of the Britons. I took her files to a local quick printer and spent several hours duplicating them at a self-serve copier (Xerox of course). Even though I no longer worked for Xerox, I couldn't help but ask the printer how his color copier was doing and felt a certain pride in hearing he loved the product that I had helped bring to the market.

Next day I took the train to Gatwick Airport for my flight to New York. My carry-on luggage contained all the new documents and tapes I had obtained in London. As the plane lifted off the runway, I pulled out the Scotland Yard report and began to read.

17

JIHAD BRITANNIA

By midsummer 2000, I had sold my home in Rochester and moved in with Ray. As my files expanded, I found Ray's tiny spare bedroom, which also accommodated his fly-tying bench, was no longer big enough for my work. I rented an office in a small commercial building near his home. There, I was able to pin up on the walls all the pieces of the puzzle I had so far been able to gather.

On a huge whiteboard, I drew all the connections between players and events that I had uncovered. There were still many gaps and question marks but the material I had gathered in London filled in many uncharted areas of my map. Most valuable was the Scotland Yard report that explained how young Muslim men growing up in London and Birmingham had come to be affiliated with the Aden Abyan Islamic Army in southern Yemen. I was able to combine information I had gathered about Hassan's activities in Yemen during 1998 with Scotland Yard's record of the Britons' movements during the same time frame and see how the two groups ultimately converged. I discovered that while I was celebrating my forty-fifth birthday in Rochester on September 2, 1998, the AAIA and the young British men were three days away from their first direct contact with each other. The meeting resulted from the religious zeal of two like-minded men—Abu Hamza in London and Abu Hassan in Yemen.

After his mentor al-Fadhli recovered his lands and defected from the leadership of Yemen's Islamic Jihad, Abu Hassan began to see himself in a new role. It was he, Zein al-Abidin abu Bakr al-Mehdar—not Tariq al-Fadhli—who would fulfilll the Prophet's prediction and lead twelve thousand men from Aden's Abyan. In the name of Allah and his messenger, Abu Hassan would be a leader of men, a mighty warrior for God against infidels and crusaders. He separated from Islamic Jihad to form his own organization. According to Hassan's own account, he formed the AAIA in June or July 1998, and its membership "did not exceed several scores." Other sources suggest AAIA existed a year or two earlier and attracted as many as two hundred members. One of the earliest public reports of an organization by this name occurred in August 1998, when the Aden Abyan Islamic Army sent a warning through Agence France-Presse declaring "total war" on American presence or activities in Yemen.

In preparation for building his army, Hassan set up a training camp near the town of Habban in Shabwah province. Often such camps were an irritant to local tribal people, who would complain about the presence of foreigners and the disruption of normal agricultural and livestock-grazing activities in the area. No doubt some of these militant groups were little more than local bandits and thugs embarking on a life of crime, much the same as gangs operating in western cities. Others were motivated by religious or political agenda, and in some cases their leaders were well known to—and under surveillance by—both provincial and national governments.

Through the network of Afghan-Arabs in Yemen, Hassan attracted to his camp men capable of instructing his recruits in the use of guns, light artillery, landmines and explosives. Among them was an Egyptian, Osama al-Masri, an explosives expert and a former member of the Egyptian Islamic Jihad. Al-Masri—an alias that simply means "the Egyptian" in Arabic—had lived in Yemen since 1992 after serving with the mujahiddin in Afghanistan. He was well known to authorities in Cairo, where he was wanted in connection with past terrorist activities. Al-Masri had affiliations with Dr. Jawahiri, the leader of Egyptian Islamic Jihad who would later be well known as the right-hand man of Osama bin Laden and the chief strategist of al-Qaeda. Using information in the Scotland Yard report as well as the story told by the five hostages taken to the front line of the battle, I realized that Osama al-Masri was the kidnapper I thought of as Bandit, the one who may have triggered the rescue shoot-out when he launched a rocket-propelled grenade into the oncoming troops—and who was himself killed in the battle.

Between 1996 and 1998, Hassan claimed responsibility for several bombings, which he described as deterrent strikes against the government in Sana'a or against foreign-owned facilities. His purpose was to destroy buildings, he said, not to harm fellow Muslims. I noted with interest his concern about killing Muslims. It matched a comment I heard from one Middle East scholar, who pointed out that Yemenis were cautious about killing a member of another tribe. They knew it would unleash retribution on their own tribal group. These facts helped explain Hassan's reticence about shooting at the oncoming soldiers during the rescue. Not being a Yemeni, Osama al-Masri would have felt no such reservations.

Algerians, Tunisians, Somalis, and Sudanese were among the nationalities that came through Hassan's camp for training. One of the Tunisians was Hussein Mohammed Salih, known to fellow militants as Abu Haraira and to the hostages as Yellow Pants. Unlike many of Hassan's foreign followers, Yellow Pants was not an Afghan-Arab. He had left Tunisia in 1989 and spent three years learning English and French in Mauritania. After stints in Libya and Sudan, he arrived in Yemen in 1996 and took up teaching. Then, apparently, he fell into the company of Abu Hassan and the AAIA, and visited various parts of Yemen with them. The Tunisian's knowledge of English would prove useful to Abu Hassan when it came time to deal with his hostages.

The Yemenis who were attracted to the camps also included religious idealists, antigovernment dissidents, and unemployed young men with time on their hands to seek some fun and adventure. One of them, Abdullah Salah al-Junaidi, was the kidnapper I called Grenade. In his statement to police, he described how he first met Abu Hassan at a house in Aden where he was doing some work for the owner. After meeting Hassan a few more times in Sana'a during 1997, he joined the AAIA at the beginning of 1998, taking the *nom de guerre* of Abu Hadhifa. Grenade explained that the aim of the AAIA was to establish the Sharia because state law was not complying with Islamic law: "The Yemen government had imported democracy from infidel countries and was imposing American and British interests on Yemen," he said. (Interestingly, in his statements to Yemen authorities, Grenade mentioned being present at a meeting between Hassan and a man called Harithi—presumably the same al-Harithi who would be identified as a key al-Qaeda leader and eliminated by an American heat-seeking missile in the war on terror three years later.)

Beyond recruiting and training new members, the primary activities of AAIA and its parent Islamic Jihad organization were sporadic attacks on government or foreign facilities. In June 1998, rocket-propelled grenades were launched in the Jaar directorate of Abyan, striking several targets including a telecommunications center, a political security office, an electric power station, and the home of the Attorney General. During September of the same year, three separate attacks were made on the security headquarters building in Abyan's capital of Zinjibar. The agenda behind these attacks was the destabilization and downfall of the Yemen government in order to pave the way for a true Islamic state and the elimination of all western influence in the country.

By mid-1998, Hassan had formalized the beginnings of his "army," which would come, as prophecy forecast, out of "Aden's Abyan." There was a long way to go, however, from a ragged group of two dozen initial recruits to the twelve thousand-strong army of heroic and shining warriors he thought the Prophet Mohammed expected from him. Abu Hassan likely faced human resource and organization development problems that would challenge any early-stage entrepreneur. Presumably, though, the network of Islamic militants around the world operates with the effectiveness of an international executive-search firm and provided him with access to a new pool of recruits. Where sweeter to find a new generation of holy warriors than in the heart of Britain, the nation responsible for Aden's colonial past?

Hassan sent one of his followers to London on a recruiting mission. By arrangement with his official AAIA spokesman, Abu Hamza, a recruiting seminar was held at the mosque in Finsbury Park on September 5, 1998. It provided the critical event that brought young British Muslims into the sphere of the AAIA. One of the invitees was Shahid Butt. Another was Hamza's stepson Mohsin Ghalain.

In 1995, Butt had become a projects coordinator for the Convoy of Mercy organization, a British-based charity founded by a Pakistani electrician to provide food and clothing to Muslim civilians in war-torn Albania and Bosnia. Reports that Butt fought with mujahaddin in Bosnia have not been confirmed, even though the videotapes from his trial showed him handling weapons there in 1994. The Convoy of Mercy clearly does carry out genuine humanitarian projects, but inevitably some of its volunteers are exposed to hard-line Islamic militants in the course of their work in war zones. The influence of extremists, combined with direct exposure to the suffering of Muslim civilians persecuted for their religion, no doubt prompted some volunteers to embrace more violent solutions in defense of Islam. One British student, convicted of kidnapping three British and one American tourist in India in 1994, claimed he moved on to terrorist activities after working with the Convoy of Mercy in Croatia during 1993.

At some point, Shahid Butt had met Abu Hamza, perhaps after hearing one of the mullah's sermons at a Birmingham mosque. Subsequently, Butt visited Abu Hamza in London and reportedly asked for help to fund work in Kosovo. Abu Hamza responded that Butt should first help the Supporters of Sharia by distributing its literature and promoting its message among Muslims in London and Birmingham. Butt was invited to attend the September 5, 1998 meeting at the Finsbury Park mosque.

The guest speaker was a man introduced simply as Amin, who spoke about the new organization formed by Abu Hassan, the Aden Abyan Islamic Army. Abu Hamza encouraged those present to consider Yemen as the site of their jihad efforts because "Yemen is the place most like Afghanistan" and it would be possible to "accomplish big things there." In particular, Abu Hamza advised Butt that he should go first to Yemen for training before continuing his involvement in Kosovo. Training in Yemen would involve the use of assault weapons, landmines, and artillery, unlike the more limited survival training offered by SOS in Britain.

The Supporters of Sharia routinely advertised military training for Muslim youth through announcements at the mosque and on its Web site. Some of these events were weekend family affairs in London, despite the hand grenades depicted on the promotional literature. Other training events were held in remote areas of Britain and involved more rigorous survival skills and hands-on use of deactivated military weapons. I learned from the Scotland Yard report that these courses were taught by former British army officers located through an organization called the World-Wide Special Forces Association (WWSFA), which advertised its services in military-interest magazines such as *Combat and Survival*.

In July 1998, a man who gave his name as Frank Etam had contacted Alan Ashes, the leader of WWSFA, to arrange a survival training course for ten adults. Once a price was agreed upon, Ashes, who had retired in 1981 from the British army's Pioneer Corps, engaged three ex-army colleagues to assist in running the camp. One of them was Roy Mobsby, who had spent twenty-two years with a parachute regiment before transferring to the Royal Corps of Transportation. Since his retirement from active duty in 1993, he had continued as a sergeant with the territorial army. Mobsby and Ashes, who had been friends for a number of years, were joined by two other instructors, who were also members of WWSFA.

According to Scotland Yard's report, Ashes arranged to meet his students outside the British Legion Club in Colway Bay on the north coast of Wales on September 26, 1998. Only six of the expected ten trainees showed up. Among them was Shahid Butt. His five fellow trainees were later described by their instructors as ranging in age from twenty-five to thirty-five and Asian, except for one who seemed to be from North Africa. During the first few days, the six trainees learned basic outdoor survival skills, first aid, and map-reading techniques on the grounds of the Old Swan Boys Club at Rowen, Merseyside, about six miles from Colway Bay. The second half of the course, which focused on building physical fitness, involved hiking with packs in the rugged Welsh mountains. Some instruction in the use of air pistols and rifles was included. Satisfied with the program, Butt requested a second one-week training course on bodyguard training and close protection skills.

All but one of the original trainees returned for the second camp, which began at Sopley Camp, Dorset, on October 19. The second course concentrated on close-combat skills and handling weapons such as a Mk II

Bren gun, a Sten gun and an AK-47 assault rifle. Training was also provided in the use of hand grenades and antitank weapons but, according to the instructors, only deactivated, nonfiring weapons were used. At the conclusion of the course, trainers acknowledged their pupils' accomplishments with a graduation parade where they issued black berets to the five participants. Frank Etam returned to the camp for the graduation ceremony and asked Ashes and his colleagues to repeat the course in three months' time.

Following these preliminary training sessions in Britain, Shahid Butt made arrangements to travel to Yemen on November 27. He was accompanied by Abu Hamza's son Mohammed Mustafa Kamel, and by Algerian Kamil Sagheer, who traveled with a false French passport under the name "Ali Merksen." (Kamil Sagheer may have been the same man who had participated in the training in Wales as Hassan Sargir or Sargi.) The three men arrived in Aden on November 28 and were met at the airport by Malik Harhara, a twenty-six-year-old with dual British and Yemeni nationality whom Butt had first met in Britain.

Like Butt, Harhara had grown up in Birmingham and had attended meetings of the Supporters of Sharia. He had graduated with a bachelor of science degree in information systems engineering from the University of Westminster, but was unable to find work. He traveled with his mother to visit relatives in Aden and in his mother's home village of Yafa in July 1998. After his mother's return to Britain on August 20, Harhara stayed on with an uncle in the Crater district of Aden before renting his own villa in the Khormaksar district. Two of his schoolfriends from Birmingham, Shazad Nabi and his cousin Ayaz Hussein, flew from Heathrow Airport to Aden on November 13 to join Harhara at his villa. Neighbors noticed that the young men were visited from time to time by their relatives from Britain, including Valerie Fleming, Abu Hamza's exwife. They also noticed that a new 12-foot-high brick wall was constructed around the villa.

Arriving on the same flight as Hussein and Nabi was Abu Hamza's stepson, Mohsin Ghalain. His friends in Birmingham described Ghalain as not in the least religious, a party boy who drank alcohol and dyed his hair red. However, he is believed to have participated in the September 5 SOS meeting at the Finsbury Park mosque.

This was not Ghalain's first trip to Yemen during 1998. A few days after the September mosque meeting, he received a phone call from Harhara in Aden and, with funds of $2,000 provided by Abu Hamza, flew to Yemen. Ghalain was accompanied by an Algerian, Abd al-Rahman Said 'Amr, who was engaged to marry Ghalain's aunt. The Algerian had used multiple aliases since obtaining political asylum in Britain in 1997; he traveled to Yemen as "James Lebourdiec" using a French passport obtained through a Tunisian member of the Supporters of Sharia. Between his arrival in Yemen on September 9 and his return to Britain on November 4, Ghalain, together with al-Rahman, traveled to a home in Habban where he met Abu Hassan. From there, Hassan took both men to his camp for a two-week training session.

On his second visit to Yemen, Ghalain brought not only the usual SOS videotapes and publications but also the satellite phone that was acquired in Britain by his stepfather. Ghalain was instructed to deliver it to Abu Hassan and to train him how to use it. This information was consistent with what Abu Hamza had told me—the satellite phone was needed so Supporters of Sharia could keep in touch with developments in Yemen. Presumably, Yemen's national phone service did not yet extend to isolated terrorist training camps.

By the end of November, six Britons and two Algerians—with connections not only to each other but also to Abu Hamza and the Supporters of Sharia—had arrived in Yemen. Two more British nationals would join the group in the third week of December. Ghulaim Hussein may have met Abu Hamza in Birmingham's Islamic Cultural Center. At some point soon after his flight to Yemen on December 18, he met up with Ghalain and al-Rahman. Hussein claimed he met them by chance and they offered him a place to stay in their hotel room.

The last player to join the British contingent gathering in Yemen was Sarmad Ahmed. Born in Birmingham in 1977, Ahmed studied accounting at Kingston University in Surrey and worked part time as a security guard. Butt and Ahmed were occasionally seen together in Birmingham and Ahmed's involvement with the Supporters of Sharia was well established. According to his friends and family, Ahmed planned to holiday in Yemen and attend a friend's wedding, as well as study Arabic.

At various times during the last months of 1998, at least some of these men met Abu Hassan and spent time at his training camp near Habban. Most of the Britons did not speak Arabic, but several of them already had some experience in the use of weapons and explosives. Hassan's strategy of recruiting followers from Britain through Abu Hamza was yielding fruit.

As he added headcount to his army, he would be increasingly capable of disrupting the Yemen government and gaining publicity for his grievances. More publicity would increase his reputation, encourage more devout young men to join his cause and accelerate the pace with which he could carry out destabilizing actions against the government.

I had now formed a fairly clear picture in my own mind of who the British men were and how they came to be associated with the AAIA. Having met Abu Hamza and encountered a couple of his followers, including the young American who escorted me to the door, I knew that there were men of many nationalities who might be attracted to the prospect of adventure in terrorist training camps. Some of Hassan's recruits, like Butt, were genuinely devout Muslims, intent on carrying out their religious duty of jihad to restore Sharia in Islamic lands. Others, I suspected, were simply looking for some excitement, an alternative to a tedious job as a security guard or a software programmer, or perhaps just an alternative to no job at all. Some, like Ghalain, may have simply been mercenaries, willing to train and conduct terrorist acts for pay. Whatever the individual motives of these young Muslim men, the jihad recruitment process tapped into their passions and fears, attracting them to Hassan's training camp like moths to a flame.

I added this new information to my whiteboard map and leaned back in my chair, staring at the maze of arrows and circles. Some loose ends still dangled, mocking my efforts. The Yemeni sheikh al-Atwi remained mysteriously disconnected from any of the other events. Where did he fit in? And who was Nankly, who had been mentioned in one report? I suspected he was the Spaniard that Abu Hamza had mentioned, but did he have any significance in the kidnapping? Were these two men just red herrings?

Although the Britons were already tried and convicted for a bomb plot, it was not clear what the point of that conspiracy had been. Was it just routine terrorism to register displeasure with the Yemen government, like earlier bombings conducted by the Islamic Jihad? Was there some special reason why British recruits had been selected to carry out these particular attacks? Through my office window, I looked out upon a snow-covered village and the steeple of a church. Yemen and upstate New York—the two worlds could not have been more different. It was becoming increasingly clear that my search for a more complete understanding of the kidnapping and why it had happened would require another journey. I knew in my heart that the story would remain unresolved unless I returned to Yemen.

I did not immediately tell Ray that I was thinking of going back to Yemen. I knew the idea would worry him. His job search was progressing, but several promising leads had failed to materialize. He was still working at Bausch & Lomb with the understanding he would leave the company at the end of 2000. Unlike me, Ray did not want to take time away from his career and hoped to move straight into a new position. These were difficult days for him, as he had to cope with the company's decision to reduce his staff and he was fighting hard to get a fair deal for these employees before he left.

Meanwhile, I was struggling with the decision I had made to give up my own home. I expected to be in Ray's home on the outskirts of Rochester for only a couple of months before we would move. Ray's two daughters both moved back home to live with him for several months as they made their own transitions from college to jobs. Much as I liked Kate and Amy and enjoyed getting to know them, I was wondering if I had made a big mistake giving up the independence and space of my own home. Most of my furniture was in storage and my files and some of my clothes were stored in Ray's basement.

In spite of all the inconveniences, I loved being with Ray and enjoyed our outdoor activities together. Ray had taught me to fly fish over the summer and, in search of fishing spots, exposed me to rural areas around Rochester I had never seen. When the snows returned at Thanksgiving, we continued to take time outdoors every weekend by getting out on our cross-country skis. Ray was religious about maintaining his weight and fitness and would work out several times each week.

He was a good influence on me, as I began to exercise more regularly. Our favorite times were simply having dinner together on Saturday nights, enjoying fine wine, classical music and conversation about every subject imaginable. We had opposite views on many aspects of politics, which spurred some passionate debates. The conservative, Republican, midwestern former Marine wondered how he had ever let a foreign liberal Democrat and feminist into his home—and his heart.

18

CONTROLLING THE CAMPS

After the bombing of the USS *Cole* at Aden in 2000, I set aside any thoughts of returning to Yemen. It was not a matter of being afraid to go back—I already knew just how dangerous the country could be—but a host of American investigators had descended on Aden, working with local authorities to seek out those responsible for this act of terrorism. I knew government and military personnel would be preoccupied, making it difficult for me to gain the attention of anyone familiar with the kidnapping.

Since the USS *Cole* attack had taken place near the anniversary of Abu Hassan's execution and on the home turf of the Aden Abyan Islamic Army, it seemed likely to me that at least some of its members might be implicated in the attack. As I followed news reports about the search for suspects, I discovered the Yemen government was questioning individuals believed to be affiliated with the AAIA, but it was too early in the investigation to establish any definite accountability. In the course of following these news reports, however, I encountered a whole new set of online documents concerning relations between the United States and Yemen. The role of American foreign policy was an aspect to the kidnapping I had not previously explored. Following links related to these documents, I also discovered new reports about events involving Abu Hassan during 1998, reports that at last shed some light on the role of Sheikh al-Atwi. Unexpectedly, it was the USS *Cole* tragedy that opened my eyes to the broader context of the kidnapping. Through this line of investigation, I came to appreciate how

America's military and political dealings with Yemen played a direct role in the events leading up to the ambush of my tour group.

By 1998, Ali Abdullah Salih was firmly established in his second term as president of a reunified Yemen, having garnered 96 percent of the vote in the 1997 elections. Although Salih's overwhelming majority might suggest otherwise, the election process was generally viewed as fair by both national and international observers. Renowned for his pragmatism, President Salih was well positioned to move ahead with his agenda for the country, which encompassed four overriding goals: economic growth; the establishment of democratic institutions and infrastructure; national security; and, of course, the retention of his own political power.

Economic growth would require foreign investment, expanded tourism and the formation of strategic alliances with wealthy western countries, especially the United States. During the Gulf War of 1991, when he had supported Iraq, Salih had learned the cost of aligning himself with enemies of the United States (and also earned the intense displeasure of Saudi Arabia). He was ready to mend those fences and so were the Americans, albeit for different reasons. In spite of its sympathies for Iraq and its political instability during the early years of the 1990s, Yemen was now strategically important to the United States.

High on the American agenda was the establishment of an alternative port for refueling U.S. navy ships in the Persian Gulf. The Americans also wanted access to Yemen's shipping lanes for enforcing UN sanctions against Iraq and they hoped for assistance with tracing the flow of funds and manpower supporting terrorism. Finally, the United States needed a backup ally on the Arabian Peninsula in the event that other relationships in the region deteriorated.

A refueling contract with the port of Djibouti, located just across the Gulf of Aden from Yemen, had expired in 1997. Djibouti's facilities were inadequate and its location on the Horn of Africa made it an even higher risk than Aden. In May 1998, General Anthony Zinni, commander-in-chief of the United States Central Command and responsible for U.S. security interests from the Horn of Africa to Central Asia, made the first of several visits to Yemen. The outcome of warming relations between the two countries was a broad set of agreements.

The United States would conduct joint military training exercises with Yemen's army and assist in operations to clear landmines left from the 1994 civil war. Yemen would allow U.S. navy vessels to use its shipping lanes. The United States would ensure Yemen was able to obtain spare parts for its American-made military hardware, including F5 planes purchased in the 1970s. The United States also engaged in a contract to store fuel and refuel U.S. navy ships. Although Zinni had concerns about security in Aden, the alternative ports in the region, such as those in Djibouti and Saudi Arabia, presented equal or graver threats. In 1998, Aden was the best of some unattractive options in the Persian Gulf.

Security in Yemen was an even greater concern for President Salih and his government than for the United States. A country considered dangerous by foreigners would be unable to attract foreign business investment. Tourism, with its enormous potential to create jobs and bring in foreign capital, would remain limited to budget adventure travelers. And Salih's political future continued to be threatened by the country's extremist elements. A campaign to eliminate sources of political violence and acts of terrorism was a top priority. Pressured by the United States and spurred on by his own political agenda, Salih determined to increase Yemen's national security. Primary targets were the militant Afghan-Arabs and the training camps used by antigovernment fundamentalists.

The rugged Maraqisha mountains provided an almost impregnable site for the most important of the camps: the Huttat camp located 20 miles north of Zinjibar. Many of the instructors were said to be non-Yemenis, presumably recruited from among the Afghan-Arabs and from the network of pan-Islamic fundamentalist organizations. The Huttat camp, operated by the Abyan branch of Yemen's Islamic Jihad, was believed to have some support from Osama bin Laden. Following Tariq al-Fadhli's renunciation of his militant past, a well-known revolutionary from Abyan had taken over the leadership of Islamic Jihad: Sheikh Salih Haidara al-Atwi. Theoretically, al-Atwi was under the tribal control of Sheikh Tariq al-Fadhli, who had recovered his lands and his sultanate title on the understanding he would control subversive anti-government activities in his territory. In return for al-Atwi's cooperation, al-Fadhli appointed him sheikh of the district of al-Hisn, from where he ran the Huttat camp. At this camp al-Atwi first met Abu Hassan, who came to Huttat in search of help for his own ongoing problems with provincial authorities.

As a result of General Zinni's visits to Yemen and the resulting need to demonstrate a higher level of national security, the government made it a priority to eliminate the Huttat camp. In May 1998, the security forces attacked it with heavy artillery and helicopters, but failed to destroy it. Turning to less direct anti-terrorist methods, the government quietly identified and deported non-Yemeni Afghan-Arabs. Arab passport-holders were also denied admission to Yemen unless they arrived on flights directly from their home countries, a policy that made it more difficult for terrorists to avoid arrest in their own countries by seeking safe haven in Yemen.

Following the bombings of the United States embassies in Kenya and Tanzania in August 1998, the Yemen government came under even greater pressure from the Americans to eliminate the Huttat camp, once and for all. Huttat was considered to play a role similar to the Afghanistan training camp that had been bombed by the United States in retaliation for bin Laden's suspected role in the embassy bombings. Since America was building a strategic alliance with Yemen and using its ports, a direct U.S. military attack on the Huttat camp by its forces, as had happened in Afghanistan, was not an option at that time.

Instead of attacking Huttat again, the Yemen government embarked on a strategy of negotiation with the Islamic Jihad. A deal was proposed in which Islamic Jihad members would be integrated into Yemen's armed forces in return for disbanding the camp. The Yemeni newspaper *Al-Umma* reported in November 1998 that Islamic Jihad had issued a list of twenty-eight demands in return for closing down the camp. One of these proved particularly difficult for the government: the demand that all Arab veterans of the war in Afghanistan should receive political asylum in Yemen, including those wanted in their home countries for terrorist crimes. Granting asylum would create serious problems for Yemen's relationships with Arab countries that sought to bring these Afghan-Arabs to trial. An assistant to Osama bin Laden is said to have arrived at Huttat in early December 1998 to try to resolve the dispute about the future of the camp.

When efforts to reach agreement finally broke down, the security forces launched an attack at al-Hisn on December 18, just three days before I arrived in Sana'a for my vacation tour. Hearing of the attack, Abu Hassan drove seven hours from Markha in Shabwah province to the district of al-Hisn in an attempt to help al-Atwi fight off the security forces. When Hassan reached al-Hisn the clash was over. Al-Atwi and several of his followers had been arrested and were in police custody. Even efforts by Tariq al-Fadhli to intervene on al-Atwi's behalf were unsuccessful.

At last my research had shown me who al-Atwi was and how he was connected with Abu Hassan. The leader of the AAIA clearly felt some obligation to try to secure al-Atwi's release, perhaps because al-Atwi had assisted Hassan in his earlier struggles with provincial authorities, or perhaps through friendship or tribal allegiance. The arrests of Yemeni militants and the government's policies of deportation and passport control were making it difficult for Hassan to retain non-Yemenis in his organization and to recruit them from overseas. His rage at Salih's government was compounded by his anger about the military strikes on Iraq by American and British forces.

It was time to take more aggressive action, and Abu Hassan had just the right people available to help him do it. The British men he had recruited with the help of Abu Hamza were in training in Yemen. Hassan would pay them to bomb foreign-owned targets in Aden during the Christians' year-end holidays, a time when the blatant drinking of alcohol in hotels especially angered Islamic fundamentalists. The attacks would damage Salih's efforts to build relationships with the foreign infidels and pressure him to stop arresting and deporting Hassan's colleagues and supporters. Perhaps the bombing would even force the government to release al-Atwi.

On the night of December 23, 1998, Hassan met up with the Britons behind a gas station and transferred the weapons and explosives they would need for their mission into their rented white Daewoo. What he did not anticipate was that the rental car would be stopped by police at a roundabout on the outskirts of Aden.

When word reached Hassan that the bomb plot had failed and that six of his UK recruits had been arrested, he sent Hamza's son and two other Britons into hiding with one of his most trusted men, Abu Muhsin. Hassan loaded his pickup truck with all his available weapons and ammunition and left the town of Habban in Shabwah province. He headed for Mudiyah in Abyan. Along the way, he picked up several of his followers, including Osama al-Masri (Bandit). On the evening of December 27, Hassan called an emergency meeting of the AAIA at the home of his second-in-command and closest friend, Ali al-Khadar al-Haj. The man I would know as Purple Skirt had grown up in the village of Kokab, just a few miles from Mudiyah. When not busy with his responsibilities as AAIA's field commander for Abyan province, al-Haj earned a living as a taxi driver.

According to interrogations of Hassan by the Yemen police, which I obtained from Scotland Yard, the plan to kidnap a group of foreigners was hatched that night in al-Haj's home. The AAIA knew that foreign tour groups used the main road from Habban to Aden on a regular basis and that vehicles carrying foreigners would certainly travel the road the next day. Hassan decided to waste no time. Al-Haj called up his local AAIA supporters. They knew the area well and selected an ambush spot on the road a mile or so past the village of Lahar. One man was assigned as a lookout, with instructions to fire his rifle as soon as a suitable tour group passed through Lahar. Hassan and several of his men would wait at the side of the road in their pickup truck. Others would hide in the bushes at the side of the road, ready to help take control of the tour vehicles as soon as Hassan blocked their path.

While Hassan was laying his plans at a house in Mudiyah, I was watching the moonlit desert spread out far below me from the roof of my hotel on a hillside in Habban. As I watched the ghostly outline of three camels moving across the valley that cool December night, my life had already become a bargaining chip. I and my fellow travelers were Hassan's last desperate chance to force the Yemen government to free Sheikh al-Atwi and the British recruits. For us, the war of terror had already begun.

On the whiteboard in my rented office, I sketched in my new knowledge of all the events leading up to the kidnapping. General Zinni was the significant new name listed on the board. Until the 2000 bombing of the USS *Cole*, I had not recognized the extent to which U.S. foreign policy and military strategy in the Middle East had contributed to the circumstances leading up to the kidnapping. Certainly, Abu Hassan had made clear his anger over the bombing of Iraq by the U.S. and Britain and had included an end to those attacks as one of his demands. That link between United States policy and the kidnapping was obvious even as we were being held hostage. What I had previously overlooked was how the American interest in refueling its ships in Aden induced the Yemen government to destroy militant bases such as the camp at Huttat. Without those events, perhaps Sheikh al-Atwi would not have been arrested; Hassan would not have paid his British recruits to carry out a bombing conspiracy; the Britons would not have been arrested; and Hassan would not have escalated his personal jihad to include the kidnapping of foreign tourists. I would have returned home from a pleasant, exotic but uneventful vacation to life as usual, my career on course in the familiar world of corporate America.

At last I was able to put what I had personally experienced into a broader political and historical context, and to appreciate the unplanned but inevitable sequence of events with which my life had collided. At an intellectual level, I could have stopped there but, emotionally, the story remained incomplete. I knew it was not a question of whether I should return to Yemen but how soon I could go.

During a trip to Washington DC for a CEDPA board meeting in December 2000, I scheduled a few extra days in the capital. I had arranged meetings with Afghan women and the Feminist Majority Foundation as a follow-up to the summer conference in Dushanbe. I also stopped in at the FBI to speak with Brad Deardorff. Brad was interested to hear about my meeting with Abu Hamza, but was limited in what he could tell me. The kidnapping and its perpetrators were still the subject of an open file, he explained, and he could not disclose developments that were part of an ongoing investigation. But he did mention that Margaret Scobey, the deputy ambassador to Yemen who had been so supportive of me after the rescue, was now in Washington and working at the State Department. Brad gave me Margaret's phone number and I was delighted to find she was free to meet with me. I wanted to let her know how much I had appreciated her thoughtfulness in the three days between the kidnapping and my departure from Yemen. During our meeting in her office, I told Margaret that I was thinking of going back to Yemen. She suggested I contact Yemen's ambassador to the United States for assistance.

I had only one day left in Washington and immediately called the office of His Excellency Abdulwahab Abdulla al-Hajjri. Somewhat to my surprise, I was invited to meet with him that very afternoon. He was an outgoing and charming man, a few years younger than I. After expressing his regrets at what had happened to me in Yemen, he offered to contact the office of the prime minister in Yemen and make arrangements for my visit. He recommended that I wait until the end of Ramadan because it would be easier to schedule meetings and make travel arrangements outside the one-month period of fasting. Ambassador al-Hajjri gave me his personal e-mail address so that I could keep in touch with him.

I booked a flight to Sana'a for January 10, 2001, a few days after Eid al-Fitr, the end of Ramadan. Ray was not happy about my plans, but declined my invitation to accompany me. His reason was simple: "They're killing Americans over there."

Knowing he could not dissuade me from making the trip, he did the next best thing he could think of to protect me and called a gun dealer from whom he had purchased hunting rifles and supplies over the years. We visited the gun shop so that the dealer could show me the basic operation of an assault rifle.

An upstate New York gun dealer does not carry any AK-47s, of course, but he demonstrated how to load and fire the most similar weapons available.

"At least the next time you find yourself grabbing an AK-47, you'll have some idea of what to do with it," Ray muttered as we drove back home.

19

INSIDE AL-MANSOOR PRISON

A little over two years had passed since I had first waited to pass through immigration at Sana'a international airport. Standing in that line of arriving passengers, I had had no idea of the events awaiting me on the other side, events that would change my life in so many ways and that now brought me to Yemen again. Ambassador al-Hajjri had assured me by e-mail that someone would meet me and that "everything had been taken care of." I wasn't sure what "everything" meant, so I had booked into the Taj Sheba Hotel, and simply expected someone would be waiting on the other side of immigration with my name written on a placard. Sure enough, a man in a white ankle-length robe and dark sports coat approached me. "Mrs. Quin? Please come with me."

I followed him to the head of the line where he spoke a few words of Arabic to the immigration officer, then whisked me directly out a side door into the baggage area. I could feel the curious looks of other passengers condemned to wait their turn in the slow-moving line. The man turned out to be a driver with a local tour company, which provided travel services to visiting dignitaries and government guests. His name was Mohammed. Somehow that didn't surprise me. Just as my luggage arrived we were joined by another man, who introduced himself simply as Sameer. He was tall and dressed in a western business suit, white shirt and dark tie. His manner reminded me of the security agents who hover around the American president in public places.

Sameer told me that Prime Minister al-Iryani had asked him to make sure I was able to do everything I wanted to do during my visit. I discovered that Sameer, who spoke excellent English, was the private as-sistant to the prime minister. We headed out to the airport parking lot and drove off in Mohammed's Land Cruiser, the vehicle of choice for touring in Yemen. I soon realized we were not heading toward the center of town where the Taj Sheba was located. Instead, I was driven to the peaceful Shahran Hotel on the outskirts of the city and shown to the top-floor presidential suite.

In the course of our conversation, it became clear there was some mis-understanding about the purpose of my trip. Mohammed and Sameer were under the impression I was in Yemen as a tourist, to complete the trip that had been cut short by the kidnapping. I explained that I was not interested in sightseeing. Rather, I had come in the hope of speaking to people who had knowledge of the kidnapping and could help me understand the full story of what had happened. I showed Sameer the list of people I wanted to meet: senior security officers, the governors of Aden and Abyan, the lawyers for the British men and for the kidnappers. "And, if it can possibly be arranged, I would very much like to meet the British men and the kid-nappers who are serving prison terms," I added. My intentions clearly came as quite a surprise to Sameer and Mohammed, who consulted each other at length in Arabic. Sameer then assured me he would see what could be done, and asked me what time I wanted to get started in the morning. We agreed Mohammed would pick me up at 9:00 AM.

I spent nearly a week in Yemen, with Mohammed and his car at my disposal. Sameer was ever present, sometimes seeming a little anxious and possibly, I thought, slightly irritated at being assigned to babysit this American woman. However, he was always courteous and responsive and, as we got to know each other better, seemed to become interested in my investigation. It would have been impossible to accomplish what I did on that trip without Sameer and Mohammed and, behind them, the gener-ous assistance of Prime Minister al-Iryani.

I had an opportunity to meet briefly with the prime minister on the first day. Sameer told me we would be stopping at the Presidential Palace be-cause al-Iryani wished to welcome me back to Yemen. We drove through the heavily guarded main gates and were escorted into the imposing building by several soldiers. The corridors bustled with civil servants and military personnel as we made our way to an empty, elegantly appointed sitting room. Rich velvet curtains, gilt-edged coffee tables and crystal chandeliers gave the room the feeling of a European royal court. I was invited by Sameer to sit in a specific seat, which was just as well because the room was lined with about forty velvet chairs, challenging my limited knowledge of ministerial protocol. "How should I address the prime minister?" I asked Sameer.

"You can just call him Prime Minister," he replied.

If the setting was intimidating, al-Iryani, who arrived about ten minutes later, was not. The diminutive man who strode briskly into the room, accompanied by several staff and a photographer, simply stretched his hand out to me and welcomed me with a broad smile. I liked him instantly. We had a short conversation in which he expressed his deep regrets at the tragedy that had befallen our tour group and his hope that this return visit could, in a small way, make up for it. We talked a little about his own years spent studying in the United States and the fact that his son was now a student in Oregon. In closing, Prime Minister al-Iryani said he would like to see me again at the end of my visit and would be interested to know what I had learned. He was a charming and intelligent man. With such leadership in the country, I felt hopeful for Yemen's future.

I had hoped to speak with David Pearce at the British embassy in Sana'a, but found that he had been transferred to Durban, South Africa, the previous year. Instead, I met with Martin Lamport, a diplomat at the embassy, who was willing to share his knowledge of events leading up to and following the kidnapping.

According to Lamport, the governor of Aden had long been familiar with Abu Hassan's training camp and had infiltrated the AAIA with his own men. The presence of informers within Hassan's organization confirmed my suspicion that it was not by chance the Yemen police had stopped the white Daewoo as it made its way towards Aden with a trunkload of weapons. Security forces had probably been watching the British recruits all along, monitoring their trips back and forth between Aden and the training camp. They watched and waited until the night of December 23, 1998, knowing that three of the Britons were now transporting weapons and explosives in preparation for the bombing conspiracy.

Lamport went on to explain that British embassies did not take a position on the guilt or innocence of British citizens arrested overseas. The role of the embassy was to make staff visits to the arrested Britons and ensure they had adequate treatment and medical care. Five of them were still serving sentences for the bombing conspiracy charges, and there were two issues that sustained political tension between Britain and Yemen. One was that the British government continued to advise against tourism and business investments in Yemen, out of concern for the safety of its citizens. The second issue was the human rights criticism of Yemen expressed in the publicity raised by the prisoners' families and supporters.

According to Lamport, the embassy staff worked behind the scenes with both the prisoners' families and the Yemen government to try to find a diplomatic solution. If the families continued trying to promote their cause in the British press, they might find little public interest or sympathy, even among British Muslims. Recognizing this, the families had an incentive to cooperate with more diplomatic strategies to bring their relatives home. The Yemen government would just as soon put the whole episode in the past and resume normal relations with Britain, but it had public opinion to consider. Releasing foreigners convicted of terrorism would imply either that the Yemeni justice system was mistaken in its original guilty verdicts or that it was giving in to pressure from the British government. The British embassy hoped both the families and the Yemen government would pursue a middle ground—an appeal for clemency. It was traditional in Yemen for the president to grant clemency at certain times of year, such as the end of Ramadan. Granting clemency would not revoke the guilty verdicts, but it would allow the men to return home to their families.

I was intrigued by this insight into diplomatic negotiation and gained a new appreciation for the fine line embassy staff must often walk between supporting their own citizens and maintaining constructive relations with other sovereign states. As our conversation concluded, Lamport suggested that I contact Mustafa Rajamanar, a diplomat at Britain's consulate in Aden. He was the person who maintained primary contact with the

British prisoners and would be a mine of information about the events following the kidnapping.

Back at my hotel, I waited in the lobby to meet Khaled Tarik, an attorney with a local law firm. Originally, he had been contacted by the British embassy to assist with the legal representation of the detained Britons. The man who approached me was dressed casually in a black nylon bomber jacket and blue jeans. He had been educated from high school onwards in Britain, eventually completing his law degree at London University.

After he had interviewed the young British Muslims, Tarik told me, his firm declined to represent them. "The boys were not frank with us. We found they were not truthful so we couldn't defend them." Tarik gave some examples. "We asked the boys about the videotapes. They claimed they were just holiday and family tapes. Later, we found out the tapes showed them in Bosnia, using guns. The boys denied at first it was even they who had run from the [abandoned rental] car. Then later, they said, 'Yes, it was us but we didn't have any weapons.' They were kept separated in the prison so they couldn't coordinate their stories."

I asked Tarik whether he thought the men were given a fair trial.

"The judge was very fair. He gave [the defendants] the benefit of the doubt where possible. The verdicts and sentences were consistent with other trials. The prosecution's case was comfortable." But Tarik agreed there had been mismanagement of evidence.

"In cases of national security, issues are handled differently. It isn't the same process of trial." Tarik pointed out this was also true in Britain. He described a case in 1991 when a number of Arabs were rounded up and put in Chester prison without formal charges, claiming it was a matter of national security.

"I think when the boys were picked up, [the Yemen police] weren't anticipating a trial. That affected the handling of what later became evidence. They saw themselves as preempting a national security threat. Only the publicity led to the trial. The government panicked because they didn't know if there was a much bigger organization involved. Were the Britons alone? How many more were there? They didn't know what the targets might be, whether there were later shipments [of weapons] coming." Tarik said he felt that in terrorism situations, there should be some room for "quick action" powers. "The far-reaching consequences of a terrorism event justifies it." His words foretold the much-debated Patriot Act in post-9/11 America.

Tarik also had an opinion about what motivated the Britons. "It's plausible they were just mules. They were not the types to carry out a bombing—they lacked experience. A sense of belonging to a 'gang' motivates them, not religious zeal. The gang is their tribe." Then he added sadly, "It is hard even for Muslims to know what motivates people who commit terrorism." Although Tarik's involvement had been primarily with the British men, I was curious to know what he could tell me about the kidnappers. In particular, I was interested in what he made of the private execution of Abu Hassan.

"A public execution would have led to bloodshed and riots," Tarik replied. "It had to be private. In Yemen, some executions are public, some private. It depends on security versus the need to set an example."

After two days in Sana'a, Sameer arranged for me to travel to Aden. On the morning of January 14, we left the Shahran Hotel in Mohammed's Land Cruiser, Sameer in the back seat and me in the front passenger seat. At each security checkpoint, Mohammed handed over a photocopy of a letter giving us permission to be traveling. Security forces would call ahead to the next checkpoint to make sure the route was safe and to find out if a police escort were needed. I quickly realized that Yemen authorities were going to make absolutely certain nothing happened to me on this trip. At one small town, I commented to Mohammed about a police car parked at the side of the road. "Is he watching for cars speeding?" I asked, with my western interpretation of the world.

"No," Mohammed laughed. "There is no speed limit in Yemen. That car has been posted there to check our vehicle has passed through this area OK."

In spite of the security concerns, I greatly enjoyed the day's journey. It was a day in which I could resume being a tourist in Yemen, seeing a route from Sana'a to Aden that I had not traveled through on my original visit. We shared the road with brightly painted trucks and tractors. Ploughed fields, dotted with flat-roofed mud houses, filled the valleys between eroded, treeless mountain ranges. Women walked along the roadside in colorful dresses and scarves, some with faces hidden behind black veils. In the fields, they worked under the shade of wide-brimmed straw hats while children guarded flocks of sheep and goats. We stopped for tea and bread in the town of Yarim, then continued up into the mountains. Sameer pointed out the prime minister's tiny home village, lost in the shadows on the far side of a broad valley. At Jibla, we stopped at the centuries-old mosque and palace built by the famed Queen Arwa. The palace was now in ruins, but was said to have contained 365 rooms, one for each day of the year. As we left Jibla, I noticed a pickup truck mounted with a machine gun parked outside a neat, single-story compound.

"That is the American Baptist hospital," Sameer explained. "The machine gun is for their security." The security would prove sadly inadequate two years later, when four Americans working at the hospital were gunned down by a Yemeni militant. Only one survived. No one had checked whether a man entering the hospital with a blanket-wrapped bundle really was carrying a baby.

In Aden, I declined to stay at the Golden Moghur Hotel. This four-star hotel overlooking the Gulf of Aden was used by American military and government visitors, including the FBI, and had already been the scene of one bomb attack. I decided the much shabbier, but atmospheric, Crescent Hotel in town would be a lower-profile place to stay. Sameer arranged for me to meet two key government figures who were involved in the decision to rescue us. The office of Nasser Mansour Hadi, permanent secretary for political security in the provinces of Aden, Abyan, and neighboring Lahij, was in a military-style government building opposite the hotel. I took a seat across a low coffee table from Hadi, noting his obviously dyed black hair, graying moustache and ostentatious gold watch. He wore green army fatigues and his fingers worked over a string of prayer beads as he spoke. Hadi told me that he had personally gone to the town of Mudiyah, along with the governor of Abyan, immediately after they received word of the ambush.

"If the government did not act," Hadi assured me, "all of you would have been killed . . . Someone representing the governor of Abyan went to see Hassan. Hassan told him, 'We don't want anything. We will kill these people.' " Hadi's account was superficial and hardly credible. He told me that he personally had given the orders to attack. "Hassan's people were on a hilltop, pointing guns down to shoot us. The security forces were afraid he would kill us." Then, as if to justify his version, Hadi added, "Hassan said in court that he killed tourists before the security forces attacked, that he wanted to kill more." I asked Nasser Mansour Hadi if he had any knowledge of Abu Hassan before the kidnapping took place. "No," he replied. "I never heard of Abu Hassan before the kidnapping. I would have caught Hassan earlier if I knew."

The government liked to play down the existence of militant groups but, given Abu Hassan's bomb attacks throughout 1998, it was not credible that the most senior official responsible for security in Abyan and Aden had not heard of him and of the AAIA. I concluded there was little prospect of learning the truth from this man. Before leaving, I asked him if it would be possible for me to meet the imprisoned kidnappers. I would need to get permission from the governor of Aden, he replied. Sameer, who sat in on the meeting, promised he would make inquiries on my behalf.

Through placing my own phone calls from the hotel, I managed to reach the office of Badr Basunaid, the lawyer who had represented the Britons. Basunaid agreed to come to my hotel, and on January 15 we talked together in the lobby. I had no intention of holding any meetings in secrecy, even if that had been possible. Sameer was aware of everyone I arranged to speak with, although he did not insist on being present. Only when I visited senior government officials through meetings he had arranged did Sameer accompany me.

Badr Basunaid was a serious man with gray, curly hair who seemed weighed down by the many legal battles he had fought. A Yemeni journalist told me later that he was a good man with a passion for the law and for fair trials, no matter what. Basunaid headed up a Yemeni human rights organization and wrote excellent rebuttals in court, calling on his knowledge of Yemeni law, international law, and the Koran. His deep sense of the injustice suffered by southerners at the hands of President Salih's northern regime quickly came through in his comments to me. "Yemen is not a state in the usual meaning of a state. Southerners are slaves to the north; they lost their land and jobs to northerners . . . I have two sons, a geologist and a lawyer. There are no jobs for them in the south."

"Socialists took my father's land," Basunaid told me, "but the president's regime is worse. Unity was done quickly and southerners' rights [lost under the socialists] were not restored. Aden people were better off under Britain. Salih wants to discredit Britain in local eyes to bolster his presence in the south." I recognized that Basunaid's political views, as well as his commitment to a fair and just legal system in Yemen, would have predisposed him to offer legal representation to the British men. He confirmed he had been the defense attorney for all of them.

Like any good defense attorney, Basunaid never conceded to me the possible guilt of his clients. He stressed the gross violations of due process during the trial, and offered explanations for why the Yemen government would seek to make scapegoats of the arrested Britons.

"They were tortured severely—hit, hung by their legs and hands on a stick . . . Mustafa [Kamel] was raped in Sana'a before being brought to Aden. Mohsin Ghalain was also raped." I already knew that the particularly harsh treatment of the two youngest Britons was because they were the son and stepson of Abu Hamza, who was on Yemen's version of a "ten most wanted" list. According to Basunaid, the government had tracked young Kamel because of the statements his father had made encouraging jihad against the regime in Yemen.

"Ayaz Hussein was asked to sign a confession under threat of being hit by four soldiers if he did not sign the Arabic document. Hussein took the pen and wrote the word "false" on it, not his own name. The judge did not even see what had been written.

"There was no evidence against these boys," Basunaid insisted. "The police took their car to Khormaksar police department and next day said they found explosives. They didn't open the car until the next morning." Basunaid's contempt was palpable. "The boys were not at a training camp but stayed at the home of a sheikh in Shabwah. This sheikh was never called to testify." I probed further as to why the government should go to such trouble to trump up charges against half-a-dozen British visitors if they were innocent. Basunaid explained that it was not unusual in Yemen for a man to be falsely accused of terrorist actions by someone else, either to take revenge or to take control of his assets. He described a case in which a Yemeni, who had declined some kind of business partnership, was later accused of participating in terrorist training courses with a man called Nankly. Fortunately, in this case, Basunaid concluded, the accused was found innocent and returned to Indonesia, where he had a home. The example did not sound particularly compelling to me as an analogy for the charges against the Britons, but I was intrigued to hear the name of the mysterious Nankly surface again.

The two lawyers I met in Yemen presented dramatically different views of the Britons and their guilt. I began to wonder if I would ever be able to resolve the maze of opinions, and separate fact from political positioning. Before Basunaid left, I asked him whether he thought Hassan might still be alive. He replied simply that he did not know.

Another source who did have a strong view on the fate of Abu Hassan was a journalist, Bashraheel H. Bashraheel, whose father, Hisham, was editor of the *Al-Ayyam* newspaper in Aden. Authorities had arrested the senior Bashraheel on more than one occasion for publishing views unacceptable to the Yemen government. Most recently, the government had detained and questioned him after he published a phone interview with Abu Hamza. His health was now failing, and Hisham's brother and son carried on most of the *Al-Ayyam*'s day-to-day operations. I first met with his son at the newspaper office, and we continued our conversation over dinner that evening at a restaurant in town. Bashraheel chose a quiet table upstairs where the only other patrons were a family group on the far side of the restaurant from us. Normally, only men sit at tables on the street level of restaurants. Tables are often available for women or family groups on an upper floor, where women feel comfortable removing their veils so they can eat.

Like Abu Hamza, Bashraheel strongly suspected Abu Hassan had not been executed. "Yemen executions are usually public, especially in high-profile cases," he told me. "Even if the execution is not public, the body is handed over to the family."

"Why would the government claim an execution had taken place?" I asked, more curious than ever about this theory.

"The execution would have ignited another civil war, which would break Yemen into three parts: the north; the Shabwah/Hadramawt region of the south; and the rest of the south, including Aden. The tribal leaders know Hassan is still alive and have been bribed to persuade their followers not to rebel." I believed Bashraheel was sincere in his theory and, certainly, he was vastly better informed about Yemen politics and history than I would ever be. However, I remembered Abu Hamza saying Hassan must still be in prison somewhere or he would have made contact. Could Hassan really keep his mouth shut and lie low if he were free? I doubted it: not the Abu Hassan I had met on the road to Aden; not the Abu Hassan who boasted of his prowess as the leader of the AAIA in the Zinjibar courtroom; certainly not the Abu Hassan who believed he was divinely appointed to lead thousands of men out of Aden's Abyan. Only maximum security imprisonment or death would keep such a man quiet.

Bashraheel also shed light on the role of Nankly, a Syrian with a Spanish passport who was among the foreign militants rounded up by police during 1997. After his arrest, Nankly had turned informant. In return for supplying the government with information about insurgent groups, he was particularly well cared for in prison. During his trial in late 1997, however, he began disclosing information in court that the government preferred not to make public. The trial was immediately closed to the press. When public attention was diverted to the kidnapping and the Britons' trial, the government quietly released Nankly to Spain, where his wife and children had already been deported. Bashraheel did not know of any significant link between Nankly and Abu Hassan.

This new information helped me discover further details about Nankly in later online research. His full name was Nabil Nanakli Qasebati, and he was considered the ringleader of a group that had carried out a number of bombings in Aden. Nankly was arrested following a shooting incident at a hotel in Sana'a. Along with twenty-six associates, he was put on trial in Aden, the trial commencing in November 1997. According to his reported testimony, Nankly claimed in court that he had been paid $150,000 by Saudi intelligence to kill Prime Minister al-Iryani, who was then Yemen's foreign minister. Nankly testified that he had been trained by the Saudis in

Jeddah, Saudi Arabia, and worked for them in Spain, where he was paid to spy on Algerian Islamic militants. The Saudis, of course, denied Nankly's story and he was sentenced to death in October 1998. Considering the dispute between Saudi Arabia and Yemen over their shared border, there is some basis for Saudi ill will towards its southern neighbor. It seems plausible that Yemen preferred not to stir up trouble with the Saudis and, as Bashraheel had suggested, Yemen was happy to deport Nankly to Spain once attention was focused on the British men. Intriguing though this story was, I concluded that Nankly was not a significant factor in the kidnapping story, even though Hassan may have included Nankly's freedom in his demands. Determining what factors to discard in my investigation was as challenging as uncovering the real issues.

The fate of Abu Hassan was still uncertain in my mind but, by the end of my dinner with Bashraheel, the convictions of the British prisoners' seemed overwhelmingly justified. This journalist, who like Basunaid had no reason to love the Yemen government, nonetheless was convinced the men had not been set up. Bashraheel told me that he had been in a position to see the files on a laptop found in the Britons' hotel room. The files unequivocally identified the intended bombing targets and the roles each of the men was to play. Shahid Butt, Bashraheel recalled, was assigned to bomb the Anglican church along with one other man. If they could not get inside the premises, they were to attach the bomb to the wall of an adjacent clinic. Sarmad Ahmed and Mohsin Ghalain were to bomb the British consulate. The other men were responsible for driving the car or remaining back at the Al Wafa and Rock hotels. Photos of the targets were found by police in their Rock Hotel room, along with a grenade hidden behind a curtain.

"Our newspaper *Al-Ayyam* was not permitted to publish any stories about the Britons' trial, but we did supply information for stories published in *The Times* and by the BBC. That way, we could quote those newspapers without directly reporting the stories ourselves," Bashraheel told me.

While Yemen is striving for democracy, it continues to control the news media and intimidate journalists with arrests and prison sentences. It made me appreciate all the more the rights to free speech and freedom of the press enjoyed in the United States, New Zealand, and many other democracies. Yemen still has a long way to go.

Sameer was as good as his word, and gained an introduction for me to the governor of Aden. I had a brief midday conversation with the governor, whose dress and office would not have distinguished him from any American businessman. In the course of our short dialogue, I requested his permission to meet the British prisoners and the kidnappers who had been captured. He could do nothing with respect to the kidnappers, he told me, because they were not held in Aden. They were under the jurisdiction of Abyan. He then spoke briefly to Sameer in Arabic and turned back to his work. Sameer indicated we should leave.

"Quickly, we can go. We have to go now." Sameer spoke urgently, as he hurried me along the corridor from the governor's office.

"Go where?" I asked, confused.

"To the prison. The governor has given permission, but we have to go there at once."

As we raced through Aden's streets, my mind was also racing. I suddenly realized I had not really expected to get access to the prison or its inmates. Virtually no one, according to Bashraheel and British embassy staff, had been allowed to see them. Even some relatives arriving from Britain were denied visiting rights. Twenty minutes later, we suddenly stopped in the middle of a typical commercial street congested with cars and donkey-drawn carts. Small one-room businesses, repairing tires or selling auto parts, lined the left side of the street. On the right was a brick wall with a large metal gate. Only the curl of barbed wire across the top of the wall clued me in that this was al-Mansoor prison. The gate opened to admit Mohammed's Land Cruiser and I found myself inside a large courtyard. Two watchtowers were now visible at each end of the building. After some formalities with a uniformed guard who was seated in an entryway, Sameer, Mohammed and I were taken through some dimly lit corridors and up an open metal stairway to a room lined with well-worn chairs. A cheap office desk was positioned at the far end of the room and a yellowing map of Yemen was pinned against the opposite wall. Several officials came in, including one who was introduced to me as the superintendent of the prison.

We were exchanging the usual pleasantries, which felt anything but usual or pleasant under the circumstances, when there was a bustle at the door. Guards escorted five men into the room. I recognized them at once from the photos I had seen in British newspaper articles. They were definitely not "boys." They stood inside the doorway, obviously confused. No one seemed about to make introductions so I stood up and walked over to them, extending my hand to Shahid Butt. He was a big man with a thick bushy black beard and a knitted hat pulled down over his shoulder-length hair. A wart marked the outer edge of his right eyebrow.

"I don't shake hands with women," Butt dismissed me, as he took one of the empty seats along the wall. Mohammed Kamel followed Butt's lead, also declining to shake hands. His resemblance to his father was striking; yet, with teenage acne, a shaven head, baggy basketball shorts and T-shirt, he could have passed for any streetwise kid in New York. The other three prisoners were apparently less strict in their interpretations of Islam, and I shook hands with each of them. They took seats along the wall opposite me, except for Malik Harhara who came and sat in a seat to my right. He had a delicate, sweet face, framed by hair that fell in ringlets. Sarmad Ahmed had the look of an academic, an intelligent face behind his full beard and glasses. Farthest from me, seated just inside the door, was Mohsin Ghalain, feigning a look of bored disinterest as he leaned back in his chair and stretched out his legs. All but Kamel wore Yemen-style futas with white T-shirts. The five men stared at me, obviously puzzled about who I was and why I had been allowed in to see them.

I told the five prisoners that I was one of the tourists taken hostage by Abu Hassan. Butt abruptly stood up and walked toward the door. "We have nothing to say to you," he told me. "We did not know Hassan. We were framed. We are innocent." Kamel quickly followed Butt, as if afraid to do otherwise. The other three men stood and looked uncertainly at each other.

"Of course you do not have to talk to me," I said. "I just thought you might be able to help me understand more about the events that happened before and after the kidnapping."

"We are pawns in a political agenda between the Yemen and British governments," Butt's eyes flashed angrily. The guards in the corridor outside had opened the door to check on what was happening.

Sameer looked distraught. "You should not have mentioned Hassan," he whispered to me. "Now they will not talk to you."

"Don't worry, Sameer," I reassured him. "They will talk to me." I was counting on the fact that these men received few visitors. The sheer novelty of my visit would entice them into some kind of dialogue. I doubted they would just leave.

"I met your father in London, Mohammed. I told him I would try to visit you." Kamel looked over at me, and I knew only his need for Butt's approval held him back from speaking to me. Malik Harhara suggested that they discuss the matter among themselves. I waited while they huddled together in whispered conversation at the far end of the room.

After a few minutes, Butt turned to me. "We will talk to you about Islam," he said, "but we will not discuss anything about Hassan. We don't know anything about him." I agreed to that and said they could talk about any topics they wished. In the company of government officials, I never expected them to give me any information beyond the claims they had made during their trial. I was more interested in understanding what kind of people these British Muslims were and trying to determine whether the views I had formed about their guilt were reinforced, or undermined, by meeting them in person.

No sooner had the five men sat down again than Butt launched on to his soapbox promoting the cause of Islam. His view was that all the world should be one Islamic state. Only then, Butt extolled, would peace, happiness, contentment—all the things that Allah willed for us—be possible. I asked if he really expected the entire world to become Islamic, and pointed out that even Abu Hamza had told me his focus was on restoring Islam in traditionally Muslim countries.

"Yes, we should start in our own backyards, with our own families, our own countries," Butt conceded. They were curious about my meeting with Abu Hamza. I told them how surprised I was to see young children playing on the floor around Hamza's feet. For the first time, Ahmed and Butt cracked a smile and started to relax a little.

"Those children are really secret miniature fighters, like transformer toys. Don't underestimate them," Butt cautioned. We all laughed. In spite of his obsessive ideology and intimidating physical presence, Butt had sparkling eyes, an engaging smile, and a sense of humor. I could see how some would find him charismatic. Sarmad Ahmed and Malik Harhara began to ask me questions about where I was from and where I worked. When I explained I was a business executive in an American corporation, Butt leaned back with a knowing air. "So, that is why you know how to communicate, to read our body language." I nodded. "It helps."

"What do you think of Islam?" Ahmed asked me.

"I think there are many positive values and messages in Islam, as there are in most religions."

"Does it interest you to become a Muslim?" Butt fired the question directly at me.

"I could never accept your version of Islam," I fired back. "It is too limiting on choices for women. I value my freedom and independence too much."

I expected another sermon from Butt, but he simply nodded. "At least you are honest." Periodically, I would try to slip in an indirect question about Hassan or the AAIA, but they were not easily led into making an unguarded remark. They joked with me about my attempts to get them to talk. Their initial hostility had faded, but they remained cautious. In the course of the dialogue, Kamel had casually moved from his chair on the opposite wall and sat in the empty chair beside me, on my left. I tried to direct some questions to him, but sensed he was very much dominated by Butt and nervous of expressing his own views. Intuitively I felt this teenager, in spite of his involvement in terrorist training camps, desperately needed his mother. Perhaps he moved across the room to sit next to me because I represented the reassurance of a mother figure.

Looking over to the silent and aloof Mohsin Ghalain and back to Kamel, I asked, "Tell me, what do you call your father, Abu Hamza? Do you call him Dad?" They were both surprised and amused by the question. "Of course we call him Dad," Ghalain replied. "What did you think we would call him?"

I happened to have with me the first page of the story entitled "Terrorists or Tourists?" published in the *Guardian* newspaper. It had portrait photos of each of the Britons. They were visibly excited to see it. Apparently, they had seen very little, if any, of the publicity in the British press about their trial. They passed the photocopied page from one to another, joking about the title and their photos. They asked if they could keep it. I knew I could obtain another copy and agreed to leave it with them.

"What do you think of us, now you have met us?" Ahmed asked me.

I replied with honesty, "I did not expect to find you as likeable as you are." In fact, it disturbed me that I did not instinctively dislike these men, as I had the Taliban prisoners.

"Do you think we are guilty?"

"I am still trying to understand what really happened. I haven't fully made up my mind yet." Out of the blue, Ghalain initiated his only question, his only sign of interest in the conversation.

"When you went to see our father, what did he say about us?" My answer was deliberate and truthful. It was also intentionally cruel. "He said he didn't know that you were coming to Yemen. That you are green and inexperienced. If you had asked his advice, you wouldn't have screwed up so badly."

Ghalain tried to hide it, but his face showed his disappointment. I guessed that impressing their father was a big part of what motivated the two youngest prisoners. His criticism would hurt them.

I had no illusions about these "boys." Whether for money or for religious zeal or to impress a militant father, they had chosen to associate with the AAIA, to participate in terrorist training and, I believe, had intended to carry out bombing attacks against ordinary civilians. Their actions had resulted in the deaths of Margaret Whitehouse, Ruth Williamson, Andrew Thirsk and Peter Rowe. If I was civil to them, it was purely to be able to draw them into conversation, to get them to open up a little, so I could assess for myself what kind of men they were.

Butt asked me how we had been treated as hostages by Hassan and the AAIA. I said that, until the rescue started, none of us had been harmed.

"You were better treated by the kidnappers than we were in jail," Butt responded.

How can he say that? I thought. All of you are alive but four of us are dead.

At no time during the hour I spent with these five convicted terrorists did any of them express any regret over the deaths of four innocent tourists and the injuries of two more. I did not want to even mention my murdered fellow travelers to them. It felt as though the memories of the dead hostages would be dishonored by speaking of them in this despicable company. Under my humor and casual bantering with these terrorists was a deep anger towards all that they stood for, the crimes they were willing to commit, regardless of who suffered.

It was clear that the superintendent was getting ready to end my session with his prisoners. I asked them what they intended to do when they were eventually released. Once again Butt spoke for them all. "We will fight to prove our innocence. We will say nothing publicly about what has happened to us here until every one of us is freed. Then, there will be fireworks."

It was a relief to return to the fresh air and blue skies outside the prison. Only when I was on my way back to the hotel did I realize how emotionally stressful it had been to actually meet these men whose names and faces were so much a part of the story I was trying to unravel. These British men were contradictions in themselves. Intelligent, well-educated, amusing, on the one hand. Willing to kill for their cause, or for cash, on the other. Nothing they had told me, nothing I had seen in them, changed my conclusions that they were guilty as charged and belonged right where they were—in Aden's al-Mansoor prison.

I didn't have much time to dwell on my reactions to the British prisoners, however. There remained an even more important goal to accomplish during my time in Yemen and, according to Sameer, it had been arranged for the following day. Two years after the kidnapping, I would now return to the remote desert in Abyan where it had all happened.

20

RETURN TO ABYAN

On the morning of January 16, Mohammed, Sameer, and I stopped at the British consulate to pick up the vice-consul, Mustafa Rajamanar. I had had an initial meeting with Mustafa soon after reaching Aden and found him not only enormously helpful but also a fascinating character in his own right. His family had lived in Aden for several generations since emigrating from India. Mustafa, who is rotund and cheerful, knew everything and everyone in Aden. Located in a residence on a quiet suburban street, the consulate was protected by ten-feet-high, whitewashed walls and an armed guard at the entrance gate. A life-sized brass statue of Queen Victoria dominated the courtyard garden. Mustafa has an endless knowledge of Aden history. He explained that the statue had been thrown into the Aden harbor when the socialists took over the city from its colonial rulers and then recovered and refurbished following the reunification of north and south Yemen. I couldn't help but notice, in a photo taken of Mustafa and me beside the statue, that the vice-consul and the queen shared the same portly physique.

In my introductory meeting with Mustafa, I had told him of my hopes to return to the scene of the kidnapping and to lay a wreath there for the four tourists who had died. Wreaths of fresh flowers, as we know them in the West, are not part of Arabic tradition and Sameer had been unable to help me obtain such a thing. Mustafa, however, had the idea of ordering a wreath of red paper poppies arranged on a circular wooden frame, similar to those the consulate used for military memorial events. I had agreed that would be a fitting substitute and Mustafa obtained two wreaths, one for me and one as a tribute from the British embassy.

We set off from Aden on the flat, straight road that heads east towards Abyan along Yemen's southern shore. The froth of breakers, rolling in from the Gulf of Aden, caught the morning light. The water provided a cool, clean contrast to the gritty desert terrain. After about an hour, we stopped at an isolated military complex. Here, Sameer explained, I would have a chance to meet the governor of Abyan, Ahmed Ali Mohsen, and we would pick up our armed escort for the journey. I was shown into a large, crowded room. It appeared to serve as both an office and a conference room. Military staff and civil servants talked in small groups, while others hurried in and out of the room with documents and briefcases. Administering Abyan required quite a bureaucracy, it seemed. Sameer motioned to me to take a seat at one corner of a large coffee table surrounded with chairs.

The governor moved away from his desk and came over to join us. He was a tall man in his mid-fifties with graying hair. He wore a blue business suit, a light blue shirt and red tie. With a ready smile, he welcomed me back to Abyan. "You probably don't remember me, but I remember speaking to you right after the rescue. I was wearing my military uniform," he said.

With a dozen onlookers listening in with interest to our conversation, the governor began to answer my many questions. At last, I had found someone who seemed willing and able to tell me what had happened during the twenty-four hours of our captivity. Based on Governor Mohsen's input, and additional details from other sources, I reconstructed what had gone on between the time of the ambush and the attempt to rescue us.

Word that sixteen tourists had been kidnapped near Mudiyah reached the governor of Abyan at his office. Ahmed Ali Mohsen immediately sent a security force to the area to find out who was involved and where the hostages had been taken. Discussions with traders who had seen the ambush, and with leaders of the local al-Fadhli tribe, revealed that some of the kidnappers were local men. One was known to be local taxi driver Ali al-Khadar al-Haj (Purple Skirt). Several others who had taken part in the ambush were also from the al-Fadhli tribe. More troubling was news that men from outside the area, and even foreigners, were involved. This was not a typical Yemen kidnapping concerning a local tribal grievance.

Governor Mohsen determined that he needed to intervene personally, and he traveled to Mudiyah to oversee the operation. Also involved were Colonel Nasser Mansour Hadi, the political security secretary for the governorates of Aden, Abyan, and Lahij whom I had met earlier in Sana'a, and General Mohammed Salih Turaik, Aden's chief of security. The location of the hostages was no secret. The route the captured convoy had taken across the desert had been observed by local villagers and nomads grazing their goats.

An elderly tribal leader, Haythemi Aishal, volunteered to try to talk to the kidnappers and find out what they wanted. During the afternoon and evening of Monday, December 28, Aishal, accompanied by two younger men, made round-trips to the grove of trees on the al-Ghanfa plateau where the tour drivers' vehicles were parked. Each round-trip took two hours or more, and at no time was Aishal allowed to see or talk to the hostages. Based on his reports back to authorities in Mudiyah, the governor and the security heads slowly developed a picture of what was happening. They learned the kidnapping was instigated by Abu Hassan and his group of extremist followers, calling themselves the Aden Abyan Islamic Army. Some of the al-Fadhli tribesmen involved were committed members of AAIA, but others seemed to be little more than boys caught up in the excitement of the ambush. With no shelter and limited means of managing such a large number of hostages, the AAIA seemed ill prepared to sustain prolonged negotiations, yet Hassan's list of demands became longer and more irrational as the day progressed.

According to the governor, the top priority for Hassan was the release of the six British nationals who had been arrested a few days earlier in Aden. The release of Sheikh al-Atwi was also mentioned, as well as that of an imprisoned Spanish national known as Nankly. These demands for an exchange of prisoners were conceivably within the bounds of negotiation for the Aden and Abyan authorities. However, some other demands were simply impossible to address. Hassan insisted upon an end to the bombing of Iraq by American and British forces and an end to UN sanctions against Iraq. Escalating his demands even further, Hassan said that release of the hostages was contingent on a complete change in the governments of Abyan and Yemen as a whole.

As the night dragged on, and Hassan's demands escalated, little progress was made. Hassan's only concession was that he agreed to release the nine female hostages the next day, but retain the seven men. Governor Mohsen realized there might be no way to resolve the situation through negotiation. He called in Lieutenant Colonel Mohammed Salah Ali, deputy chief of police for Abyan province, to prepare for the possibility of an armed rescue. The governor anticipated that the next day Hassan might attempt to take the hostages into the more remote regions of the mountains. He wanted security forces to encircle the kidnappers' campsite and prevent that possibility.

At dawn, Lieutenant Colonel Ali began to move over two hundred troops in the direction of the kidnappers' camp. The tribal elder Aishal made yet another journey into the camp, bringing packets of cookies and small boxes of orange juice for the hostages. It was the breakfast meal we hostages had shared among ourselves that morning—the simple, last meal of their lives for Ruth and Margaret, Peter and Andrew. Hassan refused to negotiate any more, telling Aishal that he was not interested in talking further with low-level local authorities. He claimed he had been in touch by phone with far higher levels of government and was awaiting their response back at midday.

"If you come back here again, you will be killed," he told the kindly and bewildered Aishal. Hassan sent one last chilling message back to the governor of Abyan: "If our demands are not met, we will begin killing the hostages. I will send you, every two hours, the head of one of the hostages." The governor believed that if any of the tourists were to be saved, he had no choice but to send his troops in.

As troops approached the defense post on the hill where Hassan had based himself and several of his men, the security forces encountered some initial gunfire. These were probably the opening shots fired by Osama al-Masri (Bandit)—the first distant gunfire we hostages heard from our seclusion in the wadi. One of the tour drivers came toward them in his Land Cruiser, horn blasting and headlights flashing. Mad Mohammed told the soldiers that four hostages were about to be killed. He had observed several hostages being taken to the defense post and assumed Hassan intended to kill them.

My meeting with the governor of Abyan had greatly added to my understanding of why the rescue attempt was launched. I knew our meeting would not last much longer and probed for further background, asking the governor about Sheikh al-Atwi.

"Yes, al-Atwi was captured in a battle after he resisted a warrant issued for his arrest. That happened two weeks before the kidnapping incident. The battle was at al-Hisn, a small town in the protectorate of Ja'ar." "For Hassan, al-Atwi was a lower priority," the governor added. "The British prisoners were the top priority. We know that Abu Hassan took the British men in his own car to Shabwah for training on how to use explosives. Hassan was briefing Abu Hamza in London every two hours before the kidnapping. It was a well-cooked plan. If Hassan had only wanted to release the prisoners it would have been a simple matter, but his main demand was a complete change of state in Yemen. He began demanding many things that could not be delivered."

Sensing I had only a few minutes left with the governor, I thanked him for making time to see me and facilitating my return to the rescue site. I also told him that I knew I owed my life to one particular soldier, the one who had shot Ali al-Khadar al-Haj (Purple Skirt).

"I have one last request, Governor. Would it be possible for me to meet the kidnappers who are imprisoned? I understand they are being held in Abyan."

"I regret I am unable to help you with that," the governor replied. "The kidnappers are in a prison in Sana'a. You will have to get permission there."

The governor stood up. Our meeting was over, but he had answered several of my unresolved questions. I could now see how the rescue had become inevitable. I understood now the confusing and unusual circumstances the Yemeni authorities were facing. The situation did not lend itself to resolution in the same way as the usual tribal kidnappings. The flow of information was slow and subject to misinterpretation. Previously, I had imagined that Abu Hassan was negotiating on his satellite phone with authorities in Aden or even in Sana'a, but that was not the case. He had no direct phone link to the governor.

While concern for the hostages' lives was a key factor in the rush to rescue us, I still suspect that the elimination of Hassan and his AAIA followers was an important objective for at least some of those involved in the rescue decision. A military strike against the leaders and key members of the AAIA would have been an important step towards President Salih's (and America's) goal of dismantling the militants' camps. Reinforcing my view was a comment made by the deputy foreign minister, Abdullah al-Saidi, who was quoted in mid-February 1999 as saying, "We are not tolerating these groups. What happened in Abyan was a reaction to a crackdown on these people."

With my new knowledge about the rescue, I was all the more anxious to return to the scene of our captivity and see the place again. How would I react to it now with the perspective of time and the benefit of all that I had now learned? I would only find out by going there and experiencing once again the scene of the ambush and the terrifying gun battle.

On the day of the ambush, our tour group had approached Abyan from the east, starting out from the town of Habban in Shabwah province, with Aden as our destination. On the day of my return, I started out from Aden and approached Abyan from the west. The first time, I was in the company of seventeen fellow tourists, our trip leader and five Yemeni drivers. Now I was accompanied by the British vice-consul, the personal assistant to the prime minister of Yemen, a Yemeni driver and about two dozen Yemeni soldiers. As we left the governor's headquarters, a pickup truck full of armed soldiers traveled ahead of Mohammed's Land Cruiser. A second truck traveled immediately behind us carrying more soldiers and a .50 caliber machine gun. This time, I had no illusions about the danger of driving through Abyan. I remembered Abu Hamza's warning: Next time there will be no hostages—they will fire a rocket from the hills; you will not even see it coming. I knew no escort could protect us from such an attack. My misgivings were for those who took the risk to accompany me.

After a long stretch of featureless, flat desert marked only by the occasional dilapidated village, the road began to zig-zag into the mountains.

Desert sand gave way to black volcanic rock, streaked with yellow-red. We passed through a township of tents called al-Jaheen, where most of the inhabitants were African. I knew Yemen had accepted refugees from the wars in Ethiopia and Sudan and guessed that this community was a refugee camp. After the uphill climb, the land leveled out again into a volcanic plateau and began to resemble the terrain I remembered from the scene of the ambush. Watermelons were piled high at the roadside, protected from the sun by blue tarpaulins held up by sticks. The land became more fertile, with prosperous farmhouses and whitewashed mosques dotting the landscape.

"The districts of Abyan are named after parts of the body," Mustafa explained. "El-Ein is the eye, al-Surrah the navel, al-Rukba is the knee and al-Arkob the ankle. Beyond al-Arkob is Habban." Mustafa was knowledgeable about medicinal uses of many of the trees and plants of Yemen. The leaves of the margoza tree have a bitter taste, he told me, but are used for a variety of ills—everything from an antiseptic during childbirth to a wrap for arthritic joints. As a result, each household likes to have a margoza tree growing nearby. I discovered Mustafa loved to cook and was planning to publish a cookbook of traditional Yemeni recipes. Throughout our journey, he commented on the history of the area, describing how the Chinese had built the bridge between Aden and Zinjibar in 1970. The bridge was destroyed by war, then rebuilt in 1984. As we approached the district of Mudiyah, Mustafa explained how, during the British colonial era, the tribal people from Mudiyah and Shabwah were much liked by the British for being both brave and trustworthy. Many of them had been employed by the former colonial administration, and even now Mustafa was responsible for overseeing the distribution of pensions for twelve thousand retired employees. Residual rays of sunlight still shine on the British empire.

Shortly after 11:00 AM we arrived at Mudiyah, the town where Claire and Margaret had been treated at the hospital and from which we had been evacuated by helicopter. The houses were built of multicolored stone. Donkeys and tractors mingled with cars and pedestrians crowding the streets lined with market stalls. Along the main street were two-story stone buildings with small shops at street level and courtyards on the roofs. Access to the residential areas of the buildings was from the side-alleys. Mudiyah did not seem familiar to me. There had been too much else on my mind the last time I was there, and I had paid little attention to the town itself.

Ten miles beyond Mudiyah, our convoy came to a stop. I recognized at once the stony track leading from the road into the desert plateau. This was the place where our hijacked convoy had left the main road. I got out of the vehicle to take some photos, quickly snapping a couple of shots of the soldiers' trucks before an officer shouted at me that photos of the soldiers were not permitted. I waved apologetically to him, as if I didn't know.

As we traveled the rutted track across the desert, I noticed that my heartbeat had increased and adrenaline was surging through me in readiness for danger. A nomad woman with a herd of goats stopped to stare at us, and a cluster of beehives was stacked at one side of the track. As we continued across the desert, it no longer seemed familiar to me but I realized the rains may well have changed the terrain, even the route of the track, in the two intervening years. It was about ten minutes after twelve when we stopped and turned around. Our military guide had taken a wrong turn somewhere and was lost. He explained that it was well over a year since he had last been in the area. The terrain seemed even bleaker than I remembered. After another twenty minutes, we came to the foot of a low-sloping rise. The vehicles stopped again and we all got out and started walking up the slope. Nothing seemed familiar to me. I could not get my bearings, but I followed our guide, a military officer. At the top of the rise, he pointed down to the valley below us. I saw it immediately. The two open fields, defined by low dirt walls; the cluster of trees where our vehicles had been parked by the kidnappers; the steep drop-off to the left of our campsite; and, in the distance, the hill we had climbed to enter the wadi beyond.

"Yes," I turned to Sameer and the officer guiding us. "This is the place."

When I reached the two open fields, I stood again in the place where we had faced two hours of gunfire as human shields. I stepped up on the low dirt wall, this time by choice, not at gunpoint. Thirty yards ahead of me was the second dirt wall where al-Haj had been shot as he forced me toward the oncoming soldiers; beyond that, the thirty yards more I had run with the AK-47; then the last dirt wall where I had found shelter from the bullets. The distance seemed much shorter than I remembered, the area much smaller. My reactions surprised me. I had expected some intense emotional response to the place. Instead, I felt a sense of relief, like a child who sees there is nothing to fear when the light is turned on in a darkened room. A tension I did not even know was with me fell away, like a cloak slipping off my shoulders to the ground.

"It's just a field." I spoke the words quietly to myself. "It's just a field." The soldiers accompanying me moved out and encircled the area to ensure security. Sameer and Mohammed were still making their way down the slope, assisting Mustafa, who was having difficulty walking on the jagged rocks. Sameer and Mohammed had the wreaths from the Land Cruiser. Sameer approached me with one wreath. "Where would you like to put this?" he asked.

I took it from him and placed it at the foot of the dirt wall where Ruth and Peter had died. "Rest in peace. Wherever your spirits might be," I told them.

Crossing the open field I came to the second dirt wall where I had felt the pressure of Purple Skirt's gun barrel fall away from my spine. The army officer came over to me. He did not speak English, but Sameer translated my questions. I found out this officer, who was now guiding us back to this place, had been in the front line of the rescue. He explained to me what had taken place in those final minutes before my escape.

After Hassan's defense post was overcome by the soldiers, and Hassan himself was captured, the soldiers advanced toward the open field where we were still standing on the dirt wall. They took Hassan along with them, insisting that he order the rest of his followers to cease fighting and surrender. I realized then that the shouts exchanged back and forth between Purple Skirt and the advancing forces must, in fact, have been an exchange between Purple Skirt and Hassan. Evidently, Purple Skirt was unwilling to surrender. It was this dialogue that prompted him to hold a gun to Eric's head, to force Catherine to the ground and fire a ring of bullets around her. Now I understood what had motivated Purple Skirt to grab me by the shirt and force me forward at gunpoint. In those chaotic, terrifying moments, when I was forced forward with his gun at my spine, unable to fathom his purpose, Purple Skirt was using me as a shield to reach his leader and friend, Abu Hassan. He made it only halfway, to the crest of the next dirt wall, when he was hit by a bullet. The officer told me that when they reached al-Haj, the terrorist was already dead. Not only had he been shot in the left side of his chest but he had also been hit in his left leg, which was fractured.

More soldiers gathered around us, and I described to them what had happened at that very spot: how I had engaged in a tug of war with Purple Skirt over his Kalashnikov and stepped on his head to wrest it from him. Their eyes widened and they grinned at me, as Sameer translated my words.

I walked around the area, the place where we had laid out our sleeping bags and the place where I had seen our drivers sheltering under rocks from the gunfire. There was no time to retrace my steps into the wadi. Sameer explained we would not be able to stay long. The soldiers were concerned about security in the area and were intent on returning to Zinjibar before nightfall.

We crossed the second open field to the place where I had tossed the gun and bounded over the last wall to safety. There was much denser foliage around the area now. The place where I had thrown myself against the dirt, protected at last from the gunfire, was overgrown with shrubs. I walked through the bushes and found that Mohammed's Land Cruiser and the army trucks were waiting just beyond. We drove about a half mile and stopped at an isolated hill. This was where Abu Hassan had first engaged the security forces; the place where Margaret and Andrew had died. A small pile of rocks had been formed into a cairn at the spot. Mustafa laid the second wreath at this site. I knew that Margaret and Andrew would both be glad someone had returned to mark the place. I would have been glad, had it been me who died. It so easily could have been me.

We spent less than an hour at the site. The soldiers were back on the trucks and I knew we had to leave. From inside my bag, I grabbed packages of cigarettes and candy I had brought with me and handed them up to the soldiers. Their faces showed their appreciation. We lacked a common language but small gestures communicated our mutual goodwill.

On our way back to Aden, we stopped in the provincial capital of Zinjibar. I had asked Sameer if I could briefly visit the courthouse where Abu Hassan had been tried and convicted. The white colonial-style building faced a square lined with small cafes. The sidewalks were crowded with tables where men talked and chewed qat. A one-story-high, whitewashed wall enclosed the courtyard in front of the courthouse. I was only able to glimpse the building through the green gate in this wall. To the left side of the gate, a camel chewed lazily on a pile of straw.

Sameer called to me: "Mary, we cannot stay here."

I took a couple of quick photos and jumped back in the Land Cruiser. The soldiers' trucks had already left. The sun would soon be setting and it was too dangerous to be on the roads of Abyan at night.

On my last day in Aden, I returned to the consulate, where Mustafa kindly searched through files for documents that might be helpful to me. His administrative assistant photocopied a stack of letters and reports, and he included some local Arabic-language newspapers. We then took a tour through the city and Mustafa pointed out the two hotels where the British men had been arrested and the villa they had rented in the upmarket neighborhood of Khormaksar. The villa was a three-story building tucked down a driveway off a residential street. It looked fairly typical of other multiunit buildings in the area.

"The wall around the villa was constructed after the Britons rented the villa," Mustafa noted. "The suspects in the USS *Cole* bombing also had a wall built around the place where they lived." Although Mustafa never gave an opinion about the Britons' guilt, I sensed that he and other embassy staff considered the evidence against them to be convincing, and that he also believed these men had not come to Yemen for Arabic language instruction or for the social life.

Back in Sana'a, I had a second meeting with the prime minister, Abdel Karim al-Iryani, this time during the evening at his home. He was as gracious as ever and pleased that my time in Aden had been productive. I asked him about his hopes for the future of Yemen.

Al-Iryani replied, "Yemen has three great opportunities: the energy of its people, its oil and gas, and its cultural history. We need to develop all three to make Yemen a more vital, active partner in the regional economy and trade. We need to build economic ties and greater influence with Ethiopia, Oman, Saudi Arabia, Eritrea, and the United Arab Emirates." He went on to list the challenges the country faced.

"Education levels are one obstacle. We need to create a much more educated workforce, with business and technology skills. We need to control our population growth. And we need to build people's confidence in having jobs and in the stability of the country." He pointed out the progress Yemen had made. "Defining our border with Saudi Arabia was our number-one obstacle but that has been taken care of now." He referred to a recent agreement between the two countries to accept the survey results of a German engineering firm.

"We have also passed a big test in dealing with the USS *Cole* bombing. After some difficulties, I feel we now have a good level of cooperation and our relationship with the United States has survived."

I took the opportunity to raise the cause of women's rights with the prime minister and described CEDPA's interest in introducing its programs in Yemen. Improvement in women's education and reproductive health, I told him, automatically brings down population growth, one of his key areas of concern. Al-Iryani appeared supportive of my view and commented that the World Bank had provided Yemen with $60 million in funds, which were being used for the education of females.

I had one last question to ask the prime minister. Could I meet the kidnappers who had been arrested, tried and sentenced to prison terms? "That would be very difficult," he told me. I knew it was his polite way of saying no. To my knowledge, no foreigners had ever been able to interview the AAIA prisoners, not even the FBI or Scotland Yard investigators. Through the support of the Yemen ambassador to the United States and the prime minister, I had already had more access to information than I dared hope.

I suspected that al-Iryani would have authorized my visit to the kidnappers unless there were reasons preventing it. I could only guess at what those reasons might be. Perhaps it was simply a sense of protecting the sovereignty of Yemen's justice system. Perhaps it was to protect something else—or someone else. Respecting his response, I did not pursue the matter. A number of reports have speculated that protection of senior officials in the government is the main reason Yemen did not allow the FBI or Scotland Yard to question any of its homegrown terrorists directly. The control of information disclosed in the trials of terrorists such as Hassan, al-Atwi and Nankly is also attributed by some to the fear of disclosures implicating senior public figures.

One candidate for such protection is Ali Mohsen al-Ahmar, a general in the Yemen army and half brother to the president. He had commanded troops of Afghan-Arabs in Yemen's 1994 civil war and was widely believed to have facilitated Osama bin Laden's subsequent funding of training camps. I knew that al-Ahmar was one of the people Abu Hassan had reportedly called immediately after the ambush. Apparently, Hassan was sufficiently well connected to the general to seek his intervention. Al-Ahmar—who is said to have ambitions to be Yemen's next president and to resent the possibility that President Salih is grooming his own son for the job—may well have wanted the Islamic fundamentalists to back his future bid for the presidency. Al-Ahmar is married to the sister of Tariq al-Fadhli, who founded Islamic Jihad in Yemen; another reason he might be willing to intervene on Hassan's behalf. Hassan may have used that family connection to gain al-Ahmar's help, both at the time of the hostage negotiations and after the sentencing to avoid execution. If Hassan were in fact still alive, could it have been al-Ahmar who had intervened to save him? I realized I would probably never know the full story. In Yemen, the political, tribal and family entanglements are too complex, their origins too deeply embedded in the past, for an outsider to ever grasp. This reality was confirmed when I had dinner the next night with Barbara Bodine, United States ambassador to Yemen.

The ambassador lives within the heavily fortified complex of the American embassy in Sana'a. She had also had the experience of being taken hostage—during the Iraqi invasion of Kuwait, where she was deputy chief of mission. Sitting in the warm evening air on the patio of her elegant residence, we were able to compare notes on our experiences and reactions to captivity. The ambassador was sympathetic to my struggle to figure out the political machinations behind the Abyan kidnapping, but explained that even foreigners who have lived for many years in Yemen still find it impossible to unravel the web of family and tribal allegiances behind the country's complex politics.

On my last afternoon in Sana'a, I took some time to wander by myself through the markets of the Old Quarter. Martin Lamport had advised me not to walk alone in quiet areas of the city, but felt I would be safe enough in the busy commercial streets and crowded souks. The embassy had just sent out an advisory to all expatriates, warning that some disgruntled tribal groups had arrived in Sana'a and they might use the kidnapping of foreigners to press their demands on the government. I took his warning seriously. Getting kidnapped twice would be much too embarrassing.

In those final hours before my evening flight home, I rediscovered the magic of the souks. Weaving my way between huge sacks of spices and stopping to purchase frankincense and myrrh, I reveled in the exotic sights and sounds of a world that has changed little in a thousand years. A short alleyway led to a shop full of exquisite cashmere shawls and scarves from India. The prices were one-third of what I would pay in America, so I purchased scarves for Ray and his daughters and a shawl for myself. In a tower house that had been converted to an art gallery, I climbed six stories to the rooftop where I could look out over the entire city. It was a scene more beautiful and mysterious than you would find in any fairy tale, a sight no one should miss. Sana'a truly deserves its status as a World Heritage Site and deserves to be protected from the ravages of weather, time and war. In spite of all that had happened to me in this country—perhaps because of all that had happened—Yemen and its people had found a permanent place in my heart.

"One day I will be back," I promised myself.

21

NORTH TO
THE FUTURE

By the time I returned from Yemen, Ray had made a breakthrough in his search for a new job. It was a breakthrough in a direction I did not expect.

"I've been invited to interview for a job," Ray told me cautiously. "It's in Anchorage."

"You mean Anchorage, as in Anchorage, Alaska?"

"Yes, that's the one." Ray's dream come true: the place he thought he could live only after he had retired.

"I guess you better go check it out," I told him. The idea of Anchorage did not thrill me. What was the deal we had made? A location where he could have good hunting and fishing and I could get an easy nonstop flight to Los Angeles for connections to New Zealand. I checked on the Internet for flights between Anchorage and Los Angeles. There were no nonstop flights. It would take three and a half hours just getting to Seattle. It was as far from Anchorage to LA as it was from Rochester, New York, to LA. Well, there was no point in losing sleep over it yet. Maybe the interview would not lead to a job offer, or maybe the job offer would not be acceptable to Ray.

There was a job offer, of course, and it was acceptable.

Ray had the opportunity to become the director of treasury operations for the Arctic Slope Regional Corporation, Alaska's largest native-owned corporation. He was thrilled.

"I won't take the job unless you are willing to move there, too," he told me. Sure, what was I going to say? Pass up on your chance to live where you've always wanted to live? Hadn't I learned from my close call with death that life is way too short, way too uncertain, to pass up on a chance to live your dreams? But this was Ray's dream, not mine. I hedged.

"Let's go out and take a look at the place together, check out the housing market, see what business possibilities there are for me." We arrived in Anchorage in mid-February. The sun did not rise until 10:30 AM and it set again at about 2:00 PM. The city streets were sanded not salted, and deep, icy ruts had formed from periodic thawing and refreezing. Large tracts of the city looked as charming as an overgrown, neglected trailer park. Major artery roads came to a dead end at empty lots, before starting up again several blocks away.

"They are still building this city," I told Ray. "I can't run a company from here and I can't get a job as a CEO here. I don't know anything about oil or gas or construction." Then the weather changed. The heavy clouds cleared and the low-slung sun bathed the city in its weak light. A massive mountain chain emerged, forming the eastern border of the city. I couldn't tear my eyes away from the Chugach mountains. They were huge, magnificent, extraordinarily beautiful. We looked at a house set up on the hillside overlooking the city and the Turnagain Arm of Cook Inlet. Every room of the house had a view of the water or the mountains. On the downside, the icy driveway was so steep the real estate agent couldn't drive up it in her BMW.

"It's usually not a problem," she said apologetically. "I should have brought my SUV." Then we saw the moose. It was huge, as big as a horse, and grazed casually on willow bushes at the side of the road, indifferent to passing vehicles. Moose, bears, bald eagles, mountains the size of the Rockies outside our back door, an inlet of the Pacific Ocean visible from nearly every room. So what if I couldn't find a job here? A quarter of a million people made a living in Anchorage. I could figure something out. Professionally, it was a huge risk for me. But what was the point of surviving the kidnapping and rescue, if I had learned nothing from it? If I went back to life as usual and didn't experience something entirely new? This life I had now was a pure bonus because I could just as easily have taken the bullets that hit Ruth or Margaret or Andrew or Peter, and be dead now. Then what would a career path matter? Life was what mattered, and Alaska represented a whole new way of life—a life that would never have happened to me if I hadn't been kidnapped, hadn't met Ray, hadn't said yes to selling my home and leaving Xerox and living with this man. My life was now heading in some direction I'd never planned, but no way was I going to miss going along for the ride. How else would I find out where the ride might take me? "OK, I'll move to Alaska with you," I told Ray. "But if I can't find a job there I'll have to commute to some other city."

Our first year in Anchorage was a period of constant learning about this last frontier and the many new skills needed to fully experience living here. Ray had taught me the basics of fly fishing when we still lived in upstate New York. Now we both had a lot to learn about how to fish in Alaska. In our first summer, Ray bought a cataraft, two fourteen-feet-long inflated tubes joined by an aluminum frame. We used the raft to explore the rivers, especially the mighty Kenai. By trial and error and asking questions, we learned about the salmon runs and how to attract the trout with pink plastic beads that resemble salmon eggs. We learned where to put the raft in and where to take it out, and I developed a real talent for falling off the raft into the glacial water. I learned the hard way always to have a second set of clothes on the raft with me in a dry bag.

Rakaia, with his short-haired coat and obvious distaste for getting wet, did not initially look like a promising breed of dog for Alaskan fishing expeditions. But by the end of our first summer, he too had learned new skills. He happily plunged into rivers and streams in pursuit of spawned-out salmon or seagulls. In spite of the dog constantly getting in the way of the oars, we could not imagine going on a rafting adventure without him as our frisky third mate.

In our second summer, Ray added a 21-foot aluminum hull boat to his big-boy toys, and we set out to explore the many islands and coves of Prince William Sound. Ray learned from his brother, a long-time Alaskan, how to construct hoochies, bright-colored plastic squid that attracted the ocean king and silver salmon. We learned how to bottom-fish for halibut, bringing up fish that are sometimes so big that, we were told, you have to shoot them with a pistol before you can safely bring them onto the boat.

For my forty-eighth birthday on September 2, 2001, Ray gave me a hunting rifle, a Winchester Model 70 custom-built for me by Wild West Guns in Anchorage. The bolt was positioned on the left because I shoot left-handed, and the barrel was fluted to reduce its weight. Ray had ordered a synthetic stock, rather than wood, to withstand the harsh Alaskan weather. Designed for 7x57 mm cartridges, it would handle most of Alaska's big game.

"When you know how to use this," Ray told me, "we can go hunting together." Never in my pre-Yemen life could I have imagined receiving a rifle for my birthday. It was an extraordinarily generous gift and I knew it expressed Ray's love for me better than any jewelry could have. He wanted to share with me one of the great passions of his life—hunting. As with any other new experience, I was more than willing to give it a try. Both of us love to eat venison and by now I had developed my own pretty good stew recipe using white-tailed deer or mule deer from Ray's past hunting trips. I had no interest in hunting for trophies to mount on the wall—with Ray's lion, zebra skin, cape buffalo, bear skin and assorted antlers on display, our house already looked like a museum of natural history—but the idea of hunting to put meat on the table appealed to my sense of independence. Hunting would also give me the opportunity to explore the true wilderness of Alaska, far from its few cities and roads.

As the months passed, I found myself feeling surprisingly connected to Alaska. One evening over dinner Ray asked, "Do you feel at home here?"

"Yes, I do. More than any other place I've lived in the USA. How about you?" Ray paused, and I knew he was less sure. In some ways, Alaska had met all his expectations. In other ways, I suspected, he was less sure this was where he would stay for the rest of his life. Experiencing all Alaska has to offer requires a certain physical strength and, fit as he was for a man in his midfifties, Ray already realized he didn't have the same power and stamina he once took for granted. It was just as well he had not waited until retirement to seek out the last frontier.

My biggest challenge during 2001 was figuring out how I could earn a living in Alaska. Since our first house-hunting trip, I had networked with the Anchorage business community. I was quickly invited to join several nonprofit boards, but prospects for employment looked grim. I knew I was not interested in having a boss again. Only the top job would tempt me to go to an existing company. But the prospects for a CEO position at a for-profit company of any size in Alaska were minimal. I could look for a CEO job in Seattle or another city with reasonable flight connections to Anchorage, but that would be unlikely to involve any time in New Zealand. The more I explored my options, the more I knew I would have no choice but to start my own company. Throughout my career, I had compromised life to fit business. Now I was determined to make business fit my life. But what kind of business would fit a life based in Alaska and New Zealand?

For months, I read business and technology magazines looking for ideas. I assumed I would come up with something technical, consistent with my background in high-tech manufacturing companies. Ideas emerged but I felt no real passion for them. Meanwhile, my savings dissipated as the stock market crashed. The Alaskan state motto is "North to the Future." I had come north, all right, but to what kind of a future? The direction my life was now taking remained more of a mystery than I cared to admit.

On September 11 I was due to fly to Chicago for a board meeting and to attend a governance seminar. Our alarm clock had not yet woken us that morning when the phone rang. Ray's younger daughter Amy was calling from Connecticut in tears, telling us that two planes had crashed into the World Trade Center buildings in New York. Ray got up at once, but I lay under the covers a few more minutes. As long as I stayed there in bed, the world was still the same as it had been the night before. I had known, ever since Yemen, that a day like this would come—had been surprised that it had not come even sooner. But now it was here and I did not want to face it.

When I did get up and turn on the television, the twin towers were still standing. In real time, the buildings crumpled in front of my eyes. All I could think about were the people inside, ordinary people who had gone to work that morning, who were doing the typical things I had done on so many days of my own corporate career—sitting at their computers, or talking in conference rooms, or getting a cup of coffee. They were now perishing in an unimaginable hell.

I watched that terrible day unfold on television, about as far from New York and Washington—the other city hit by terrorist action that day—as it is possible to be in the continental United States. It was awesome in its horrifying simplicity. Use a passenger jet, fully loaded with fuel, as a guided missile. Use our own technology and tools as weapons against us. The words quoted later from a Yemen sheikh, who knew in advance about the plot, foretold my reaction: "The man who planned this is a genius and a madman. It will turn you to ice." The front line of terrorism was now here in America, on our own turf. One no longer needed to be on some exotic or foolhardy trip to the Arabian Peninsula to face the terrorist threat. I had simply had a taste of it nearly three years before most Americans.

The search for the perpetrators quickly focused on Osama bin Laden and al-Qaeda, and the Taliban that protected them. Afghanistan, whose plight under the Taliban was largely ignored when I traveled there in the summer of 1999, was now the center of media attention. In the strategy sessions I had engaged in with Afghan women, we had struggled with ideas for getting the United States government to take more action against the Taliban. Never had we imagined the action would be so swift and decisive. In a matter of weeks, the Taliban was gone from power.

Many Americans were shocked to see a filthy, half-starved young man from Marin County, California, staring out of the rubble of Mazar-e-Sharif. They wondered how there could be an American among the Taliban forces; I was surprised there were not more like him. Perhaps other Johnny Walkers had escaped earlier, or never made it into Afghanistan in the first place. Where was the young American man I had talked to in the mosque at Finsbury Park? Had he also found his way to Kabul, only to discover himself at war with his own country?

As details began to emerge about the men who had hijacked the four aircraft, one name stood out among the nineteen: Khalid al-Mihdar, a

Saudi with Yemeni roots. Could this al-Mihdar have any connection to Zein al-Abidin abu Bakr al-Mehdar, better known as Abu Hassan? Arabic names are spelled in various ways when translated to English. Al-Mihdar and al-Mehdar were almost certainly the same family name in Arabic. It was too incredible to think that Abu Hassan might indeed have been released rather than executed, and had now shown up as a hijacker on American Airlines flight 77, which struck the Pentagon. As soon as photographs of the hijackers were published, it was evident that Khalid al-Mihdar was not Abu Hassan. Nonetheless, I was curious about the possibility that they were related, perhaps as cousins or even brothers.

I resumed searching on the Internet, this time for information about Khalid al-Mihdar. Over the course of several months, I discovered scraps of information about his background. Apparently, al-Mihdar had been identified as an al-Qaeda suspect by the FBI some eighteen months before the September 11 tragedy. He was photographed meeting a Yemeni by the name of Tawfiq Attash in Malaysia in January 2000. This in itself did not mean much to me until I continued to research more broadly the events that had taken place in Yemen in the time since the kidnapping.

One of the two suicide bombers in the USS *Cole* attack was a man called al-Khamri. He was among the suspects arrested for the AAIA conspiracy to kidnap Americans from the Jibla hospital in 1999 and exchange them for the imprisoned Abu Hassan. There was another name among those arrested in the Jibla affair: Abdulaziz Attash, brother of Tawfiq Attash. I now had two links between the hijacker and Hassan. Khalid al-Mihdar had met in Malaysia with the brother of a known AAIA member. He was also a suspect in the USS *Cole* bombing, an attack for which several AAIA members had already been arrested. Khalid al-Mihdar may not have been a card-carrying member of the Aden Abyan Islamic Army, but he was certainly an affiliate.

Another link between the hijacker and terrorist cells in Yemen emerged some months after 9/11, when a terrorist suspect blew himself up with a grenade while being chased by Yemen police in Sana'a. He was Samir al-Hada, who turned out to be the brother-in-law of Khalid al-Mihdar. Al-Hada's father operated a safe house in Yemen for visiting militants, and it was this safe house phone number, belonging to his father-in-law, that Khalid al-Mihdar used to communicate messages regarding the bombing of the U.S. embassy in Nairobi in August 1998. Khalid al-Mihdar was a busy man, it seems, involved in major acts of terrorism ranging from Kenya to Yemen to Washington DC itself. I found no evidence that Khalid al-Mihdar and Zein al-Mehdar were related, but wasn't it Abu Hamza who told me, when I interviewed him at the mosque in London, that Abu Hassan had a big family? If they were not brothers in blood, they were certainly brothers in bloodshed.

Against the background of the war on terrorism, I continued to struggle for a path forward in my professional life. In addition to researching the kidnapping, I was busy with consulting assignments, volunteer work and service on the boards of directors for several organizations—but none of this was providing much income. My Xerox stock had crashed from over $60 a share to $4.50. Like most Americans, my retirement portfolio had been hammered. There were days when I wondered if I had made a terrible mistake giving up my former life, my well-paid job at Xerox, my beautiful home in Rochester.

In response to a call from a headhunter, I was interviewed for the top strategy job at a Fortune 500 company on the East Coast. Still lacking a compelling idea for my own company, I agreed to meet with this corporation's top executives, including the CEO, to see if there might be a fit. The moment I walked into the hushed executive office suite at the company's headquarters, I felt I was suffocating. The all-male senior vice presidents sat in their huge, wood-paneled offices with their all-female secretaries sitting like sentries, guarding access to their domains. The atmosphere reminded me of the top floors of Kodak's headquarters building in Rochester, a place that always felt remote in time and touch from the real world of employees and customers. As I went from one interview to another throughout the day, I knew there was no possibility I could return to this stultifying corporate world.

During our first year in Alaska, I traveled back to New Zealand twice and networked with New Zealand's business community. I was approached about several jobs, but none of these positions would allow me to operate even part time from Anchorage—and I knew Ray would not yet give up Alaska to move to New Zealand. My dream of a life that encompassed working in both the United States and New Zealand—with opportunity to travel worldwide and participate in causes I cared about, plus a secure financial future—seemed as ephemeral as ever, yet I still believed it must be possible. I just had to figure out how to do it: how to create the life I wanted in my second chance at being alive. And where better to feel truly alive than in Alaska, where adventure beckoned from mountain, sea, and sky?

22

BECOMING THE HUNTER

The shadow of the single-engine Beaver floatplane was reflected in the silver-gray waters of Cook Inlet as we crossed from the Kenai Peninsula westward, towards the massive, snow-covered Alaska Range. Ray and our friend Gerry occupied the seats behind the pilot and me, while our gear filled all remaining space in the four-seater aircraft. My headphones blocked out the noise of wind and engine, as well as any prospect of conversation. It was my first flight in a floatplane, a form of transportation that is as routine to bush Alaskans as driving SUVs is for those of us who live on the state's limited road system. We were on our way to hunt caribou.

Throughout the summer of 2002, Ray had coached me on the use and care of my rifle. Every few weeks, we had staked out two adjacent shooting benches at the Rabbit Creek Rifle Range in Anchorage and worked on improving my shooting accuracy. Ray showed me how to fine-tune the alignment of the telescopic sights and use a chronograph to compare the speed and consistency of different bullets. To build up my fitness and strength, I had worked out at the gym several times a week. On weekends, we had regularly hiked ten or twelve miles through the mountains and valleys of Chugach State Park on the eastern boundary of Anchorage. Poring over hunting catalogues, I had found camouflage gear to fit me, bemoaning the limited choices in women's sizes compared with the vast array of hunting clothes for men. By the end of August I felt ready to tackle my first hunting trip.

We were blessed with a clear, calm day for our flight, which afforded spectacular views of the forbidding Alaska Range. Its snow-capped peaks and steep slopes of bare rock face soared above the braided river valleys far below, reminding me of the mountains of Afghanistan. At least I didn't have to worry about being shot down by the Taliban's Stinger missiles on this flight, I reassured myself, while trying not to think about the possibilities of weather, mechanical failure, and pilot error, which contribute to the regular demise of bush planes in Alaska. As our pilot maneuvered his small aircraft through a pass in the mountains, it seemed we could almost reach out and touch the jagged peaks and snowfields on either side of us. I was relieved to emerge an hour later above the vast rolling tundra of southwest Alaska. The land below us was already turning from green to every imaginable shade of gold, rust, and sienna, mixed with deep reds, scarlet and purple. The pilot picked out our destination among the myriad small lakes glinting in the sunlight, and landed smoothly on Fox Lake, where our outfitter Jeff waited to greet us. A second plane—bearing another of Ray's hunting friends, Bill, and his two sons—had landed ahead of us and was tied down near the shore.

The accommodation could hardly be described as luxurious. Jeff's camp, tucked away in a gully a few hundred yards from the lake, consisted of two canvas-walled cabins with plywood floors and a couple of pitched tents. The larger structure was a dark, windowless single room, which served as kitchen, mess and sleeping quarters for three hunters. Bill and his sons claimed those three beds, which offered the warmth of a wood stove in compensation for lack of privacy. Ray and I dropped our gear on beds in the smaller cabin, which would serve as our sleeping quarters, and Gerry occupied one of the tents. An outhouse was set off to one side of the campsite and a makeshift shower stall had been constructed just beyond Jeff's tent. This would be our home for the next seven days.

After serving up a meal of caribou chili in the larger cabin, Jeff explained to us the recommended techniques for hunting caribou. Our group of six had signed up for an unguided hunt, so Jeff would not be accompanying us, only providing accommodation and meals, but he was happy to give us the benefit of his experience.

"The worst thing you can do is go walking all over the place," he observed. "You want to find a high spot that gives you a clear view over the surrounding terrain and wait for caribou to come into view. Then, when you see a caribou you want to go after, you watch it for a bit, see which way it's going and figure out a path to intercept it." Jeff was in his thirties, overweight, with dirty blonde hair in need of a decent cut. His camouflage pants and blaze orange fleece sweater looked as though he had lived in them all summer. He sat near the propped-open door as he talked, periodically leaning out to spit chewing tobacco onto the muddy ground outside.

Alaska is home to an estimated one million caribou that roam the state in about twenty-five distinct herds. The best known of these is the Porcupine herd, the fate of which is often argued in the debate over drilling for oil in the Arctic National Wildlife Refuge. The Mulchatna herd, which we were seeking, migrates between winter and summer feeding grounds across an area of 16 million acres between the Alaska Range and the Kuskokwim River, northeast of Dillingham. We had heard from the bush pilots that the huge Mulchatna herd seemed to have followed a different route this year, taking it further west than usual from the area of the camp. A change from the well-worn migration routes was an inconvenience for us, but might once have meant disaster for native Alaskans, who were dependent on the caribou for food, clothing and tools.

"There aren't so many caribou around here this year," Jeff agreed. "You'll see enough of them, though. There's a small group of a dozen or so up on Cadillac Ridge." He gestured in the direction of the northern skyline. "And you'll see others coming through in ones and twos." When we planned the trip, I had imagined we would see thousands of caribou spread out across the tundra, like the zebra and antelope herds I had seen during my travels in Africa. Not this year, apparently. In the words of Eskimo wisdom, no one knows the ways of the wind and the caribou.

Anticipating an early start next morning, Ray and I headed back to our cabin, where the temperature had dropped close to freezing. By the light of a gas camping lantern we set out the gear we would need the next morning and crawled into our sleeping bags. I slept badly, never able to get my feet warm in spite of two pairs of thick socks. Next time, I promised myself, I'll bring my hot-water bottle with me.

The terrain around our campsite was not as difficult as I expected. It was a rumpled land like an unmade bed, with hills and ridges, mostly less than one thousand feet in height, separated by stretches of open land, small lakes and streams. In the distance, steeper mountains rose to about three thousand feet, but we did not expect to walk more than one or two miles from camp in pursuit of the caribou. As we set out toward Cadillac Ridge, I noticed that the low springy bushes underfoot offered a smorgasbord of berries, the favorite fall food of grizzlies and black bears.

Typically, Ray, Gerry and I would set out from camp together at daybreak and choose a lookout spot about a mile from camp. Gerry would often split off on his own but regroup with us from time to time. Multiple crisscrossing paths, worn by the hooves of generations of caribou, provided the easiest walking trails. We avoided fighting our way through the stands of stunted spruce trees and the dense thickets of alder, which were not only hard to penetrate but would also make handling a rifle difficult if we should stumble upon a bad-tempered grizzly.

Settled on a hillside overlooking a valley, Ray and I would sit for hours, scanning the area with binoculars. From time to time, a caribou would come into view and we would discuss its size and the shape of its antlers, deciding if it were worth pursuing. My personal goal was to bring home good venison for eating, not the biggest set of antlers. On the assumption that a younger animal, with less well-developed antlers, would provide more tender meat, I saw big antlers as an undesirable feature. Not so my male companions, who were all intent on outdoing each other in the "mine is bigger than yours" department.

Gerry was the first to bring down a caribou. At the end of our first day, Ray and I were considering heading back to camp when we heard a gunshot. After a few more seconds, a second shot rang out. When we found Gerry twenty minutes later, he had already begun to butcher a good-sized bull caribou. Its blue eyes stared from its motionless head and a small pool of vomit had spilled out of its mouth.

"Do they always throw up when you shoot them?" I asked Ray.

"No, it's probably because one bullet penetrated its stomach." He pointed out the neat hole in the animal's hide. I felt the velvet on its antlers and the surprisingly soft fur, still warm to my touch. Much as I wanted to come on this hunting trip, I was still unsure whether I would actually shoot a caribou myself. Ray and I set about helping Gerry dress the caribou. By Alaskan law, all edible meat must be recovered by the hunter and the antlers must be the last thing taken from the kill site. I had seen animals butchered in third-world markets, so I was not shocked by the process, but I was surprised to discover how strenuous it was—and how messy. The stomach contents spilled out in a mass of thick brown goo, mixed with straw-like material. Ray stepped back quickly to avoid the murky, stinking flood.

"That is why you try not to shoot an animal in the stomach," he said grimly. Ray rolled up his sleeves and plunged his arms up to the elbows inside the caribou to work on cutting out the internal organs. I worked on skinning the hide, while Gerry removed the lower legs. After another hour's work, all the meat was stored in four cotton game bags. Daylight was fading, and we still had to carry the venison and our gear several miles back to camp. Hunting, I decided, was hard work.

Next morning, I remained in camp while Ray headed out to help Gerry bring back the rest of the caribou. My plans for a leisurely few hours' reading were soon interrupted by a shout from Jeff.

"Mary! It's a wolf! Come take a look."

I ran out of the cabin to where Jeff was peering through his spotting scope. About a mile away, a wolf was pursuing two caribou across the face of a low ridge of hills.

"Grab your rifle. We're going after it." Unsure if I really wanted to hunt a wolf, I raced back into the cabin for my boots and loaded five rounds in my rifle. Jeff was already following a trail out of camp, his own rifle slung over his shoulder. As I caught up with him, I recalled his comments about how the growing wolf population had already wiped out every moose in the valley and was having a significant impact on the caribou population.

"I'll shoot a wolf any chance I get," Jeff had told us, "and I encourage you all to do the same." Wolves were a threat to his livelihood.

At the top of a hill just outside the camp, Jeff stopped and scanned the distant hillside with his binoculars. We had lost sight of our prey. Jeff cupped his hands around his mouth, emitting a howl that sent shivers down my spine. He waited several minutes, then howled again. It sounded realistic to me, but I couldn't believe a wolf wouldn't know the difference. We followed the trail a little further along a hill face. Jeff suddenly stopped and pointed across an open area to where the land rose up towards the ridge on the other side of a valley. Through my telescopic sight I could see the wolf, more than 500 yards away. Jeff let loose another howl. To my amazement, the wolf looked up, immediately changed direction, and began loping through the brush straight towards us. As we crouched down on the trail, Jeff whispered to me.

"Keep extremely still and quiet. As soon as the wolf suspects something, it will be gone. I'll let you take the first shot at it but, if you're not ready, I'll shoot." I eased myself into a sitting position, with an elbow resting on each knee. I aimed my rifle towards the wolf, watching it still loping towards us. In spite of Jeff's concerns about their impact on game animals, I wasn't at all sure I wanted to kill a wolf. Yet I knew Jeff would shoot if I didn't. As a former instructor at the Marines sniper school in Quantico, Jeff was unlikely to miss. The wolf was now 300 yards away. My heart was pounding as I followed it in my sights. Suddenly, it disappeared into thick alders.

"When it emerges, you'll have a split second to shoot before it sees us," Jeff whispered. I watched in the direction I had last seen the wolf, but there was no sign of movement in the bushes.

"Over there." Jeff was pointing in a direction 90 degrees from where I had been looking.

BOOM. A mass of white fur flew into the air from the edge of the bushes barely 50 yards away. I was surprised how close to us it was. We headed down the slope to where the animal lay.

"That is one huge wolf," Jeff commented, after approaching cautiously to make sure it was dead. "Must be close to 120 pounds." I looked at the pool of blood staining the thick white fur, and felt glad it was not me who shot it. Even if I had been ready, even if I had located the wolf in my sights before I heard the blast of Jeff's rifle alongside me, I had no cause to kill this wolf. I would rather have watched it run free. Killing, I started to understand, was not so much about knowing how to do it, but knowing why we do it. Under what circumstances would I shoot a wolf? Under what circumstances would I have shot Ali al-Khadar al-Haj? The problem is that the circumstances can come upon us without warning, sweeping us too fast for thought into an adrenalin-charged moment of decision. I once asked Ray if he thought I should have used al-Haj's gun to kill him. For the trained military man, the choice was clear: "He was an armed enemy combatant on a field of battle. He was still a threat. Yes, you should have shot him." To Jeff, the wolf was a threat to his way of life and his livelihood. Without moose and caribou in the area of his licensed campsite, Jeff could not survive as a professional hunting guide. I could understand his reasons, but his reasons did not apply to me.

In spite of the physical effort involved, and the moral dilemmas, I discovered I loved hunting. Prior to the trip, I had always thought of hunting in terms of aiming and firing a rifle. In reality, that moment was a tiny part of the hunting experience. In the wilderness, in vast empty spaces eighty miles from the nearest road, I was content to sit for hours scanning the terrain. I found myself paying attention to the thousand different shades of color in the tundra, the slow movement of the sun across the sky, a small change in direction of the wind against my face. Hunting for caribou was the first time I could remember being able to just sit outdoors and observe the world around me for hours at a time. Even the day we spent in relentless rain, never sighting a single caribou, I was glad to be out there.

"I think of days like this as earning preference points," Ray encouraged me, as we finally returned towards camp, looking and feeling like two drowned rats. "There are times in hunting when you have no luck at all for days at a time. Then, when you least expect it, the animal you've been waiting for appears right in front of you, like a gift. It's as though you've earned that gift, from all the preference points you stacked up on the bad days."

My perception of time had changed since my close encounter with death as a hostage. In the face of death, I had learned that time is the only truly scarce resource in our lives. Ultimately, our lives are about what we do with the time we have. So many of us let ourselves be held hostage to careers that are not satisfying, relationships devoid of love, or locations we do not really enjoy. What a terrible waste of time. You do not need to be kidnapped by terrorists to be held hostage. We let ourselves be kidnapped constantly, our lives held to ransom in return for companionship or pay-checks, approval or prestige, ambition or expectations.

By the fifth day of the hunt, all five of the men, including Ray, had taken a caribou. The pressure was on to show that I could do it, too. On the eve of my forty-ninth birthday, Gerry, Ray and I spent another long day scanning from several different lookout points. Midafternoon we sighted and stalked one animal but, after our long chase to intercept it, the caribou spooked and ran into a thickly treed gully, before disappearing up a steep hillside. We turned back towards the camp and repositioned ourselves on a flat plateau overlooking a dry lake bed. Ray and I glassed from one end of the plateau and Gerry from the other. Ray and I took turns watching and napping.

It was approaching 5:00 PM when Gerry came running toward us.

"I've just spotted a caribou. Over there, on the left end, the second ridge over." He pointed in the direction where we had attempted our ear-lier stalk. The thought of crossing all that terrain again, in a direction tak-ing us further away from the camp, had little appeal. Ray handed me the binoculars. The caribou was a young adult bull, perhaps two or three years old, with relatively small antlers. Just the kind of animal I was seeking. A few minutes later, a second caribou, similar in size but a female, also ap-peared over the ridge. Caribou are the only deer where the cows as well as the bulls grow antlers each year, using them to access plants and lichens under the deep winter snows. The two animals appeared to be moving to-gether. We watched them as they grazed along the ridgeline, moving slowly in our direction.

"If we head over that way, I think we could intercept them where the ridge tapers out." Ray pointed towards the right end of the ridge. "Are you up for it?" I was already tired from a long day crossing hills and valleys, but tomorrow was my birthday. I did not want to spend it running all over the tundra again. The idea of resting the next day, with a caribou in the bag, had a lot of appeal.

"OK, let's do it."

Ray and I left our packs with Gerry and took only our rifles. We reached the first ridge, but both caribou had already disappeared. We moved along the valley to where the ridge started to taper out. Eventually, Ray caught a glimpse of the two caribou again. They were traveling together along a flat plateau beyond the second ridge, grazing as they moved toward us. Bent low, we crept quietly from one clump of bushes to another until we could clearly see both caribou. They were still about 300 yards away, and I knew my odds of dropping one were not good at that distance.

Ray and I discussed in whispers whether I should attempt to move closer. At closer range, I was more likely to hit my target but I also increased the risk of spooking the animals before having a chance to shoot. Then, to our surprise, the two caribou suddenly folded their legs under themselves and settled down for a rest. Was this what Ray called the gift? The animal giving itself to the hunter, as the native Alaskans would say? We moved another 50 yards to the next clump of small trees. The caribou were still lying down, facing away from us. The wind was blowing sideways across us, muffling the sound of our movement and preventing the caribou from catching our scent, which I'll admit was none too fragrant by that stage of the trip. Only a small, steep gully now separated us from the plateau, where the caribou were sitting. I figured I had nothing to lose by trying to cross the gully and get to the edge of the plateau, where I would have a clear line of sight at a comfortable distance.

"You won't be able to aim for the usual point behind the shoulder," Ray whispered to me. "Because he's lying down and facing away from you, you'll have to aim for the spine." Ray and I crossed the gully and went up the other side. I eased myself carefully up onto the edge of the plateau and Ray stayed behind me just below the drop-off. With his range finder, he checked the distance—130 yards. Both caribou were still oblivious to our presence. I settled into the sitting position that I had practiced at the rifle range, elbows resting on knees. Even after all the target practice, and watching Ray's and Gerry's hunts, I still wasn't sure I could do this. I looked back at Ray. He nodded. I reminded myself of everything he had taught me at practice.

"Take a slow deep breath. Don't try to fix the target in the crosshairs, just let the crosshairs move a little around the target. When you squeeze the trigger, it should be so gradual you don't even know yourself when the rifle is going to fire." I aimed for the top of the bull caribou's shoulders. This was it—the moment of truth.

BOOM! Instantly, I saw the caribou drop over on its side like a rock. I heard the shot but hardly felt the recoil. I looked back at Ray. His face showed his amazement.

"Bodacious shot. Wow. You don't see a shot like that very often." Ray later told me he had been ready to shoot if I had missed or, worse, if I wounded the animal and it started to run. His backup wasn't necessary. We stood up and approached the two caribou. The cow stood and watched us. To my surprise, she didn't move away, just watched us approach. She seemed confused, and I wished she hadn't been there to see it. The bull caribou was motionless. An entry wound in the back of its neck, an exit wound in its left cheek.

"That caribou never even knew what happened," Ray commented. "Instant lights out." I pulled out my knife, the one Ray had brought me back from a former hunting trip in Montana. I made the first cut just above the genitals, the way I had seen Ray and Gerry skin their caribou. There was no sound but the wind across the vast empty tundra. I felt strangely detached from time, as though this moment might have happened at any point in a million years of human history. For the first time, I felt connected to the earliest generations of humankind who hunted mammoths to survive. For the first time, I had a sense of why American Indian and Eskimo cultures give thanks to the animal spirits, thanks to the animal that has given itself. Hunting for food, for survival, felt as basic to being human as breathing, eating, making love. I did not know what I had expected hunting to feel like, but I never expected this—an experience profoundly spiritual.

With Gerry and Ray carrying most of the meat, and the caribou's antlers attached to my pack, we began the trek back towards camp. It had been a long, exhausting day and we moved slowly without speaking. Toward the west, the skyline was rimmed with liquid gold spilling from a setting sun. All around us, the rolling hills glowed pink and deep shadows filled the valleys. The long Arctic twilight would give us time to find our way across the tundra.

As we walked, I instinctively checked the safety catch on my rifle, then eased the sling into a more comfortable position. The rifle on my shoulder, which had initially seemed so heavy and awkward to carry, now felt a natural part of me. My relationship with guns had certainly changed, I reflected, since the day I had relieved Purple Skirt of his AK-47 nearly four years earlier. Even now, I could still vividly recall the feel of his gun barrel against my spine as he forced me toward the soldiers. I could still clearly remember my surprise when I turned to find Purple Skirt on the ground behind me, and the intensity of my aggression as I fought for possession of his gun. I remembered the moment I had wrenched the rifle from his grip and had known for the first time that I could kill. The prey had become the hunter.

Such transitions are the ultimate purpose of any journey, of course—whether it is a vacation tour through Yemen, a human-rights expedition into Afghanistan, or a hunting trip into the Alaskan wilderness. The best trips are those in which we discover something new, not only about the world but also something new about ourselves. Journeys force us beyond the familiar. Faced with the unfamiliar, we have no choice but to find new ways to respond. Our responses may surprise us—we may not even like them—but we come home more fully human. It is the price and the prize of a journey.

On the night of the summer solstice, Ray and I climbed to the top of a mountain called Flat-Top with Rakaia. We can see this mountain, with its distinctive squared-off profile, from our Anchorage home. Flat-Top is a traditional location for celebrating the longest day of the year, and we joined a steady stream of climbers on the well-used trail. Pulling ourselves up and over the last steep rocks, we reached the broad plateau on the summit at about 10:30 PM and found ourselves a secluded nook overlooking Anchorage and Cook Inlet. On the far western horizon, the Alaska Range and two volcanoes—Iliamna and Redoubt—were sharply defined against the pink tinge of evening sky. City lights twinkled far below us, in anticipation of the brief Arctic night. Ray opened our bottle of red wine and we leaned back against a rocky outcrop to enjoy the last hour of sunlight. The sun would not finally set until 11:45 PM and it would rise again four hours later, as prolonged dusk transitioned into dawn.

Looking out across the foothills of the Chugach mountains toward the sea, I thought back to that day when I looked out across a different sea toward the land of Yemen. From Abyan to Alaska—it had indeed been a strange and unintended journey. On that mountaintop, watching the midnight sun, I remembered again the question that had overwhelmed me when I threw myself against the desert floor, safe at last from the crossfire.

"Where does my life go from here? Where can I possibly go from here?"

I now knew the answer to that question. It was simple. My life has come here—to Alaska, to Ray, to a different view of the world. I do not know what the future holds for me here and where else the journey of life might take me, but I would not be on this mountaintop tonight, in the arms of the man I love, if I had not first traveled on the road through Abyan.

AFTERWORD

By April 2004, the last of the jailed British men and their two Algerian colleagues had been released from al-Mansoor prison. Abu Hamza's son was freed in January 2002, after serving his three-year sentence. In December 2003, Shahid Butt and Sarmad Ahmed completed their five-year sentences and were freed along with Algerians al-Rahman and Ali Merksen. In April 2004, Malik Harhara and Mohscn Ghalain were given early releases from their seven-year sentences. Yemen authorities expressed their hope that these early releases would help to fully restore bilateral relations with the UK. Attorney Rachad Yaqoob was quoted as saying the released men remained intent on proving their innocence and that Shahid Butt had "some cards up his sleeve." I recalled Butt's final comment to me at al-Mansoor prison that there would be "fireworks" when all the men were released. So far, his only reported activity has been speaking engagements at events such as those organized by the Stop the (Iraq) War Campaign. Interestingly enough, Butt's accused accomplice in his 1995 conviction for social security fraud was a British national named Moazzam Begg who later turned up in American custody at Guantanomo Bay, having been arrested in Islamabad and turned over to the U.S. by Pakistan.

Abu Hamza continued to be the object of intense investigation, not only by the British Metropolitan Police but also by the FBI and the southern district of New York's antiterrorism unit. After review of the evidence by a grand jury, the U.S. Attorney General's office submitted an extradition request for Abu Hamza in May, 2004. He was charged with eleven counts, the first two of which were the kidnapping of American citizens, Margaret Thompson and myself. Abu Hamza was also charged with trying to set up a terrorist training camp in Oregon; sending at least one individual to Afghanistan to train at terrorist camps; and supplying funds and resources to terrorist organizations. British authorities once again arrested Abu Hamza, who was already appealing a British Home Office decision in 2003 to revoke his citizenship. Hamza was taken to Belmarsh Prison and, after preliminary hearings during the summer, a date of October 19, 2004 was set for his formal five-day extradition hearing. In an unexpected development, just days before the hearing was due to begin, the British announced that they too were bringing charges against Abu Hamza and the extradition proceedings would be put on hold pending the prosecution of those charges. The outcome for Abu Hamza remains uncertain but American allegations suggest his involvement in the kidnapping may have been more direct and proactive than I had previously suspected.

Back in Yemen President Salih continued to conduct his own war on terror, not only because militant groups such as the Aden Abyan Islamic Army represented a threat to his political goals but because he feared Yemen would suffer the same fate as Afghanistan and Iraq if he did not convince the Americans of his genuine cooperation. Little was heard of the AAIA for a period of time following the arrest of Abu Muhsin who took over its leadership from Abu Hassan. Senior government officials would occasionally comment that the group had been eliminated. That wishful perception was shattered when a military medical convoy was attacked by AAIA gunmen in June 2004, leaving seven soldiers wounded. Yemen security forces immediately launched an attack on a camp where the gunmen had taken shelter. The camp was none other than Abu Hassan's old stomping ground at Huttat, now home to an estimated eighty militants associated with AAIA, Islamic Jihad, and al-Qaeda. Six militants died and eleven were captured during the attack. A dozen more were rounded up in mop-up operations but over 50 were believed to have escaped. Khaled abd al-Nabi, leader of the AAIA at the time, was initially reported to be among the dead. His appearance some months later, sporting an official pardon from the president, suggested reports of his death had indeed been exaggerated. Apparently al-Nabi was among those terrorists who had engaged in the Yemen government's latest amnesty program that offered militants a pardon on condition they, and their families, promised to conduct no further attacks on foreigners or government facilities in

Yemen. At the beginning of Ramadan in 2004, dozens of detainees in Yemen's prisons were set free after they convinced a committee of clerics that they had truly seen the error of their ways and would renounce the militant ideas of al-Qaeda. The Yemeni judge who headed up the committee was quick to deny rumors that the men who were convicted of kidnapping the sixteen tourists in Abyan in December 1998 were among those released. Presumably Yellow Pants and Grenade are still serving out their prison sentences.

My own life became settled in Alaska with Ray. After exploring dozens of new company ideas and several intriguing job opportunities I took the risk of launching my own company. My first venture is Tuliqi LLC, a retailer of upscale natural and organic bed and bath products. I opened my first retail store in Anchorage in November 2004, featuring products from New Zealand and around the world. The name Tuliqi (pronounced tooly-key) originates from the Polynesian word tuli and the Inupiat Eskimo word tuliq meaning birds which migrate between the South Pacific and Alaska. Like the tuli I seek the best of all worlds, balancing my love of travel with time spent in New Zealand and Alaska, the two beautiful places I am lucky to call home.

SOURCES

The material in this book is a blend of three broad sources of information: my own personal experience of events; interviews and conversations I conducted; and information gleaned from Web sites, newspapers, magazines, reports, and books.

In the third category I reviewed over 1,200 documents drawn from approximately 200 Web sites and printed publications. Many of these originated from reports distributed by Reuters, Associated Press, Agence France-Presse and United Press International. I would like particularly to acknowledge the value and scope of information sourced from the *Guardian* (UK), the *Telegraph* (UK), the *Yemen Times*, *Al-Ayyam* (Yemen), ArabicNews.com, Yemen Gateway (al-bab.com), bbc.co.uk and various news sites on yahoo.com.

A report provided to me by the Antiterrorism Branch of the UK's Metropolitan Police Service and correspondence provided by the British consulate in Aden were especially useful to my research. Background information on Yemen was sourced primarily from Paul Dresch's *A History of Modern Yemen* and Lonely Planet's 3rd and 4th editions of their Yemen guidebook. General information about terrorism and kidnapping came from Bruce Hoffman's *Inside Terrorism* and Ann Hagedorn Auerbach's *Ransom*.

Permission to reproduce the photographs of Abu Hassan in his prison cell and the British and Algerian defendants in the Aden court was provided by *Al-Ayyam* in Yemen. Permission to use the photograph of Abu Hamza was provided by the *Guardian* in the UK. All other photographs are my own. Permission to use the map of our tour route was granted by Explore Ltd, and Random House (NZ) Ltd kindly allowed the use of all three maps in the form created for their New Zealand publication of this book.

The interpretation of events and impressions of people disclosed in *Kidnapped in Yemen* represent my best efforts to understand and describe the causes and consequences of the kidnapping. I make no claim to be an expert on the history, politics, or military matters addressed in this book. Information does exist that I have not been able to access, and new information about the kidnapping may become available in the future. For now, this is the story of what I believe to be true.

Appendix

RELEVANT NAMES

A. Tour Group—Hostages
(Occupations as known at time of
  kidnapping)
Chris Cheeseman
British, warehouse worker, life partner
  of Gill

Gill (surname omitted by request)
British, occupation unknown,
  life partner of Chris Cheeseman

Eric Firkins
British, high school teacher

David Holmes
British, retired high school
  headmaster

Claire Marston
British, university lecturer, wife of
  Peter Rowe

Sue Mattocks
British, high school teacher

Pat Morris
British, musician with orchestra

Mary Quin
New Zealand and American
  citizenship, executive in copier
  industry

Peter Rowe
Canadian and British citizenship,
  university professor, husband of
  Claire Marston

Brian Smith
British, postal worker

Catherine Spence
Australian, occupation unknown

Andrew Thirsk
Australian, management
  consultant

Margaret Thompson
American, project manager in oil
  industry in UK

Laurence Whitehouse
British, high school teacher, husband
  of Margaret Whitehouse

Margaret Whitehouse
British, elementary school teacher,
  wife of Laurence Whitehouse

Ruth Williamson
Scottish, trainer in healthcare
  industry

B. Tour Group—Others

Dave Nott
Tour leader, employed by Explore

Mohammed Babiker
British of Sudanese descent, physicist,
    husband of Susan Babiker, escaped
    ambush in lead vehicle

Susan Babiker
British, occupation unknown, wife of
    Mohammed Babiker, escaped
    ambush in lead vehicle

Carolyn Gay
American, left tour before kidnapping

David Leadbetter
Independent tourist accompanying
    Carolyn Gay, left tour before
    kidnapping

C. Tour Group—Drivers

Sammi (full name unknown)
Driver of lead vehicle, fluent in
    English

Abdul (Abd al-Khaliq Yahya Biza)
Driver of second vehicle (when
    convoy ambushed)

Mad Mohammed (Mohammed Ali
    Saleh, aka Little Mohammed)
Driver of third vehicle

Yellow Mohammed (real name
    unknown)
Driver of fourth vehicle

Mohammed with Glasses
    (Mohammed Naji Al-Assa'r)
Driver of fifth vehicle

D. Kidnappers

Abu Hassan (Zein al-Abidin abu Bakr
    al-Mehdar)
Leader of kidnappers and founder
    of Aden Abyan Islamic Army
    (AAIA)

Purple Skirt (Ali al-Khadar al-Haj)
Commander of AAIA in Abyan
    province, taxi driver, close friend of
    Abu Hassan

Bandit (Osama al-Masri)
Egyptian associated with Islamic
    Jihad in Egypt

Yellow Pants (Hussein Mohammed
    Salih, aka Abu Haraira)
English-speaking former school
    teacher, interpreter, originally from
    Tunisia

Grenade (Abdullah Salah al-Junaidi,
    aka Abu Hadhifa)
Fondness for fondling grenades while
    guarding hostages

Ahmed Atef (Ahmed Mohammed
    Ali Atef)
Operator of machine gun; older
    brother of Saad Atef

Saad Atef (Saad Mohammed
    Ali Atef)
Teenage younger brother of Ahmed
    Atef

Gray Shirt
Identity unknown, fled kidnapping
    after shooting at three hostages,
    killing one

Ali Ahmad Haydara
Fled kidnapping but arrested October
   2000

Said al-Fayadhi al-Maqab (aka Abu
   Nasser al-Awlaqi, aka Nasir al-
   Shiba)
Fled kidnapping but surrendered
   February 6, 1999—assumed to be
   brother of Salim al-Fayadhi al-
   Maqab

Salim al-Fayadhi al-Maqab (aka Abu
   Abdullah)
Fled kidnapping but surrendered
   February 6, 1999—assumed to be
   brother of Said al-Fayadhi al-
   Maqab

Ali Awad Barasin
Wanted in connection with
   kidnapping

Jalal al-Khadar al-Haj
Wanted in connection with
   kidnapping—possibly related to
   Purple Skirt

Salim al-Badawi
Wanted in connection with
   kidnapping for conducting
   reconnaissance of ambush site

Mohammed Ali al-Hamal
Wanted in connection with
   kidnapping

Awsan Ahmad Salah
Wanted in connection with
   kidnapping

Abu Ubayad
Wanted in connection with
   kidnapping

E. Other Militants

Sheikh Tariq al-Fadhli
Founder of Islamic Jihad in
   Yemen who later renounced
   militancy role

Sheikh Salih Haidara al-Atwi
Appointed as sheikh by Tariq al-
   Fadhli and took over Islamic Jihad
   and militant Huttat camp

Ayman al-Jawahiri
Leader of Egyptian Islamic Jihad,
   close associate of Osama bin Laden

Abu Muhsin (Hetam bin Farid)
Took over leadership of AAIA after
   capture of Abu Hassan

Nankly (Nabil Nanakli Qasebati)
Syrian with Spanish passport, arrested
   in 1997 in Yemen on charges of
   Aden bombings

Khalid al-Mihdar
Saudi hijacker of plane which crashed
   into U.S. Pentagon on 9/11,
   affiliated with AAIA members and
   USS *Cole* suspects in Yemen

Abu Ali al-Harithi (Qaid Ali bin
   Sinian al-Harithi)
Al-Qaeda suspect eliminated by U.S.
   missile attack on his car, likely the
   same al-Harithi reported by
   Grenade to have met with Abu
   Hassan

Abdulaziz Attash
Suspect in planned kidnapping of
Americans at Jibla hospital with
intent to demand release of Abu
Hassan; brother of Tawfiq Attash

Tawfiq Attash
One-legged suspected al-Qaeda
operative known to have met with
9/11 hijacker Khalid al-Mihdar in
Kuala Lumpur; brother of
Abdulaziz Attash

Samir al-Hada
Yemeni suspect in African embassies
and USS *Cole* bombings; brother-in-
law of Khalid al-Mihdar

Khaled abd al-Nabi
Leader of AAIA after Abu Muhsin's
arrest; pardoned in 2004

F. Supporters of Sharia
Abu Hamza (Mustafa Mohammed
Kamel)
Egyptian with British citizenship,
preacher at London mosque and
founder of Supporters of Sharia,
spokesperson for AAIA

Frank Etam
Owner of security business who
organized weapons and outdoor
skills training for Supporters of
Sharia

G. "British Boys"
(ages given as at time of arrest)
Mohammed Mustafa Kamel
Seventeen-year-old son of Abu
Hamza

Mohsin Ghalain (aka Abu Ahmed)
Eighteen-year-old son of Abu
Hamza's Moroccan second wife

Shahid Butt
Pakistan-born Briton, active as
volunteer in Islamic causes, 33
years old with wife and four
children

Sarmad Ahmed
Born in UK of Pakistani descent, 21-
year-old computer graduate whose
name and cell phone number were
listed as contact on Supporters of
Sharia Web site

Malik Nasser Harhara
Dual British and Yemeni citizenship,
26-year-old with a home in UK
and relatives in Yemen

Ghulaim Hussein
Security guard, 25 years old, with
English wife and baby daughter

Ayaz Hussein
Computer studies graduate, 24 years
old, cousin of Shazad Nabi

Shazad Nabi
Bus driver, 20 years old, cousin of
Ayaz Hussein

Kamil Sagheer (aka Ali Merksen)
Algerian traveling on French passport,
entered Yemen with Shahid Butt
and Mohammed Kamel

Al-Rahman (Abd al-Rahman Said
'Amr, aka James Lebourdiec, aka
Pierik James, aka James Louvre)

Algerian traveling on French passport, engaged to aunt of Mohsin Ghalain, entered Yemen with Mohsin Ghalain

H. Western Political, Diplomatic and Military

Barbara Bodine
U.S. ambassador to Yemen

Margaret Scobey
U.S. deputy ambassador to Yemen

Chuck Rosenfarb
Medical doctor on assignment to American embassy in Sana'a

Victor Henderson
British ambassador to Yemen

David Pearce
British consul in Aden

Mustafa Rajamanar
British vice-consul in Aden

Martin Lamport
Diplomat in British embassy, Sana'a

Anthony Zinni
Commander-in-chief, U.S. Central Command

Brad Deardorff
FBI agent assigned to investigate kidnapping

Mark Sofia
FBI agent assigned to investigate kidnapping

Beverly Mills
Detective constable, Scotland Yard

I. Yemen Political, Diplomatic and Military

Ali Abdullah Salih
President of Republic of Yemen

Abdel Karim al-Iryani
Prime minister of Republic of Yemen

Abdulwahab Abdulla al-Hajjri
Yemen ambassador to United States

Ahmed Ali Mohsen
Governor of province of Abyan

Mohammed Salih Turaik
Security chief for Aden

Ali Mohsen al-Ahmar
General in Yemen army, half brother of President Salih, married to sister of Tariq al-Fadhli

Sheikh Abdullah bin Husayn al-Ahmar
President of Yemen's al-Islah party

Hussein Mohammed Arab
Yemen's interior minister

Nasser Mansour Hadi
Secretary for political security in Aden, Abyan, and Lahij

Mohammed Salah Ali
Deputy chief of police for Abyan

Sameer (surname unknown)
Assistant to Yemen prime minister; coordinated Mary Quin's return visit to Yemen

Mohammed Mozeid
Driver on Mary Quin's return visit to
  Yemen

J. Legal and Media
Najib Mohammed al-Qaderi
Judge in Abu Hassan's trial

Mohammed Thabet
Attorney defending Abu Hassan

Jamal Mohammed Omar
Judge in "British Boys" trial

Badr Basunaid
Attorney defending "British Boys"

Rashad Yaqoob
Lawyer and Amnesty International
  volunteer assisting Britons on trial

Gareth Peirce
British attorney known for defending
  high-profile terrorism suspects

Khaled Tarik
Yemen attorney who declined to
  represent accused Britons

Hisham Bashraheel
Founder and editor of *Al-Ayyam*
  newspaper in Aden

Bashraheel H. Bashraheel
Editor for foreign desk of *Al-Ayyam*
  newspaper, son of Hisham
  Bashraheel

K. Others
Ray Kaufman
Finance executive and former Marine,
  life partner of Mary Quin

Shah Ahmed Masood
Military commander of Northern
  Alliance in Afghanistan,
  assassinated September 9, 2001